D1591549

THE HARMONY OF PARTS

THE HARMONY OF PARTS

John Garabedian

with Ian Aldrich

ORANGE *frazer* PRESS
Wilmington, Ohio

Published for the author by:
Orange Frazer Press
P.O. Box 214
Wilmington, OH 45177

Telephone: 937.382.3196 for price and shipping information.
Website: www.orangefrazer.com

Book and cover design: Alyson Rua and Orange Frazer Press

Front cover photograph: Cliff overlooking Race Point Beach, Provincetown,
Massachusetts, summer, 1966.
Back flap: Post Grammy Awards, Staples Center, Los Angeles, California.

Library of Congress Cataloging-in-Publication Data

Names: Garabedian, John. | Aldrich, Ian.
Title: The harmony of parts / John Garabedian, with Ian Aldrich.
Description: Wilmington, Ohio : Orange Frazer Press, [2016] | Includes index.
Identifiers: LCCN 2016009499 | ISBN 9781939710413
Subjects: LCSH: Garabedian, John. | Disc jockeys--United States--Biography.
Classification: LCC ML429.G166 A3 2016 | DDC 791.44092--dc23
LC record available at http://lccn.loc.gov/2016009499

Two roads diverged in a wood, and I—
I took the one less traveled by,
And that has made all the difference.

—Robert Frost, "The Road Not Taken"

Foreword

I like to joke that I gave John Garabedian his first big break in radio—and I'm only partly kidding!

We first met in the spring of 1957. It wasn't a planned visit, at least not on my part. In his characteristically mischievous way, John, who was only fifteen years old at the time, had forced the encounter. I was working at WBOS in Boston, an AM station that specialized in foreign language programming during the day, but at night handed the controls over to me for my Top 40 Rock 'n' Roll show, *The Night Train*. It was an outside-the-box program hosted by an outside-the-box personality. We made hits of songs that nobody else wanted to play and injected much-needed fun into the radio of the time. It was no surprise that John, an original person himself, became a fan of the show.

John and a friend had made a spoof of a record; a fake news program that spliced together the headlines and hits of the day. They had made the recording in the basement of John's family's home in Weston, Massachusetts. They came in unannounced to the WBOS studios and asked me to play it over the air.

I had my doubts. But from the moment I dropped the needle on that 45 I knew I had something good. Actually, better than good. It was entertaining, hilarious, and for a couple of high school kids who were working with a home-made recording studio, pretty slick. That night I played the record on my show. I knew right away that John had a future in radio. I should have realized also that we'd become good friends.

John's career has been exciting to watch—and certainly to be a part of it. From his dominance at my old home, WMEX, to the start of his own station, WGTR, to our partnership to launch Boston's first video TV station, V66, John has brought tenacity and talent to whatever he's touched.

He is demanding and has no time for negativity on the part of others. Most important, John has something that isn't prevalent in radio—vision. He knows what he wants and more important, knows what the audience wants. If John was solely interested in money, he would have burned out years ago. Although he is a shrewd businessman, John's real passion is radio—how it works, why it works, what it can mean as a cultural force. Listen to his current Top 40 program, *Open House Party*, and you'll understand what I mean. The same energy, drive, and love for radio that drove him all those years ago, are still there. It's why so many of us have gravitated toward his orbit and found ourselves working with him.

I'm thrilled that John has finally found the time to tell his story. It's an important one not only because it sheds light on the history of Top 40 radio, but also because it lays out the personal path of a man who despite any obstacle lives his passions to the fullest both in his personal and professional lives. John oftentimes flatters me by calling me a mentor, but I know that I've learned many things from him as well.

From that first encounter nearly sixty years ago, when a gangly teen opened the door to my studio, stuck out a hand, and showed me his record, I've loved watching the *John Garabedian Show* unfold. Thank you, John, for letting me be a part of it.

—Arnie Ginsburg
January, 2016

Contents

University of Miami, Florida, freshman year.

Preface

Sitting on the kitchen floor at age two or three playing with pots and pans, I looked up at my mother who was at the sink cleaning breakfast dishes after my father had left to go to work. This didn't make sense. How come she wore a dress and he wore pants? And why did he wear a nice suit and get to go into Boston to work in a nice office when she got stuck every day doing house cleaning?

That was the start of me feeling like an outsider, a misfit who couldn't understand the rules and customs of society. This challenge turned my life into a special adventure of seeking truth, and filled it with spiritual and career highs as well as sex and drugs and rock n' roll.

For years, after I told some story about my life, many people would say, "Wow John, you oughta write a book." So at dinner one night on Cape Cod, after my friends Shelia and Jeff Bauer said, "Wow John, you oughta write a book," Shelia reached out to her cousin, Marcy Hawley, publisher at Orange Frazer Press in Wilmington, Ohio, and the result is what you have in your hands.

The book is honest, at times graphic, and discusses personal things most people never share. As John Lennon once said, "Everybody's got something to hide except for me and my monkey." I've always felt compelled to deal with reality honestly. After all, reality is all there is. So if you live in "pretend-land" you're not going to win the game, since reality is what you're playing against.

Each chapter begins with a song title, generally from the era in that chapter. For maximum enjoyment, go to YouTube or Spotify as you begin each chapter and listen to the song. It will put you in the mood, and you just may discover or re-discover some incredibly great music.

Thanks to writer-supreme Ian Aldrich for spending over a year asking questions and listening to me babble, and another year using his skills writing and organizing a long and complex tale. I feel privileged to have worked with him.

John Garabedian

THE HARMONY OF PARTS

1. Get Together

The Youngbloods, 1967

On trips to Vermont we'd frequently camp high on Belvedere Mountain at an abandoned asbestos mine. When it got windy, this white dust blew around. We had no idea asbestos was a major carcinogen. Billy Harrison (left) and his brother Jimmy, a core part of the crew.

July 1969—Cabot, Vermont

What was I going to do with my life? That was the question that kept rolling through my brain as I sat under the fading sunset on a balmy summer evening in a mountaintop field in northern Vermont. Maybe it was the clean country air, or possibly the purple microdot acid that I'd dropped, but I felt an urgency to take on some of the confusion that had been rattling around my head the past few months.

Where had life put me? For starters, I'd been fired earlier that year by WORC in Worcester, Massachusetts. To call my relationship with the radio station complicated was an understatement. Over the last decade I'd left, come back, been fired twice, and returned again. Even after a couple of ugly endings I felt loyal to 'ORC and its owner, Bob Bryar, a mentor who'd given me my first chance in Top 40 when I was just a senior in high school and then gave me the encouragement to pursue the kind of entertaining, crazy, great radio I admired. WORC was my home. But then suddenly, unexpectedly, in early '69 Bob decided he wanted to cash in his chips and sold the station to the highest bidder. The new owners didn't exactly have an appreciation for my big personality. It was like oil and water and I got shown the door pretty damn quickly. WORC was now out of my life for good and that really felt weird. Like I'd been chucked out of my family home and told to never come back. It was unmooring.

But the drama didn't end just there. No. There was also my ongoing quest for a license to build my own radio station. Since about the time I could ride a bike I'd dreamed about being in broadcasting. For five long years I'd been battling to get the FCC to grant me a broadcast station license. And it wasn't just the bureaucratic hell that the FCC had put me through that was causing me headaches. Now, I was competing against a company with deeper pockets for the license itself. I was running out of money, time, and job prospects. Nobody

John Garabedian

who ran a Boston radio station wanted to hire a guy who'd eventually bolt to start up a competitor. I was twenty-seven years old, out of work, and had no idea what lay next.

Jesus, did I even want to stay in radio?

◀

The mere idea that I'd leave radio had seemed unfathomable just six months before. I'd been obsessed with it all my life. By the age of five I didn't just crank on the big console Philco in our living room every afternoon so I could listen to *The Lone Ranger*, I wanted to know how the thing worked. I'd peer behind it, gazing at those glowing tubes, which lit up with a warm amber glow, like a city at night. A few years later, I built my own mini-radio station in my bedroom. I blasted out The Platters and Elvis to my neighborhood buddies who picked up the little signal in their nearby homes from the long wire antenna I'd hung out my bedroom window and hooked to a tree. Then came my first paid radio job, midway through my senior year of high school.

And now I was just kind of floating. I called it my summer of freedom and was it ever. I lived in East Natick, a suburb west of Boston, and made ends meet by photographing weddings. At night I hit the clubs hard. Then, nearly every Friday I loaded

my van with buddies and we rumbled north on Route 3, making the five-hour drive to Vermont to chill.

I never made the trip alone and this hot July weekend was no different. I was there with some of my closest friends. We'd sprawl out in the clearing on the mountaintop for the sunsets and then always stayed much later. Smoking, talking, tripping into the night, it was new terrain for all of us—the big sky, thick woods, that serene Vermont tranquility and freedom—and we couldn't get enough of it. Without the endless noise and electricity of the city, it opened up a

Spectacular views and good times on Belvedere Mountain in Eden, Vermont. The asbestos deposits there are the largest in the world and once produced 83% of all asbestos mined anywhere.

John Garabedian

deep intimacy that enabled the most honest discussions about life, reality, and our future.

I'd only discovered Vermont a few months before after my friend Angus McPherson had invited me to come along on a trip to the state where he owned a thousand acres on top of a mountain. He was clearing trees to make way for a power line to a new cabin he was about to build. To me as a Boston club kid this sounded boring. All I could picture was cows, trees, and chickens. But with no other plans or responsibilities, I figured "what the hell" and said yes. So on a warm Friday morning I rode up with him and experienced my initial shock at being miles from absolutely anything. "What the hell do you do up here, Angus?" I kept asking him. Seriously, by the third day, even though I was perfectly sober, I was so high from the serenity and beauty I felt like I was on drugs.

God knows I needed the time to think. After a decade in radio—Top 40, mainly—working my ass off and just staying "on," Vermont gave me the chance to chill, open my mind, and relax. After that long ride from Boston, we'd roll into Vermont's Northeast Kingdom and say goodbye to the pavement. Up and up we'd go, following a winding circuit of dirt roads that climbed endlessly to field and sky. From the hilltop opening where we set up camp, you looked west as far as the Adirondacks in New York over what seemed like all of Vermont. There was the Worcester mountain range. Beyond that the Green Mountains, and in the distance was the high tip of Mt. Mansfield, the tallest point in the state. The lodging was modest. My buddies and I would eventually crash in a tiny camper trailer Angus owned, or sometimes just settle in on the big field itself. It didn't matter. The point was, we all bonded together in the open wilderness, and I loved that.

On this June night in 1969, the sun tucked behind the horizon, illuminating the sky with a brilliant display of deep oranges, pinks, and yellows, the sarcastic banter that had filled the air, fell silent. "Wow," said Rob Seely, never afraid to break any kind of silence. "You think it can't get any better and then it does."

I pulled a toke from a pipe, held in the smoke and nodded. "Yep," I said, holding my breath before letting out a big exhale. I handed the pipe over to Kris Carlson. "Clockwise, right?" I said with a laugh.

As the night grew older, the conversations deepened. They always did. As we smoked, we tried to tackle life's big questions: What is life? What are we here for? What kind of impact do we want to have? How can you make sure when you're pushing into old age that you can look back on your life and be proud of how you lived, what you've done, and where you ended up? That the mark you've left has real meaning.

That last question in particular carried weight for me. Throughout my childhood I'd seen my dad, a vice president at a chain of furniture stores in Boston, trudge home from work, briefcase in hand, carrying a worn look on his face. He'd gone

My buddy Rob Seely. Listening to the Bee Gees song "Israel" as he tripped on LSD, he deduced that "Israel" "is real" and concluded he immediately had to get there. Rob was arrested at Logan Airport demanding to board a flight to Israel. Our next meeting was at Lindeman Mental Health Center in Boston.

through the Great Depression and two World Wars, spending most of his life chasing security, not following his dreams. He'd dutifully spent day after day working to support his wife and children, working for people who weren't as smart or as capable as he was. From an early age I'd been cautioned by my mother not to run up to my father with questions right when he got home. "Wait until he's had his medicine," she told me. That meant a couple of Canadian whiskies on the rocks. He'd glide into the evening, have dinner, and then fade off into the night. The next morning, he'd start the routine all over again.

That was never going to be me. It looked like prison. I was a different person than my conservative father—stronger willed, more optimistic, more ambitious and confident, less scripted by society's rules. I wasn't the only one. The very questions that we tossed around during those nights in Vermont were being asked back then by seemingly everyone under the age of thirty. That suburban

John Garabedian

life our parents had flocked to had no meaning to most of us. My generation was on a quest for authenticity. The little home with the white picket fence, a couple of cars, a chicken in every pot—what the hell was that? Was that really the end game in life? We didn't think so and all you had to do was listen to the airwaves to know what the times were like. Pink Floyd, the Beatles, Jefferson Airplane, Moody Blues, Crosby, Stills, Nash, and Young—they were all singing about a new, better world, a new reality. You could feel that excitement in the way a lot of people were talking about a big concert that was scheduled for later that summer in upstate New York.

"Hey, John," Rob blurted out. "Where do you think you'll be in fifty years?"

"Homeless," I retorted.

"No, no," Mark Parenteau said. "You guys don't know? John's going to be the next king of radio. He's going to end up taking care of the rest of us. Right, Johnny?" Even then Mark was never shy about letting people know what he wanted.

Truth is, however, I appreciated Mark's underlying confidence in me. From the moment I'd first met him two years before, when as a seventeen-year-old, he'd lied his way past the receptionist into my WORC studio to meet me, he'd been one of my biggest fans. He'd grown up listening to me on WORC and became a huge fan of the kind of radio I loved doing—surprising, daring, risky, funny, human. Getting on the radio to invite people for impromptu drag races down Portland Street in downtown Worcester? Why not? Let's go for it.

As the clock pushed two in the morning everyone started to fade and pass out. Eventually, I had the night to myself. I stretched back, took in a deep breath, and gazed up at the sky. Damn, those stars were beautiful. I thought about how far that light had traveled to create this moment, the years it took for this incredible light show to reach me.

It got me thinking about life. What we were all doing as humans here on Earth? Where did we all fit in? What was our purpose? I thought about my own journey, too. Where I was headed as a person? Where would my life end up? Would I be proud of what I had accomplished? Would it matter that I had even lived?

My mind drifted back to the personal and career obstacles that had been thrown at me over the last decade, the shit that had come at me for being who

I was. The dull morons I'd worked for who didn't appreciate really great radio programming and how interactive and entertaining it could be. I'd bulldogged my way through all those things, and now, when things seemed especially hard, I was going to quit? Give up? That wasn't me. Maybe I couldn't save the world, but I could at least set an example. Maybe I could show others that if you stick to who you are and follow your heart, you can do anything you want.

Meanwhile I had to earn a living, and the one place I knew I could do well was radio. Until I could figure out a higher mission, radio was what I was good at. No, it's what I knew I was great at! As I lay under that starlit sky, a chill ran through me, an excitement.

I needed to get back to work. ◀×

2. Sunny Side of the Street

Tommy Dorsey Orchestra, 1945

A four-year-old me in the family living room, 57 Gale Road in Belmont.

The sound of the '40 black Plymouth pulling up in front of our Belmont home was a familiar one. It was like clockwork. At 3:55 every Wednesday afternoon, right on the dot, the ugly car would thunder in. I'd be in my room, playing with some toys, maybe looking at a book, and hoping like hell that this Wednesday would be different. It never was. My mother, Iris, who'd usually be sitting on the front stairs puffing on a Pall Mall, talking with her sister on the phone, would hear that damn car, too. She'd hang up, stamp out her cigarette, and then yell upstairs for me.

"Johnny!" she'd call out. "Miss Danielson's here! Time for your piano lesson."

And so it would begin. My hour of hell. I'd slowly make my way downstairs and there'd be Miss Danielson, a plain-looking woman who kept her brown hair tied tightly back in a bun and had a fondness for unflattering gray pant suits. Seeing her standing there talking to my mother struck me as funny. Even to me as a four-year-old, their contrast seemed hilarious. My mother, for whom wearing big hats and jingly jewelry felt about as natural as the need to breathe, was elegant and glamorous, with black hair and hazel eyes that glowed like jewels. Always ready for her close-up. Seeing her there next to my piano teacher, it was like looking at Olive Oyl holding court with Marlene Dietrich. The two would gab for a minute and then I'd follow Miss Danielson into the living room where I'd take a seat next to her on the bench in front of the family's baby grand Ivers & Pond piano.

"Now, Johnny," she always asked. "Did you practice every day since I last saw you?"

And like always, I'd shrug my shoulders, look down at the ground and give her my best no-comment. The truth is I hadn't touched a key. I hated the thing. It didn't make sense to me. Those black and white keys were not laid out logically. I liked machinery. Building stuff. Fixing things. Those were things I was interested in.

John Garabedian

The home I grew up in, 57 Gale Road, Belmont. Synchronicity: While visiting new Cape Cod neighbors at Thanksgiving, 2014, I met their daughter's boyfriend. We were amazed to learn that he grew up in that same house, and his bedroom is my old bedroom.

The lessons had been my mother's idea. She started me studying classical piano at three years old. I could read music before I could read English, but it was challenging. For the next four years I labored under Miss Danielson's guidance, banging away without an ounce of passion or caring. To this day, I'm not sure who was happier when I was finally given permission to quit: me or Miss Danielson.

My mother must have known early on that I didn't exactly embody the next great concert pianist. She wasn't a great pianist herself, but she was a devoted one. Every afternoon she'd sit down and attempt to get through some complicated piece like "Polonaise," "Moonlight Sonata," or "Clair de Lune" without making a mistake. The problem was, she never did. She'd get halfway through a composition, screw it up and start all over again from the beginning. It drove me crazy and eventually I'd cover my ears and run out of the room to play outside or in the basement until it was over.

But God, did she have it in her that one of her three kids would make it as a musician. The seed for that had been planted early on. Sometime in the 1930s, after she had my two older sisters, she visited a psychic in Boston. The woman told her she'd have a child who'd become internationally known in music. My mother never let that go, and so she made us all take music lessons. My two older sisters experienced the same pain I later did. Doris on the violin, Jackie on the piano. It's funny, though, because in the end the prediction came true, just not in the form she'd originally planned. "I never thought she meant I'd have a son who was a famous disk jockey," she once said.

Never letting go of that dream, no matter how little talent her children had with an instrument, was my mother. She dreamed big. As an Armenian immigrant she had seen firsthand the opportunity here. She came to America at the age of nine, fleeing with her family in 1912 from Sivas, Turkey, right before the second Armenian Genocide in which the Ottoman Turks brutally slaughtered over a million Armenian Christians—men, women, and children.

My family had been lucky. Friends in the Turkish government had warned my grandfather he had to get out, and the two oldest sons, my uncles Levon and Edward, were first sent to Boston for college to avoid the Turkish draft. A year later, my mother and the rest of the family sought refuge in America.

My mother as a toddler with her sister, Elmon, and parents, taken around 1906 in Sivas, Turkey, before they left for America. My grandfather died at age fifty-four in 1918 from the Spanish flu; the epidemic killed between fifty to 100 million people, 3–5% of the world's population.

They entered through Ellis Island and rejoined Levon and Edward in Malden, a Boston suburb, where they had started new lives.

Almost immediately my mother, enamored with her new country and the opportunities it presented, embraced her new American identity. While her three siblings never completely lost their Armenian accents, my mother spoke perfect English without a trace of her native tongue. It was a real point of pride for her. It's not that she denied her roots, but she rolled her eyes at the hardcore Armenian enclave in nearby Watertown, which to her seemed hell-bent on not allowing themselves to become Americanized. "This is the greatest country in the world," she liked to say. "You can be anything you want here. Those people who still speak Armenian in the house, listen to Armenian music, read the Armenian newspaper; if they like it so much they should go back to Armenia." My mother's appreciation for the freedoms and opportunities she found in her adopted country framed her entire life and the manner she went about raising her children.

John Garabedian

My mother's independent spirit knew no limits. After graduating from Malden High School, she bucked her family's wishes and enrolled in a women's business school in Boston in order to find work as a secretary. When her brother, Levon, who owned a Moon automobile dealership, needed to pick up new cars in Charlestown, it was my mother he hired to pick up the vehicles—she who at the age of sixteen became the first woman in Malden to get her driver's license. That's who she was: determined to go after what she wanted, damn the idea it hadn't been done before or that it might be hard.

She also had no patience for dogma. Before the 1960s counter culture made it popular, she pounded into us the idea to question everything. *Don't take what's said or accepted at face value, religion especially.* As a girl she'd suffered through several years at a French Catholic school in Turkish Armenia. My mother hated the nuns and their rigidity; the idea that you're not supposed to ask questions about what they taught you. One time, when I was young, some Jehovah's Witnesses knocked on our front door trying to sell her their *Watchtower* religious magazine. Finally, when she ran out of patience and was ready to turn them away, they tried to catch her attention by squeezing in one more question: "But Mrs. Garabedian, aren't you afraid of what's going to happen when you *die?*" My mother's eyes hardened. "Listen, dear," she said wagging her finger, "Nobody knows! Nobody knows!" And with that, she shut the door. That was the attitude of idealistic confidence and defiance I was brought up with. Deal with reality. Using a script written seventeen hundred years ago, translated and twisted dozens of times, and reciting events that happened three centuries before the first draft was written, how can that help you figure out life? You have to figure out for yourself what's right and wrong.

My father, also named John, was another story. If my mother loved pushing the envelope, he defaulted to restraint and convention. He was tall like me, and had a head of thick dark hair, which hadn't thinned and barely grayed even by the time of his death at 94. His Armenian-born father, Markar, had come to this country in 1885 as a teenager, penniless but hungry to work hard. He eventually found employment as a shoemaker in East Cambridge where he settled and met my Scottish-born grandmother, Eliza Hood.

In the early 1900s, Cambridge wasn't the trendy, intellectual enclave it is now. More working class. My grandparents' home was a brick row house on the east side, where other tradesman—masons, carpenters, small merchants—lived. Our dad was the oldest of three brothers, and the two younger ones went on to become Protestant ministers. I don't really know what my dad's boyhood was like because he didn't talk about it. He didn't talk much about any-

When the U.S. entered World War I, my dad (rear, center) was a junior at Cambridge Latin School (where Ben Affleck and Matt Damon later graduated). Though accepted at Harvard, at age sixteen he dropped out of high school to join the U.S. Army with his buddies, and by seventeen was master sergeant over 250 men.

thing, actually. He was quiet, a bit dour at times, a trait he undoubtedly picked up from his reserved Scottish mother.

But he also saw himself as a disciplinarian. It's a role that defined much of his life, first as the older brother, then as a seventeen-year-old master sergeant of over 250 men in France during World War I, and later as vice president of a major furniture retailer in Boston. It was who he was. *Keep your shoes on in the house otherwise you'll wear your socks out. Always wash your hands when you come inside.* The man was predisposed to give orders. And whereas my mother dreamed of possibilities and opportunity, my father liked to dwell on what could go wrong. "Who's going to pay for this?" was one of his go-to lines whenever he was approached by my mother about a major purchase. When I landed my first radio job at a small station in Milford, my mother gave me a smile and a big hug. My father just looked at me. "Why would they want a kid like you?" he asked.

3. How High the Moon

Les Paul & Mary Ford, 1951

With my father at Humarock Beach, Scituate, Mass., summer, 1943. World War II was underway and I remember excitedly watching the blimps on patrol, flying over the shore searching for German submarines.

My sisters joke that my arrival upended the whole household. They may have a point. My parents met and married while in their early twenties. Then, pretty quickly had two daughters, Doris in 1927 and Jackie four years later. For all my father's lack of enthusiasm for family fun, he was a good provider. Even in the midst of the Great Depression he made enough of a salary to buy a four-bedroom Garrison Colonial in a new neighborhood in Belmont. For a young family it was a great spot. The house sat on a small hill and had a small backyard shaded by several locust trees. On muggy summer nights my sisters would sleep out on the back porch, letting the breeze from those big trees wash over them. For the most part it was a neighborhood of other young families who sent their kids to the Mary Lee Burbank School, directly across the street from our home. And with the exception of my mother banging away on the piano every few days, life at the Garabedian home was quiet, joyful, and steady. No surprises.

But as my mother hit forty my dad's mother badgered my parents about having a son. *You need a boy to carry on the family name,* she kept telling them. She was old country like that. I guess my parents gave her lip service for as long as they could before finally wearing down. I was born thirteen days after the bombing of Pearl Harbor, on December 20, 1941.

Quickly, I became the tornado my sisters had never been. I couldn't stay still. During one family vacation at Humarock Beach on Boston's South Shore, my mom put me down for a nap, and then promptly fell asleep herself. I was still in diapers and had just learned to walk. No matter. I climbed out of that crib, waddled out the door, and into town. My mother was finally awakened by a ringing phone. On the line was the owner of the general store a few blocks away. Your infant son, she was told, has just walked in.

John Garabedian

Fifth grade class photo. All the other kids were Irish, Italian, or English, and I was the Armenian kid with the weird last name who was uncomfortably taller than everyone (top row, third from left). By fourteen I was 6'4".

Another time, when I was just two years old, I woke up early one Sunday morning. Everyone was sleeping, so I decided to make the family breakfast. Eggs, bacon, toast, coffee—the whole deal. When I thought it was ready, I burst upstairs and announced that it was time to eat. My parents awoke to a house filling up with smoke. After opening all the windows, my mom surveyed the kitchen to find the bacon half in the pan, eggs all over the counter and my grand-mother's prized pewter teapot completely melted on the stovetop, just ruined. She had every right to be mad, but she just shook her head and smiled. "Oh, Johnny," she said with a laugh, then picked me up and gave me a big hug.

That was my mom, extremely forgiving. I guess she had to be when it came to me. She wanted to encourage me to succeed in life and not constrain me with iron rules. I was high-energy, strong-willed, stubborn, smart. A lot like her, and she knew personally what it meant when you weren't allowed to be exactly who you are.

After the first several years of my parents' marriage, she began suffering a string of migraines. She finally saw a psychologist about the problem, who told her that she was repressing herself, holding too much in. It became liberating! From that day forward she was much more outspoken. "You go to hell!" became a popular line of hers, which would burst out whenever she and my father got into an argument. He couldn't figure out what happened to his compliant, adoring wife. She still loved him and played the part of the full-time housewife, still took good care of her family and the house. Still ironed my dad's shirts, but she no longer whistled as she did them.

Surrounded by my mother, two sisters, two mothers-in-law, and a female Russian Wolfhound, my dad ruled the house as the only male until adorable little Johnny was born. The six females treated me like their newborn prince and suddenly my dad wasn't the star any more.

She went the opposite way with me. She showered me with adoration. I was her pride and joy. "My Johnny." That was what my mother proudly said whenever I did something that amazed her. One time, when I was nine, I took an old speaker and put it inside a cardboard box that I'd turned into a baffle by poking holes into it. I secretly placed it under my parents' bed, connected a wire and ran it out the window to a record player in the basement. Early one Sunday morning, I got up before anyone and cranked it up, waking my parents up from a dead sleep blasting "How High the Moon" by Les Paul & Mary Ford. I howled with laughter as I ran upstairs to find my parents sitting up, looking bewildered. When I explained what I did my mother smiled. "Oh, my Johnny," she cooed. My father just looked annoyed.

That's kind of how it went in our household. My mother showed me unconditional love, my father largely tolerated me. Years later, as an adult, I concluded it must have been jealousy. My arrival upended my father's life more than anyone

John Garabedian

else's. Until I'd come along he'd been *the* man in the house, the only male in a household of five women. For my mother, two sisters, and the two grandmothers who lived with us, he was the king of their world. And then suddenly, he wasn't. This adorable new baby boy with curly blond hair and big blue eyes got all the attention. You can be sure as hell my father struggled with that. I don't resent him for that. It's just how it was.

But the times were also different. Back then, fathers weren't expected to be affectionate. There was a certain "manhood" they had to live up to. Get a good job, provide for your family, keep to yourself. Men didn't hug or show affection back then, it was regarded as queer. Not a lot of "I love you." Oh sure, I thought he loved me. I know he was proud of me, but he never felt comfortable saying those things. It just wasn't in him to be affectionate. He didn't feel it was manly.

Besides, it wasn't like he was absent from family life. Sometimes he took me along when he went out with his buddies to fish offshore in Marshfield, and years later after we moved to Weston, we'd all pile into the family Buick every Tuesday night and go to Chin's Village in Wellesley for Chinese food. The times where I'd see him really open up was on Sundays when they'd send me to Sunday school and he'd stay home and cook a big family dinner. Roast beef, ham or roast chicken was usually on the menu. He'd putter around the kitchen that whole morning, eventually joined by his childhood friend, Dr. Cogan, who always liked to stop by Sunday mornings for a few shots of Canadian whiskey. By the time we got home, my father was in pretty ripe shape. Cracking jokes, just laughing it up. It was a side of him I rarely saw.

Maybe it's because it was the only time he didn't think about work. We never spoke about it, but I suspect my father lived in a world of duty rather than a life of enjoyment. He'd given up the chance to enter Harvard College at age sixteen so he could instead join his buddies in World War I. When he returned from France after the war, he stumbled into the furniture business, and eventually began working for John H. Pray and Sons Furniture in Boston. There he rose to vice president. He did well, but he was stressed, constantly at the mercy of a boss who inherited the company and didn't know a thing about running a business. He was a fine example of the "lucky sperm club." As a result my dad ended up pumping most of his career into that place, and as a thank-you he lost his pension a year into his retirement when the company filed for bankruptcy.

But I realize I have both my parents to thank for who I've become. My mother pushed me to pursue my dreams and my father showed me structure and what happens to you if you don't dream. 🔇

4. Radio Gaga

Queen, 1978

Johnny Bieberbedian? School photo in fourth grade from the Mary Lee Burbank Elementary School.

If you visited our Belmont home in the middle of the afternoon in say, 1946, you no doubt would have entered a house where music played constantly. Besides her piano playing, my mother was always listening to classical and opera and my sisters were playing the pop songs of the day. My mother always wanted something playing. Common, everyday regular life, she felt, was more beautiful with a soundtrack.

She also went to great lengths to expose her children to music. She took me to my first opera when I was just four years old. Boston Symphony Orchestra concerts were a regular thing for us, as were sister Jackie's ballet performances and Boston Pops summer concerts on the Charles River Esplanade. When my sisters were both still in their teens, my mother took them to a Frank Sinatra concert at the Paramount Theater in Boston. Recent boy idols like Justin Bieber and One Direction are no different than Frank Sinatra was in 1940. The screaming girls, the sheer mayhem that accompanied his shows, and even the run-ins with the law. My mother didn't care. Amidst all that pandemonium, there she was, watching her daughters enjoying the show and taking it all in.

"He's got such a sweet voice," she gushed.

Early pop culture actually had a place in our house. When I was young and my sisters still lived at home, they were always gabbing about movie stars. Judy Garland, Lana Turner, Betty Grable, and Ingrid Bergman. My sisters went to the movies any chance they could and devoured movie magazines like candy. Those big glossy pubs would be sprawled out across the living room and I'd listen to them gossiping about the stars the way TMZ and fan sites do today. These celebrities were people who seemed important. They represented something much bigger than anything going on in quiet little Belmont.

My big sister Doris in front of our Belmont home with our pet Russian Wolfhound. Behind her is the Mary Lee Burbank elementary school, which I attended.

This bigger world entered my life in other ways, too. In the living room of our family home sat a console Philco radio, a giant walnut-encased piece of furniture. My mother's love of glamour didn't stop with her wardrobe. She was always going to estate auctions and coming home with something elegant—a crystal chandelier, fancy wine glasses, gold-trimmed plates, sets of ornate chairs. The Philco had been the product of one of her adventures. I don't remember how she got it home. It was huge—probably four feet tall and five feet long—and weighed a ton. But there was no doubting my mother's eye. The dark, polished wood, the glowing knobs, the 78 RPM automatic record changer that rolled out of one of the cabinet drawers. But its best feature was its giant center speaker. It had this rich, deep tone. When music came out of it you felt like you were standing in the middle of a grand concert hall.

Even my father was drawn to that big radio. One of the lasting childhood memories I have of him is sitting around our big dining room table every Sunday evening, combing the newspaper to look at the ads competing furniture stores were running. He'd tune the big Philco to a station playing the popular hits of the day and get to work.

For a curious six-year-old, that radio became the most important thing in the house. Every afternoon at 5 o'clock I hustled into the living room from whatever I was doing, turned the radio's big on-knob and tuned into shows like *Roy Rogers*, *The Shadow*, *Gene Autry*, and another favorite, *Bobby Benson & the B-Bar-B Riders*. Then at night after dinner it was *The Lone Ranger*. Those hoof beats would fade in like a pair of drums, building up the anticipation. Then came the announcer: "*A fiery horse with the speed of light, a cloud of dust and a hearty hi-yo Silver! The Lone Ranger! ... With his faithful Indian companion Tonto, the daring and resourceful masked rider of the plains led the fight for law and order in the early west.*" I thought my heart was going to pound out of my chest. It was exciting! I'd park myself on the dark green carpet and just stare at the radio, riding along the empty plains.

That's when I first felt the power and excitement of what radio could do. It brings you life, connects you to the whole world, and can even transport you to another time and place. It was all there. People get wrapped up in stories, the drama; they want to feel the excitement and emotion, be taken somewhere. Those things are powerful, emotional, and eternal. A popular song connects you immediately to a feeling, an emotion, a sense that you are connected to something. I've never forgotten what my friend, the legendary Boston radio DJ, Arnie "Woo Woo" Ginsburg, once said, "a hit song is like a friend." It conveys things that you relate to. It transmits feelings that you can experience. It can bring back a memory or give you new feelings that nothing else has before.

For a young kid confined by the limits of suburban Boston, radio represented a connection to real life and culture. There was no Internet then, no Facebook, no Instagram. Radio and the music taught lessons about life, love, and heartbreak. Nothing else came close. You can write twenty-five pages that describe something or compose a song of thirty words that melodically, powerfully, transmits the same essence. Of course nothing as cerebral as that registered with my six-year-old brain. All I knew is that I loved the feeling it gave me

John Garabedian

School photo in sixth grade. T-shirts had become fashionable.

and that connection made me feel in touch with humanity and the world.

I was also fascinated by machines, technology, and the mechanics of radio. How the thing came together. How it all worked. I tried asking my parents about this stuff but they were useless. My father wasn't a technical or mechanical guy. If something needed fixing, even when I was five or six, I'd fix it. A doorknob which had been loose for months? A dripping faucet? I learned that a butter knife made a great screwdriver. I loved figuring out systems. Machinery, cars, electronics—I loved dissecting things. Taking something apart and putting it back together again let me learn how everything worked. Unlike my father, who didn't even own a screwdriver, I never felt intimidated by mechanical objects or machines. They're nothing but systems. The reason I struggled so badly with the piano was because it's abstract. Give me a machine to figure out and that's a different story because it's logical.

As a junior at Weston High School, for example, I became editor of the school newspaper, the *Smoke Signal*. We had an advisor, Miss McDonough, a math teacher and former nun, who was a strict authoritarian and clearly took no enjoyment in working with us. But the paper wasn't getting printed on time. Dorrington Press in Waltham was printing it as a favor to the school for fifty dollars an issue, but they'd always fall behind and push us aside because of backup caused by their profit-making jobs.

As weeks went by, the stories became out of date. Over the objection of old Miss McDonough I visited Dick Dorrington, the printing plant owner, and told him I wanted to help out. Before long I learned how to do press layouts, set hot

I was elected editor of the Weston High School newspaper, the *Smoke Signal*. To improve readership, we interviewed celebrities like Jimmie Rodgers who had three top five hits, including #1 "Honeycomb." (Left to right) Reggie Curtin, Sue Herrick, Rodgers, myself, and John Reissner.

type on a linotype machine, screen halftones, and make negatives for the lithographic plates—the whole thing. After that we began getting the paper out in time. It was rewarding to make it happen, and taught me the thrill and satisfaction of overcoming obstacles with determination and effort. To this day I still love the smell of press ink.

But it was electronics that became a real passion of mine. The basement and my bedroom were my laboratories. By the age of nine I was breaking down old radios, building amplifiers—every waking chance I could I spent trying to understand this stuff. Connections helped. My cousin Vollmer Hetherington worked at the RadioShack on Washington Street in Boston. It was the original RadioShack and at that time the only one in the world. Visiting it was as exciting as walking into a candy store—the place was filled with electronic gadgets, war surplus radios, amplifiers, and electronic parts.

John Garabedian

Even if my parents didn't entirely understand my interests, they didn't hold back in supporting them. In the fall of 1952, the same year my family bought our first television set, the first home tape recorders were introduced. Today, where making an audio recording is as simple as tapping your iPhone screen, it's easy to forget just what a breakthrough tape recording represented. Previously, if you wanted to record audio you did it on a wire or on an acetate disc. It was cumbersome, not user-friendly, and very expensive.

The recorder that caught my eye was a Revere. Packaged in a big tan case with a pair of seven-inch reels, it was beautiful. But it cost $500. Even my mother paused when I first approached her about it. "You think you really need it, Johnny?" she asked. I nodded my head. To her credit, she swallowed hard and went ahead and asked my father. I don't know what she said to him, but that Christmas I found it waiting for me under the tree. Considering my dad made, maybe $10,000 a year, it was a true sacrifice for them.

The machine was everything I'd hoped for. I'd spent God knows how many hours tethered to that recorder and the Philco, recording and listening to those early radio shows, and subconsciously schooling myself on what they did. By age twelve, radio DJs had begun to proliferate as all the big stars of prime-time network radio moved over to television.

The DJs added a new dimension to radio. I began forming opinions about what worked and didn't work. Did they talk too much? Who was saying dumb things? In the summer of 1954 one of my favorite stations was WORL in Boston. The morning announcer was this hilarious guy named Larry Welch, who called himself the "Voice of the Turtle." Unfortunately, every morning at 8:30 they cut away from Larry Welch to broadcast Archbishop Cushing and the Catholic Rosary for fifteen minutes. No matter. I sat through it just so I wouldn't miss a word Welch had to say when he came back on the air. It's why even today, even though I was never a Catholic, I can still recite the Rosary from memory.

But now with my Revere tape recorder I could actually record shows. Radio shows, DJs, television shows. It became my DVR. But I also used it to make recordings of myself practicing to be an announcer, introducing music, reading magazine ads, news, doing little segments.

With my mother on a vacation trip to Washington, D.C.

Of course, my parents weren't spared from this new technology. One spring day I happened to be sick, home from school, and figured out how to make tape loops. My mother was angry with me for something I'd done and had sent me to my room. While she was downstairs repainting trim in the living room I decided to have some fun. I took a speaker and stuck it out my door, right at the top of the stairs. Then I ran a wire to the speaker terminals inside the tape recorder. On the machine was a tape loop I'd made of me in my high-pitched ten-year-old voice saying, "Keep painting! Keep painting! Keep painting!" Over and over it played. I turned up the volume and listened.

At first she tried to ignore it, but that only lasted a few minutes. Finally, she marched upstairs, screaming and banging on the door. "Turn that thing off!" she yelled. I hit the stop button but still couldn't contain my enjoyment. I opened the door and gave my mother my best, most charming grin. A peace offering. A slight smile emerged on her face and she just shook her head. "My Johnny," she said, and then turned to go back downstairs. 🔇

John Garabedian

5. When I Grow Up

Beach Boys, 1967

On the front steps of our Belmont home. I was pretty self-conscious back then and hated being photographed.

As a kid, I always struggled to fit in. I hated standing out, but that's all I seemed to be able to do. Start with my last name: *Garabedian*. It's not a common name, and worse, it was not "American sounding." In the 1940s and '50s Boston suburbs, most people had English, Italian, or Irish names, so mine stuck out. My dark looks only made things worse. It also didn't help my self-confidence that I was tall—by the time I was fourteen years old, I stood 6'4". Which made the fact that I didn't enjoy playing sports even worse. Baseball especially bored the crap out of me. And there was a reason. At the time the Boston Braves hadn't left for Milwaukee...and ultimately Atlanta, so there were two baseball teams in Boston and only two television channels. Those dumb baseball games would take up both channels and preempt my favorite TV shows!

My mother didn't always help my self-confidence, either. On my first day of kindergarten at age four, she made me go to school dressed in a full-length camel-hair overcoat. All the other kids were in baseball jackets and shirts, but my mother wanted her precious son to look high-class. For a child who hated being different, it was terrifying and I cried in the schoolyard before finally going in.

Even today, I don't like being perceived as a showboat. Several years ago when I sold Superadio, the radio network I'd founded, I thought I'd give myself a present and bought a sharp new silver Mercedes SL500 convertible. It was gorgeous, but I soon realized how uncomfortable it made me to drive it. If I pulled up to 7-Eleven to get milk I'd half expect to hear trumpets with ruffles and flourishes announcing my arrival. I felt like a fake, like I was some pompous ass trying to be something I wasn't. Eighteen months later I sold it with twelve hundred miles on it. Now I drive a Jeep.

John Garabedian

As a boy, though, fitting in came with compromises. By adolescence I looked at most of the kids my age and didn't identify with them. Instead of playing sports I wanted to be doing stuff. Building things. Exploring. It was difficult. There was never one group I identified with. Not the jocks, not the geeks. I felt like an outsider. It was the same later in life. I struggled to find intelligent people who really cared to talk about higher-level things. It's made me realize that when you're exceptional, life can be a lonely place.

I also just looked at life, wondered and thought about things differently from most of the other kids. So many of them seemed content to just accept what came their way. Something was either black or white. I couldn't look at life that way. I was predisposed to question everything. Even as a young boy I looked at my parents and couldn't figure out why men and women had starkly different roles. In the morning my father would leave for work dressed in a fancy suit and go into Boston for work, while my mother got stuck at home doing housework in a housedress? He went into Boston to a nice office and she got to clean and cook? Why did men wear pants and women wear dresses? Was this some law? It confused me and made no sense.

 It became pretty clear to me that there was the path in life that people were following, and then there was the repressed life that people might want to be leading. Especially with sex. At a young age, I found myself with these urges that nobody else seemed to talk about, and it weirded me out. I thought I was the only person who had these thoughts. I'd be watching television and see a woman with big breasts or a cowboy in tight pants and admire his butt. Then, I'd shake myself free from the moment and wonder what was wrong with me. Why was I liking that? Sure, I liked girls, but boys got me excited, too. But this wasn't anything people talked about…ever. It was an era when men never hugged and were only supposed to shake hands and keep their distance.

And yet, I had these feelings.

When I was four, my mother had a good friend who often visited with her son, David, who was my age. They'd go off into the living room for coffee and talk, and David and I would head down to the basement to play and occasionally explore each other's bodies. It felt natural and exhilarating. But another part of me made me feel that it was wrong, that I should feel guilty about what we'd done. When David and I became a little older and met again in the eighth grade, we never spoke about it.

The confusion only deepened as I moved into my teens. Yeah, I had girlfriends, but there was this whole other side of life that reared its head. I saw it all the time. The double standards and contradictions between societal norms and reality were everywhere. You just had to look for it. You have to be perceptive enough to seek truth in the gray areas of life. While we were in high school, the Weston High School football captain and I were buddies, and occasionally while hanging out we'd take a hike through the woods by our neighborhood to the old Babson estate, and "fooled around" inside an abandoned garage. We never talked about it. One of us would suggest going for a walk and off we'd go.

This was a decade before the Stonewall riots, before the first traces of the gay rights revolution had begun. These were the very conformist 1950s. There were only white, Protestant, heterosexual role models to be seen on TV or in the movies. Gay people were viewed and portrayed as clowns, rapists, and perverts. So the feelings that swelled up inside of me had to be buried. And I knew that. I mean, I was already paranoid about feeling like an oddball for being tall, smarter than the average kid, and nonconformist. Even though I had these feelings and urges and saw others had them, too, they couldn't be allowed to surface for fear of being cast out and humiliated. I felt vulnerable, insecure. If I said anything, I worried I'd be rejected by my family, friends, and community. It felt safer to shut my mouth and pour my focus into something I loved and knew I could master.

That was radio. 🔇

6. Rock Around the Clock

Bill Haley & His Comets, 1954

We moved from Belmont to Weston in 1955 when I was thirteen. Here I am in the family TV room at fourteen.

really hate bullshit. No, I mean I really hate it. Start feeding me a bunch of religious or political dogma and I'll head the other way. On the other hand, I've always considered myself to be an extremely spiritual person. Which means I don't believe there's some white guy in a robe waiting to hug me on other side of life. But there's no doubt in my mind that there's some kind of "force," some greater master "thing" that makes the whole universe work and connects everything.

And music is a highly spiritual way to help you tune into that. A melody conveys emotion, and the very best music and songs communicate deep limbic feelings. As a small kid I remember Sunday services at the First Unitarian Church in Belmont and being sucked in by the magnificent sound that rolled out of the big 1930 Casavant pipe organ. The whole building seemed to fill with life, spirit, and feeling. It felt important, godly, and made me feel like I was connecting to something deep, big, and spiritual in the universe. Maybe it was just in me, part of my DNA, or my early music education, but music is something always I've felt, rather than simply heard.

A defining moment in my relationship to music came in the spring of 1951. Ask anyone what the first song they ever bought or downloaded was and they won't even pause. It's like the first time you have sex, or get behind the wheel of a car. It means that much. For me it was actually three records: "How High the Moon" by Les Paul and Mary Ford, the Weavers' "On Top of Old Smokey," and "The Thing" by Phil Harris.

The problem was all three songs had been issued on a new piece of technology: the 45 record. Those little seven-inch vinyl 45 rpm record players had been introduced by RCA Victor in 1949 and they'd quickly caught on. I'd first seen a 45 changer at the RadioShack in Boston and knew I had to have one. All

35

John Garabedian

through that fall of 1950 I pleaded with my parents to get me one and on Christmas morning it waited for me under the Garabedian Christmas tree.

After saving up money to pay for some records, I pestered my mother to drive me to a record store in Cushing Square in Belmont. While she waited in the car, I combed through the bins and eventually emerged clutching my first three 45s like they were newly discovered treasure.

All three of those records got played to death, but it was the Les Paul tune that I just couldn't get enough of. I'd sit close to the record player and ride along Les Paul's energetic guitar playing Mary Ford's multi-track harmonies. To this day I can still bring up that song on YouTube and it blows me away how perfectly well done it is.

But the more I listened to music and the more I dissected what I heard on the radio, the more I began to understand how songs fed off one another. That good radio isn't just a random collection of tunes strung together. There's a real art and science behind the music flow to deliver a great listener experience. I'd begun experimenting with this as early as nine years old when I built my first micro radio station. I'd been combing through the tables of gadgets at RadioShack when my eyes caught sight of a phono oscillator, a small, rudimentary electronic device that transmits a low power AM signal. It wasn't big, maybe five inches long, with an open metal chassis and three vacuum tubes sticking out of the top. Wire a turntable to it and you'd hear the music play through any radio in the house.

At the age of twelve I used that phono oscillator to build a little home radio station. I constructed an audio mixer to feed the device then wired it with faders and a mike switch, hooked a microphone and turntable to it, and began talking. The thing only had a range of a hundred feet or so—maybe the people next door could pick it up—and because it was missing a preamp you practically had to scream into the mike, but I could not have cared less. I was on the air: telling jokes, delivering the weather, just having the kind of fun I imagined every radio DJ had.

In the summer of 1955, our family moved from Belmont to Weston, and I took over the neighborhood. At RadioShack I bought a small slant-faced steel cabinet that was maybe nine inches high, fourteen inches wide, and seven inches tall. I drew a schematic diagram, drilled out the box and wired in a mike switch, four control potentiometers, and some resistors. This homemade device became my control board, so I could play one song, introduce the next one, and have it all ready to "cue in." I wired the output to my Revere tape recorder. Now I had a way to critique my DJ skills! After reading a book on antenna theory, I hooked up that old phono oscillator to a long-wire antenna that ran out my bedroom window. Now my little radio station went a half a mile!

The Johnny G. Show became the most popular radio program on Ledgewood Road. My best friend, Evan Caracostas, tuned in through a small radio he had in his bedroom. But sometimes he preferred other listening environments. Like his mom's car. Just thirteen years old, he'd wait for his mom to start one of her legendarily long showers, then he'd sneak her big white Lincoln convertible out and just cruise around the neighborhood blasting tunes.

Evans's approval was one thing. Seeing how a group of people responded to the music I played was something else completely. As a freshman in a new high school I was still a shy kid. I had friends, sure, but I was thirteen and still cringed at being the center of attention. My friends today laugh at that idea, but it's true. School dances were the worst. In ninth grade I'd muster just enough courage to go to them and then hang with my buddies along the wall, my hands stuffed in my pockets.

But what I really loved was the music. This other kid, Stu Harnish, two years older than me, was the DJ. He had two turntables and stacks of 45 records set up on this long table and soon I made friends with him. Stu also suffered no shortage of confidence. He seemed to own the whole school. Smart, outgoing, tall like me, he was a good-looking blond kid with a voice that dropped down to diplomat smooth when he needed something from you, and Stu had somehow finagled his way into getting his hands on a copy of the school's master key. The outside doors, any room in the building, any time of day, Stu's key could get you into the place. When Stu graduated high school he passed on that master key to me. But, man, I was too fearful of the repercussions to do anything nefarious. I mainly used it to sneak into the school darkroom at night, on weekends, or during school vacation and develop photos for the school paper.

At the dances, Stu had no problem sharing how he did things. Filling the dance floor was the number one goal, he kept reminding me. But pace was also important. He showed me how he picked his spots to throw in a slow song and

John Garabedian

School newspaper interviews with popular DJs were high on my list, and what a thrill it was for me to sit at the WBZ microphone, even if it was off. Here I am with (left to right) Frank Best, Andy Wolff, Susan Bump, and John Reissner.

when it was necessary to speed things up with a tune that packed more energy. Then, one night after another dance, Stu was packing up his records when he said, "Hey, John, I've got too much going on right now. I'm not sure I'm going to be able to do these anymore. How would you like to take over?"

A shot of adrenalin ran up my spine. I said yes immediately and the next Friday night I was the Weston High School ace DJ in control of the whole room. It was intoxicating. To keep people dancing, to entertain them, to control the mood of the place. One thing I learned early was that the songs I liked weren't necessarily the ones others wanted to hear, or that would get people dancing. You could quickly see which tunes worked and which didn't. It was an early lesson but it's something that is crucial in radio.

Of course, with my new responsibility as Weston High School's official DJ, I needed to make sure I had a lot of records. Every chance I got I headed to Whelpley's Music in Weston or the Music Box in Wellesley Square to expand my arsenal of 45s: Elvis, Chuck Berry, Buddy Holly, Carl Perkins, Little Richard, Lloyd Price. I quickly had an outstanding record collection.

I think I was pretty good at being a dance DJ. And it helped my own self-confidence. For the first time I felt sort of accepted in high school, respected and even looked up to. Before a big dance I'd get stopped in the hallway by kids I didn't even know, asking if I was going to be deejaying it. It gave me confidence. It also gave me permission to say no to people. I have no problem now speaking my mind and letting others know exactly how I feel. But back then it was such a struggle. I worried what people thought of me, that I might hurt their feelings if I said what I really wanted to say. Deejaying those dances helped break me out of that shell. Every dance or club DJ will tell you about the requests they get that they know will absolutely kill the scene. So to avoid quieting the dance floor, I learned to quickly say no and let people know why their idea wouldn't work. This ability has proven priceless throughout my life.

Television arrived in my life like this welcomed force, just upending everything. Our neighbors, the Leightons, an older couple who lived next door to us in Belmont, had the first TV set I ever saw. Mr. Leighton had developed terminal cancer and they bought it for his entertainment. I was around six years old and it was so early in the TV age that no Boston station had signed on the air yet.

But things moved quickly and within a year, every Monday night, my parents and I would hop into the family Buick and head over to Dr. Jameson's house in Belmont Center to watch his Dumont, a huge tabletop cabinet with a little seven-inch screen about the size of an iPad. We'd crowd around the thing at eight sharp with a crew of his neighbors to watch Milton Berle and the Texaco Star Theater. It was an event. Out Berle would come, dressed in drag, and the whole room would erupt in laughter.

For a kid like me looking to be a part of a whole world that lay far beyond Boston, TV represented this exciting connection to something huge. It was like being blind then all of a sudden having vision. It felt that transformative. Later, when I was granted the TV license that would become my music television station, V66, I got pummeled with questions about why I'd ever want to get into TV. You're a radio guy. What are you thinking? I didn't go into it but since those early days of TV, before I became wed to radio, sitting around the set at Dr. Jameson's house as part of the first TV generation, laughing my ass off, I'd always wanted to do television.

The Garabedian TV set finally arrived in 1952. My parents stuck it down in the basement playroom and that's pretty much where I stationed myself for the next few years. Radio? It seemed dead, or was on the verge of extinction. By 1955 all the big name shows and talent had migrated to TV. The Lone Ranger, Jack Benny, Fred Allen, George Burns & Gracie Allen, Kate Smith, Betty White, Amos 'n Andy. Across America, those big console radios, like the Philco that sat in our living room, suddenly went quiet.

Radio required a visionary to save it and it found one in Todd Storz. In 1953 Storz had inherited KOWH, an Omaha radio station whose ratings, like most stations in the new television age, had gone into the toilet. A couple of years later he was clobbering the competition using a song-playing formula he'd developed by paying close attention to what people actually wanted to hear. It was called "Top 40."

"While in the Army during the Second World War, I became convinced that people demand their favorites over and over," he explained in a 1957 interview in *Television Magazine*. "I remember vividly what used to happen in restaurants here in the States. The customers would throw their nickels into the jukebox and play the same big hits over and over."

Storz's idea was simple: Play the most popular songs of the day over and over and people will tune in. Mix in some station jingles and energetic deejays, and voilà, Top 40 radio was born! What began in Omaha, Nebraska, literally became the framework for the rock 'n' roll era. Top 40 transformed radio and saved its ass.

It certainly brought me back to it. My own introduction to Top 40 came when I was thirteen. Like most summer days I had plans with my best friend, Evan Caracostas, who lived just a few houses up Ledgewood Road from our house in Weston. I'd met him shortly after we moved there. I had gone exploring in our backwoods and came across a winding dirt path that ran behind our house. About a half mile away was a summer day camp bustling with teenage girls. I didn't want to be seen, so I followed the path past the campus and up this small hill where I came upon a kid about my age peering down through an outlook.

"Hi," he said looking up at me with a warm smile. Then he stuck out a hand. "My name is Evan."

"I'm John," I replied. I looked at him and then down at the camp. "What are you doing?"

Evan pointed. "If you look closely," he said turning his gaze back at the scene, "you can see through that window the girls putting on their bathing suits."

From that day forward, Evan and I became best friends and we hung out every chance we could. But executing plans with Evan was never easy. His Greek dad was a slave driver and always had some list of chores for him to do. That hot July day was no different. As I rode my bike to meet him, I saw poor Evan sweating

Evan Caracostas. With him being Greek and me being Armenian, Evan and I resembled each other enough that people always asked us if we were brothers. I was best man at his wedding and we remain best friends today.

away, pulling weeds from the giant rock garden in front of his house. "Oh, boy," I blurted out to him. "How long is this going to take?"

Evan smiled and shrugged his shoulders. He always played it mellow. "It won't be much longer," he said. "Hang out 'til I'm done."

I took a seat on one of the boulders and that's when I noticed the radio Evan had sitting on the lawn. It was this beat-up looking thing, small with a bunch of scratches on the casing, and a bent antenna. To power it he'd run this long extension cord into the kitchen. I'm sure if his dad had seen it he would have ripped it out of the wall. Yet his old man, who was known to have, let's say, a robust extramarital life, was out for the day.

But it wasn't the radio that so much caught my attention as the sound that was pumping out of it. Evan had cranked up WCOP, Boston's first Top 40 station, and through that crappy little speaker came Elvis Presley's "Heartbreak Hotel." Then it was Bill Haley & His Comets' "Rock Around the Clock." Then there were the fast-talking DJs whose energy matched the music they played. It was unlike anything I'd ever heard. It wasn't so much that the music was foreign to me—but the whole package was new and different. When the DJs talked, they were in an echo chamber so it sounded like they were in this huge auditorium. This big, exciting, new world was being piped through Evan's cheesy little radio.

I finally asked Evan, "What station is this?"

He looked up, clutching a handful of weeds, chucked them in his wheelbarrow, and shrugged his shoulders again. "WCOP 1150," he said, arching his eyebrows. "You've never listened to it?"

I still watched television after that, but I wasn't spending every waking hour at my house glued to the set. I joke that the moment I heard Top 40, I graduated from TV to radio. Timing helped. It wasn't long before most of the Boston airwaves actually became dominated by Top 40 stations. Up and down the dial you'd go and Top 40 blasted away. Lots of it was the great foundation rock 'n' roll music that formed the basis for the "British Invasion," the music revolution that followed in the sixties.

Like when I was younger, I was also listening closely to the DJs. I studied them, tried to get a better understanding for their pacing and setup. Even the newsmen didn't escape my ears. My absolute favorite was WBZ's Streeter Stuart. That guy was awesome. He had this crisp, strong delivery that projected absolute authority. Henry Brock at WKBW in Buffalo was another. Both of them could make a reading from a telephone book sound vitally important.

Another favorite was a young DJ named Dave Maynard on WORL 950. Maynard was still a few years away from beginning his forty-one-year career at Boston's WBZ. He was just a young guy, barely twenty-five years old, who was really funny, knew his music, and radiated a special warmth and informality that made you feel like he was your best friend. He'd also have big-name guest singers on his program.

One rainy afternoon while waiting in the family Buick as my mother did her shopping in Wellesley Square, I tuned into WORL and heard him interview Paul Anka. He was fresh off his first hit, "Diana." What blew me away was that he was like me, fourteen years old. For a moment, I thought, man, that's what I need: to become a singer and have a hit song. But it wasn't long before I noticed that most singers only have one or two big hits ever and are doomed to have to sing those two songs over and over again for the rest of their lives as they fade into obscurity. That seemed like a lifetime jail sentence.

At night, I could pick up distant AM stations that came blasting from all over the country via skywave. The big ones like WINS 1010 in New York City, which featured Alan Freed (who coined the phrase "rock 'n' roll") and Murray the "K," and Buffalo's WKBW 1520 whose nighttime DJ, Dick Biondi, "The Wild Eye-talian," seemed to me like the energy center of the universe. Biondi was electric, always screaming and yelling. In between songs he'd blast away at his listeners, saying things like, "Somebody bring me some pizza! Where is my pizza?" Just a total wild man. His demise in Buffalo came after he complained loudly on the air that his program director was a jerk and proceeded to describe the program director's car, where he typically drove, and jokingly told listeners to throw rocks at it. That was the end of Dick Biondi at WKBW.

But for every larger-than-life Biondi out there, there were a thousand bland, boring guys on the air. Top 40 DJs in straitjackets who obediently read slogans printed out on three-by-five index cards and had no freedom to entertain or deliver any kind of entertainment. Listeners heard the time, weather, the name of the station, some stupid slogan, and a couple of songs. Oh, and commercials. That's it. No jokes, no gossip or fun. It isn't much different today. With music streaming services to compete with, like Pandora, Spotify, and Apple Beats, radio needs to offer something more than just songs to be "sticky" to compete and attract and hold a huge audience. Unlike music-streaming services that just play tunes, radio needs to sound compelling and fun so that people don't just "listen" to a station, they actually love a station. Great radio gives listeners reasons to be loyal. Outstanding stations attract fans, not just listeners.

Boston has always been a great radio market. In the late 1950s, there were a few DJs really worth listening to. One of them was Arnie Ginsburg.

One spring morning in 1956, I had just walked into Weston High School when another kid yelled, "Hey, John! Arnie Ginsburg mentioned Weston High

With only seventy-three kids in my graduating class, Weston High School was a close-knit place where everyone knew everyone. It's where I made my public DJ debut at age fourteen.

on his radio show last night." I looked at him sort of dumbfounded and then asked, "Who's Arnie Ginsburg?"

That night I went home and listened to his show on WBOS-AM, 1600. I could barely pick up the signal through the static, but what came through was electric.

Train whistles, bicycle horns, kazoos, they were all a part of Arnie's show—I felt like I was listening to a circus. The excitement of the program came through immediately with an opening jingle recorded by the 3-Ds, a local Boston group. "Gather 'round, everybody," the tune went, "'cause you're about to hear, the show that's gonna make you, smile from ear to ear. It's Arnie Ginsburg, on the Night Train show...at sixteen-hundred, on your radio."

And then there was his voice. It was weird, nasally, and high-pitched and Arnie often made fun of it by referring to himself as "Old Leather Lungs" or "Old Aching Adenoids, Arnie Ginsburg." That's what got him noticed. Even his name was an anomaly on the airwaves. Just the hint of something Jewish and non-WASPy was unheard of. But that's exactly what made Arnie stand out and be so appealing.

Virtually everybody listened to him. Arnie became popular first from 9:30–midnight on WBOS, and then from 8 to 10 p.m. on WMEX beginning in 1959 when competing DJ Joe Smith, another Boston DJ idol of mine, left for New York to join the record industry. For the next decade, Arnie became Boston's biggest, most influential DJ. Record companies beat down his door to get him to play their music because they knew that if a song got into Arnie's rotation, there was a good chance it would become a hit. It was Arnie who introduced the world to songs like "Monster Mash" by Bobby "Boris" Pickett and Bobby Vinton's "Roses are Red."

His biggest sponsor was the Adventure Car Hop on Route 1 in Saugus, which added to its menu the "Ginsburger." It was a burger served on a free 45 record. Arnie would do a live broadcast from the drive-in and on a good summer night two thousand people would turn out.

That kind of popularity flew in the face of WBOS' standing: a seedy AM operation that specialized in foreign language programming and low audience share. But at 9:30, right after the Bulgarian music show, the keys were turned over to Arnie.

I took religiously to listening to Arnie's show while continuing knee-deep growing my experimentations with electronics, video, and audio mixing. One thing my high school buddy John Reissner and I began fooling around with was a takeoff of a comedy record by Buchanan and Goodman. Dickie Goodman was one of the pioneers of what we now know as sampling. He put out novelty comedy records about Martian invasions featuring a fake newsman doing fake interviews with politicians. When a question was posed, the politicians' responses were familiar lines cut from popular hit songs. They were fast-paced and hilarious.

Reissner was the class brain and we got along great, especially because of his deliciously dry sense of humor. We came up with a concept called the "World News Roundup" and over a few days in the fall of '57, the two of us worked in my bedroom to make our parody recording. I had the deeper voice so we decided I'd be the newsman. There was no computer editing like today so we recorded the setups on my Revere tape recorder, then spliced in the song bits, inserting sections from 45s from another reel. After editing everything together with Scotch tape, we cut the final thing on an acetate disc using an acetate cutting lathe I'd acquired. We had what we thought was a drop-dead funny four-minute recording.

Arnie Ginsburg. I shot this portrait of him around 1967.

"How can we get this played on the radio?" John asked after we finished. Which one of us actually came up with the idea of bringing that recording to Arnie to play on his show is up for debate, but I remember that on a muggy late September day, we piled into John's family's green '55 Chevy and made the twenty-minute ride to the WBOS studios on Commonwealth Avenue across from Boston University. My visions were of a gleaming radio studio with modern furniture, paneled walls, and tall ceilings. And maybe it was spectacular about two decades before. But now it was a dump with raggedy carpets, dirty walls, and dinged up furniture.

We talked our way past the secretary and made our way into the studio where Arnie was doing show prep. He was almost thirty at the time, skinny, with a conservative haircut, big nose, and large black square glasses. There was a shy quality about him, but he was still warm and friendly. I couldn't believe that we were actually in the same room with the actual Arnie Ginsburg!

"What can I help you guys with?" he asked as he combed through a stack of records.

After first gushing over how much we liked his show, we then nervously presented the acetate to him. "It's kind of a comedy record," I explained. "We did the whole thing ourselves."

I passed the acetate to Arnie, who turned the disc over a few times and inspected it closely, as though it might start playing right there in his hands. "You really made this yourself?" he asked, revealing a smile. We both nodded. "Let's give it a listen."

John and I took a seat and looked on as Arnie watched the acetate spin around and around, playing out loud what the two of us had spent hours working like hell to complete. At first he was stone-faced and unemotional, but about thirty seconds in, Arnie laughed out loud. Then he laughed some more. When the thing was done, Arnie leaned back in his chair.

"You guys have something here," he said. "It's funny. Come back around ten tonight and we'll put it on the air."

John and I shot out of those studios with so much adrenalin we probably could have run back to Weston. Those next few hours felt like days. We had hoped that Arnie would like the record, had even dared to let ourselves dream a little that he might play it on his show. But a little bit of the insecurity in me had braced me for the worst and prepared for another scenario: that he wouldn't even see us or would hate what we'd put together.

"Can you believe it?" John kept saying on the drive home. "We are going to be on Arnie Ginsburg's show!" As soon as we got back to my house, we called everyone we knew and told them to listen.

I couldn't believe it was happening. Not even as we stepped back inside the studio that night and handed the acetate back over to Arnie. But then after introducing us as high school kids, and us shyly muttering something incoherently, that recording went out over the air and four of the most exciting minutes of my life rushed forward. I sat perfectly still, one of the few times in my life I can say I've done that, and listened as my voice was transmitted on the most popular radio show all over greater Boston. It was the first time I had actually spoken over the radio!

I replayed that idea over and over again in my head on the drive back home. Something we had made had actually been broadcast on the air. People sitting in their cars and living rooms had heard a production that we'd made in my bedroom out of nothing but some equipment and blank tape. Holy shit.

The next day at school, we were treated like celebrities. "Was that you on the radio?" we were constantly asked. "Were you really on Arnie Ginsburg's show?"

"Yeah," I said, as coolly as I could. "That was us."

That whole experience cinched it for me. I was certain about what I wanted to do with my life. My parents, on the other hand, had other ideas. 🔇

John Garabedian

7. Beginnings

Chicago Transit Authority, 1970

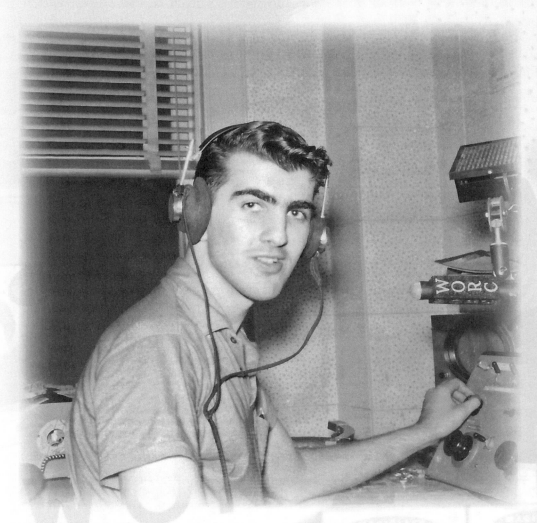

My first summer working at WORC as a seventeen-year-old, I was hired to host Saturday nights. Five decades later I still host radio on Saturday nights.

"Johnny," my mother said one Saturday morning, "your father and I would like to talk to you." I was sitting across from my parents at the kitchen table, in the middle of breakfast. Hardly a word had been said all morning. As he liked to do, my father focused his eyes on the newspaper, scouring the ads to see what kind of deals the competing furniture stores were offering. Between a few huffs and the occasional "How are they going to do that?" he looked at his half-eaten eggs, pushed them around a little, then went back to reading.

Outside of a few bites of toast, my mother had hardly touched her food. She looked anxious. A couple of long breaths here, a circling of the room with her eyes there, she didn't have to say a word. I knew exactly what was on her mind. I knew what was coming next. I pushed my plate toward the center of the table, leaned back from the table and waited.

The college talk was about to commence.

"Now it's not that we want you to do something you don't want to do," my mother said. "But we don't think you're taking this college idea seriously enough."

My father, who had finally put down his newspaper, was less diplomatic. "To get anywhere in life these days, you need a college degree. It's just that simple."

Only it wasn't. I had just started my senior year at Weston High School and I had no desire to go to college. I didn't get it. Why was college necessary to succeed in radio? And honestly, what could a liberal arts degree contribute to my life or career? School hadn't been so much a struggle for me as a bore. Slow and unexciting. Another four years of something like it seemed a waste of my time. I already knew what I wanted to do with my life. But trying to convince my parents that radio was where I was headed, that I didn't need a college degree to get there, was useless. God knows I'd tried. But my father just rolled his

When my mother became a grandmother in 1951 at age forty-nine, she had a formal portrait taken to memorialize that she was still glamorous.

eyes whenever I tried to counter their college talk, which, over the last few months, had become more frequent. "What the hell are you going to do in radio?" my father always asked. "What kind of living do you think you can make?"

I'd then counter that he hadn't gone to college and he seemed to be doing okay. But he wanted none of it. "Different times," he always said. "Today you need a degree to succeed. And besides you'll learn things in college and build relationships."

Much of the divide was generational. By the time I became a teenager both my parents were well into their fifties. They'd been born into a different era. Horse-drawn buggies had clogged the streets of the Cambridge my father grew up in. Electricity, the telephone, cars, these weren't things his parents or their neighbors had in their lives. My conservative father had come from a time when following the script was the only option.

My mother wasn't much different. Sure, she was generally my ally, but she had a traditional outlook on life as well. The thought of her son working away in a radio studio hardly excited her. She aimed high for me and had serious dreams of me becoming a lawyer or a doctor. To her, Harvard was the next logical step in my life. One time when she mentioned medical school as a possible route for me, I let out a laugh. "Why?" I said. "So I can look at people's butts all day?"

But she was stubborn. Back in Belmont she'd gone as far as to enroll me at Belmont Hill School, an elite private school, for my eighth grade year. I felt like a trained monkey. A jacket and tie were required every day and we had to attend chapel service first thing in the morning. Two hours of sports every afternoon was mandatory. And the homework was relentless, one to two hours every night for each subject. When my parents decided to move from Belmont to Weston in 1955, I was sad to say goodbye to my old neighborhood but happy that it meant my time at Belmont Hill was over. My father didn't want to pay for me to board at the school and my mother had no interest in driving me in every morning. Back to public school I went and I loved the idea.

My parents told me they'd match my money if I bought their idea of a "safe car." I wanted a hot looking '56 Ford convertible, but ended up with a boring (but "safe") '54 Buick Special. My next car would be different!

The other thing is, I'd come of age during a much more optimistic time than my parents. I believed there wasn't anything I couldn't do. Unlike my father, I felt I could do a number of different things—get into electronics, newspaper printing, be a photographer, work as a TV producer, or, of course, work in radio—and be happy. I felt like I had options. But I also knew I needed experience. I couldn't just run around telling people I was going to work in radio one day. I needed to actually do it.

So in early November of my senior year, I was sixteen and decided to try and get a job in radio. Hunkering down in my bedroom with the Revere tape recorder, I recorded a demo tape to present to radio station program directors. I read commercials, introduced songs, and summarized the news. I made twenty-five copies of the tape and then, with my mother's blessing, I took two days off from school to drive to every radio station within fifty miles of Weston and drop off copies of my tape. My car was a '54 Buick Special, and, man, I bet I put a good three hundred or four hundred miles on it. Worcester, Manchester, Boston, and Providence were all part of the itinerary.

My plan was simple. When I arrived in a city, I found a phone booth, grabbed a copy of the yellow pages and tore out the page listing "Radio Stations and Broadcasting Companies." Then I'd pay each of them a visit. News stations, classical stations, Top 40. It didn't matter. I just wanted a job in radio. If I was lucky I'd get a face-to-face with a program director. And sometimes they even asked me to fill out a job application. Many times, though, a dour looking secretary would reluctantly take my tape and say if anybody was interested they'd call me. In other words, *Thanks for the homemade demo, kid. Don't get your hopes up.* The rejections came often but with each one, easier to digest.

I was down to my last few tapes when, on a raw, rainy morning in late November, I walked into the Opera House in Milford, Massachusetts, and up a long wooden stairway into the offices of WMRC. Like so many of the small stations I'd ventured into, I'd never heard of it. It was small, transmitting with just a 250-watt transmitter and specializing in bland, middle-of-the-road music. Mitch Miller, Connie Francis, Andy Williams, Perry Como, Pat Boone—the boring stuff old white people gravitated toward. It was not a station intent on lighting the world on fire.

Then there were the studios. The old Opera House was a run-down, three-story wooden building where enough dirt had settled that it should have been charged rent. The station was the same way: dusty, with white acoustic paneling that had grayed over the years from all the grime. Not even the LP record albums had escaped the filth. They were stored in large wooden bins in the studio, and when you flipped through them you had to hold your breath because the records in the back always kicked out a fluttering of dust, which made you sneeze. Some hadn't been played in years.

"I'm here to see about any job openings," I told the secretary at the front desk, a friendly-looking woman with shoulder length brown hair and an easy smile. "Is the program director in?" I asked, showing my demo tape.

She looked me up and down for a second and then nodded her head. "He's on the air right now, but if you hold on a second, I'll ask if he wants to see you."

She disappeared from her narrow little office through a tall, wood door and then a few minutes later returned with a tall Irish-looking guy, about forty-five, with a sweep of brown hair. "Charlie McDermott," he said, sticking out his hand. He glanced at the demo tape. "I understand you're looking for a job. Come on in."

Charlie led me into the tiny studio where he was doing the midday show. I handed him my tape and took a seat. "Let's see what you sound like," he said, racking up the tape on a reel-to-reel tape machine that sat on a desk. I stared intently at the machine as it spun out my recording. He listened to about two minutes of it and only nodded here and there at certain points. When it concluded he spun around in his chair, back toward me.

"You're OK, and we actually may have something available." He grinned. "You ever do the news?"

"For two years I did the morning announcements in high school," I said. Damn, I thought, that sounded stupid. I was convinced I had just killed my job prospects, but Charlie only nodded again. He turned back toward the desk and unearthed a stack of papers from the news wire.

"Here," he said, handing me a sheet. "Go into the studio and when I give you the signal, read the news and weather."

The nerves finally kicked in. My hands were all clammy and this jolt of anxiety ran up and down my body. I waited for what seemed like hours for Charlie to give me the signal. When he finally did what poured out was this overly stiff and formal reading. I closed my eyes for a couple of seconds when I was done before getting up and heading back into the main studio.

Charlie looked up. "Not bad," he said. "I think you've got some real potential. What do your weekends look like?"

I swallowed hard. "They're pretty open," I said.

"Well, I don't know if it's anything you'd be interested in, but we've got Saturday and Sunday afternoons available," he said. "Not exactly prime hours, one to six, but they'd be your slots. What do you think?"

What did I think? I didn't have to spend a millisecond even considering it. "I'd love it," I said, sticking out a clammy hand to seal the deal. My first radio job. I didn't want to just run back to Weston. I wanted to carry my Buick back home. Even the pay wasn't horrible for 1959. A dollar an hour, plus an extra dollar for an hour of show prep.

But as much as I wanted to announce it to the world, I didn't. Outside of my parents and girlfriend—I still hadn't taken *that* kind of leap yet—I kept it under wraps. Truth is, I was afraid I was going to suck. And then get fired for sucking. How would I explain *that*? I didn't even tell Evan, my best friend. Not that it mattered. His weekends were still booked, too. His old man's pile of chores and hours working at Chimes Brownies, the family bakery in Roxbury, were never ending.

In some ways WMRC proved to be a perfect first radio job. The whole experience was trial by fire. My first day, my brain was on overload as Brian Dow, who came on just before me, walked me through how the studio worked. *Here's where you turn on the mike. Here's where you turn on the turntable. To cue it up, turn the volume pot back until it clicks.* Then there was the transmitter. To meet the FCC regulations I had to learn how to run the remote control that ran the transmitter and then log the meter readings every thirty minutes. That last part was a stupid carryover from the 1930s when transmitters were unstable and the chance for interference with other stations was a bigger issue. But those days were long gone and besides we were working with 250 watts. I mean, it had less power than a toaster. How much damage could it do?

I took in as much as I could but I soon just accepted the fact that, yeah, there would probably be some screw-ups. It helped that the guy I was replacing had been a drunk. The fact I didn't slur my words, play songs at the wrong speed, and have dead air were major victories. Sitting there, behind the big Gates control board and microphone, prepping my music, thinking about my intros, it all felt so natural. By the time I dropped the needle on the first song I ever played on a commercial station—Billy Williams' version of "I'm Going to Sit Right Down and Write Myself a Letter"—I was more than ready for the job.

Over that winter I grew into the position. Whatever WMRC could throw at me, I ran with it. I even began setting up and doing remotes for the station. In downtown Milford there was a club called The Crystal Room owned by "Boots" Mussulli, a jazz great who had played with Stan Kenton, Gene Krupa, Teddy Powell, and many of the big jazz stars of the big band era. Even in the 1950s his name still carried weight and it wasn't uncommon for performers like Dizzy Gillespie, Ella Fitzgerald, or Woody Herman to play the room. We often did live broadcasts of the Crystal Room shows and eventually they just began sending me down to set up the broadcasts. Running the cables, mixing the audio—it all had to come together fast. And for the most part, it did.

But I was also feeling more comfortable on the air. I sounded less stuffy and began telling jokes, trying to give my show a little of the flavor that I admired in guys like Arnie Ginsburg, Dave Maynard, Alan Freed, Joe Smith, and Dick Biondi. When people listened to their shows, they knew they were hearing something electric and unique; special. That's what I wanted to create. It was developing my voice and a relationship with the listener, my on-air persona. And that was no small thing for a tall, young Armenian introvert. Going on air, being charismatic and funny, it was intoxicating, like I'd broken out of a full-body cast and I could finally move around.

Which eventually made me learn I was an awful fit for WMRC. It was a conservative community station; perfectly happy to plot the boring, monotonous path it had set out for itself. I remember telling a joke on air once and then laughing at it. As soon as we went to commercial, Charlie McDermott burst into the studio. "What are you doing?" he said. I looked at the board and then around the room to see if I'd screwed up anything. "The laughing," he said. "We don't laugh here. That's not professional radio."

It was all I could do not to roll my eyes. "But they laugh on WBZ," I countered. "Don't people like to laugh?"

He had no interest in having a dialogue about it. "We're a more formal station," he said, then wheeled around and left the studio. It was ridiculous but not the kind of devastating blow to my still fragile confidence that it could have been. That's because the next day one of the ad sales guys came up to me as I was prepping my show. "Don't pay any attention to what they tell you," he said. "You're going places. You're the most talented guy here." I had just turned seventeen.

By that spring, after a winter of playing boring, shitty music and trying to temper my growing on-air personality, I needed a change. At home I was listening to all these other stations that weren't afraid to make a little noise to actually sound like they were having fun on the air. It frustrated the hell out of me to hear the kind of radio I admired and thought kicked ass, and yet not actually be able to do it.

This time, though, I had an actual air check on a real radio station to showcase myself. It meant missing more school, but my mother didn't object. I think she felt placated by the fact that I'd finally given in and said yes to giving college a try. Her thinking might have been that I just needed to get this radio thing out of my system a little more and then I could start thinking more seriously about medical or law school. That was never going to happen, but I agreed to give them a year. I'll see how I like it, I told them, and go from there. I applied to three schools: Emerson College in Boston, because it had a well-known communications school; Harvard just so I could tell my mother I'd given it a shot; and the University of Miami because it also had a reputation for a decent broadcasting program *and* Florida was some place that sounded exciting and different.

With copies of my new audition tape from a real radio station, I headed out to drop updated tapes at the major stations in Boston, Providence, and finally Worcester. The big station in Worcester was WTAG, a blue chip powerhouse owned by the *Worcester Telegram and Gazette*, which carried all the CBS network programs, including Arthur Godfrey, Lowell Thomas, Edward R. Murrow, and Walter Cronkite. I knew I was too young for such a stodgy place but felt it was worth a try. I then set my sights on a smaller place, WAAB, a Top 40 music station on Mechanic Street in downtown Worcester.

The program director, a guy named Paul Coss, had some time and invited me into the studio where we sat as he did his midday show. Just before going in, I'd sat in my car and listened to the station for a few minutes. It was the first time I'd ever really listened to Worcester radio and I was surprised at how good it was. WAAB was a slick, professional-sounding station, equal to anything you'd hear in Boston. They had great jingles, tight production, a friendly personality, and played all the big pop hits—exactly the opposite of WMRC.

Five months of actually being on the air had flushed the nerves right out of me for these kinds of sit-downs. In fact, because I had just finished reading Dale Carnegie's *How to Win Friends & Influence People*, I made a point of asking Paul questions about himself, his job, and the station. The Carnegie book taught that people like you if you get them talking about themselves.

When I complimented him on how good I thought WAAB sounded he was hopeful. "I've only been program director for a year," he said, "but we're starting to make some gains on those guys at WORC."

WORC? Who the hell was he talking about? I had memorized the list of the stations in Worcester and I'd never come across those call letters. They *must* be his big competition, I thought. I stuck around for another hour, but as soon as I felt it was okay to leave, I thanked him for his time, exited the building, found my car, and turned on the radio. It was just before noon as I slowly scanned the dial when all of a sudden—WHAM!—I hit 1310 and out leapt "Personality" by Lloyd Price. It was absolutely the loudest station on the radio. I had to turn the volume down just to be sure I didn't burn out my speakers. This was WORC!

It was just the beginning. When the song finished, this wacky little jingle came on. "Knock, knock. Don't phone, come right in and make yourself at home." Then this funky band came in and the song continued. "It's always open house at our house. There'll be plenty to eat, plenty to drink, drink as much as you want, but it'll come from the sink." I chuckled. Right after, in came the announcers, two of them, "Welcome in to the big all-afternoon Open House Party. The lines are open for your requests," then it jumped into "Hushabye" by the Mystics, with a "whoosh" cue-burn sound at the beginning.

On and on it went. The hits poured out, the energy was addicting, and in-between the songs the show's two hosts bantered and battled. They argued over what tunes to play, then yelled at the producer to see how many requests had come in for a certain hit. In the background you'd hear, "We got only five for that one," or "People keep asking for it." Sometimes even the producer jumped into the frenzy. "Why you gonna play that song? It sucked." I mean what radio station did stuff like this on-air?

It was a cool, sunny late March noontime as Worcester's downtown life buzzed around me; I leaned back in my seat and took it all in. The energy, the sound, the outrageousness—I immediately recognized that Boston stations I'd admired simply couldn't compete with the programming power and excitement of what 'ORC was doing. I loved it. It felt authentic, like I was actually listening to human beings instead of this fake, plastic formatted thing. While WMRC had banned laughing, the WORC DJs howled and hooted into the mike. Finally, after a good half hour I looked for a phone booth to find a telephone book and look up the station's address. It became pretty damn obvious why I'd overlooked their

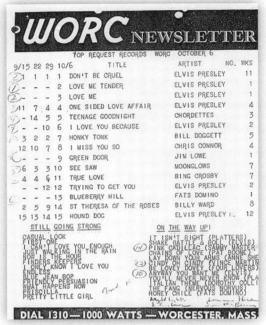

·WORC NEWSLETTER

TOP REQUEST RECORDS WORC OCTOBER 6

9/15	22	29	10/6	TITLE	ARTIST	NO. WKS
1	1	1	1	DON'T BE CRUEL	ELVIS PRESLEY	11
-	-	-	2	LOVE ME TENDER	ELVIS PRESLEY	1
-	-	-	3	LOVE ME	ELVIS PRESLEY	1
11	7	4	4	ONE SIDED LOVE AFFAIR	ELVIS PRESLEY	4
-	14	5	5	TEENAGE GOODNIGHT	CHORDETTES	3
-	-	10	6	I LOVE YOU BECAUSE	ELVIS PRESLEY	2
3	2	2	7	HONKY TONK	BILL DOGGETT	5
12	10	7	8	I MISS YOU SO	CHRIS CONNOR	4
-	-	-	9	GREEN DOOR	JIM LOWE	1
6	3	3	10	SEE SAW	MOONGLOWS	7
4	4	6	11	TRUE LOVE	BING CROSBY	7
-	-	12	12	TRYING TO GET YOU	ELVIS PRESLEY	2
-	-	-	13	BLUEBERRY HILL	FATS DOMINO	1
-	2	5	9	14	ST THERESA OF THE ROSES	BILLY WARD	8
15	13	14	15	HOUND DOG	ELVIS PRESLEY	12

STILL GOING STRONG

CASUAL LOOK
FIRST ONE
I CAN'T LOVE YOU ENOUGH
JUST WALKING IN THE RAIN
NOW IS THE HOUR
FINDERS KEEPERS
I ONLY KNOW I LOVE YOU
ENDLESS
BLUE JEAN BOP
FRIENDLY PERSUASION
WHAT HAPPENS NOW
PRISCILLA
PRETTY LITTLE GIRL

ON THE WAY UP!

IT ISN'T RIGHT (PLATTERS)
SHAKE RATTLE & ROLL (ELVIS)
PINK CADILLAC (SAMMY MASTER)
CHAINS OF LOVE (PAT BOONE)
LAY DOWN YOUR ARMS (ANNE SHE
CINDY OH CINDY (VINCE MARTIN
BE LOVEY DOVEY (FOUR LOVERS)
ANYWAY YOU WANT ME (ELVIS)
YOU'LL NEVER NEVER KNOW (PLA
ITALIAN THEME (DOROTHY COLL)
THE FANG (NERVOUS NORVUS)
HONEY CHILE (FATS DOMINO)

DIAL 1310 — 1000 WATTS — WORCESTER, MASS.

By 1960, the WORC weekly music survey became the most important influence in breaking hit music in America. Because it was an honest tabulation of actual requests from active radio listeners, it was a trusted barometer of song popularity.

listing. While every other station in the city had a display ad in big, bold type, WORC had only this tiny little one-line listing. It was like they didn't even care. Not that it affected the ratings. As WAAB managed to squeak out a five share, WORC had a twenty share. It owned Worcester.

But it wasn't just the sound that differentiated WORC. Even its offices packed a different flavor. The station was downtown across from Worcester Common in the grand old Bancroft Hotel on Franklin Street. The studios and offices were in converted guest rooms. You'd enter the magnificent lobby of the hotel, then hike up an elegant, wide staircase to the mezzanine, pass through a set of large double doors, then head down this long hallway to a tiny desk sitting in the middle of the hall. That tight little space was the domain of Lillian Brown, the station receptionist and the first WORC person I ever met. Unlike almost all the other station secretaries I had to deal with on my job search, Lillian was actually friendly. An older woman with thin hair in a weird bowl cut, she was just a jewel of a woman. "Diamond Lil" is what everyone called her. Behind her the studio thumped with sound. The music came right through the door.

My first introduction to the popularity of 'ORC came sitting in Lillian's "waiting room," right in the hallway. The main office phone lines were constantly ringing. Lillian could barely speak a full sentence without it clanging. Even though there was a dedicated request line—a totally unique thing for radio in those days—it was school vacation and loads of kids just rang up requests to the office number. Which meant those calls went straight to poor old Lillian. "Damn kids," she said, hanging up the phone after it had gone off during my second attempt to explain why I was there. After finally getting it out and weathering a few more calls, Lillian told me to sit tight. "The guy you need to talk to is Budd Clain," she said, then disappeared to find him.

Budd was the program director and a really great guy, maybe only twenty-three. Budd had worked at WORC since high school. He was also co-host of the WORC morning program called "The Early Birds." It wasn't just a cute name. There were actual canaries living at the station. The eight canary cages were in a small bathroom just off the main studio with a microphone hanging over them and a small clock radio so the birds could sing to whatever song was playing on the station. Budd, who'd probably explained the reason for the birds a thousand other times, didn't bother waiting for me to ask about them.

"When WORC's owner, Bob Bryar, was growing up in Chicago, he used to listen to this show called "The Hartz Mountain Canaries," he explained. "It was the number one morning show in Chicago, and they found out that women love hearing birds singing."

In Worcester those damn birds became as familiar a sound on the morning show as any Elvis record. The tweets went out over the air all morning while the music played. It was gimmicky, I suppose, but it added to the unique allure of the station. That WORC was innovative and didn't follow any rules, or at least any of the rules the conservative managers of most stations followed, was exhilarating. Plus, WORC blasted out at 5,000 watts. That was a big-city blowtorch compared to 250 watt WMRC in little Milford where I worked.

The station's success was only recent. It had first gone on the air in 1925 but, like so much of radio, had fallen on hard times in the early 1950s with the advent of television. WORC fell to the point where it was ranked number five in the ratings in a city that only had four radio stations. Even Boston's WBZ pulled in more Worcester listeners. And that's how, in 1955, Bob Bryar and his wife Shirley Palmer, scooped it up for $100,000.

Both Bob and Shirley were veterans of New York City radio. Shirley, a vivacious blonde with a deep voice, had had her own daily talk show on New York's WOR; Bob had been a staff announcer at WHN, the voice of the New York Rangers, and a TV pitchman. With two partners they put together the money to

John Garabedian

buy 'ORC. Since neither one of them liked to get up early, Bob and Shirley set themselves up to do the afternoon show together.

At first they didn't stray too far from the script and just continued to play the corny popular music of the day. "How Much Is That Doggie in the Window" by Patti Page, "Sixteen Tons" by Tennessee Ernie Ford, "Mr. Sandman" by the Chordettes, bland pop stuff. Just to see if people were actually listening

Unlike any other radio station in the United States, WORC employed paid request operators to tabulate the most popular songs from the always-ringing request lines ("Call SWift 9-0585.") Requests were written on large squares of paper so they could be easily sorted and filed.

to the station, one afternoon Bob and Shirley rolled out a small promotion. *Be the first person to call and we'll give you a silver dollar.* Nobody called. After trying a few more times, somebody phoned in and asked to hear Bill Haley's "Rock Around Clock." Even though it was an "extreme" rock 'n' roll song they normally wouldn't play, Bob and Shirley went for it. Then a few minutes later, another call came in asking for another rock tune. Within days things exploded.

For Bob it was a revelation: The more rock 'n' roll they played, the more requests they received. And most of those calls came from high school and college kids. They didn't want their parents' music. They connected to rock 'n' roll and 'ORC was the only Worcester station playing it. Word quickly spread and it wasn't long before the place became a teen-age hangout.

Bob and Shirley even began using some of them as regular volunteers to man the request line. Because WORC was confined to those hotel rooms, it became natural to put the request operators in the record library adjoining the main studio. You couldn't visit 'ORC without at least checking out the record library. It was enormous, nothing but floor-to-ceiling shelves packed with records. Since the station had first gone on air in 1925, everything had been catalogued and not a single record had ever been thrown out. Shelves of 78

John Garabedian

RPM records sat next to albums which sat next to even more shelves of newer 45s. You could find almost anything. That forgotten Sinatra song from '42? It was there. Right across the room from the newest Elvis single. One day in 1955, not long after Bob and Shirley started taking song requests, one of the interns shuffling through the library found this red 78 record by Benny Strong and the Orchestra called "Open House." Bob played it once and fell in love with the tune. So much so that the opening stanza of it became the theme song and name for 'ORC's new afternoon show: *Open House Party*.

By the late 1950s, the whole 'ORC scene exploded. It became so crazy they decided to hire paid phone operators to manage the request line because the kids were unreliable and some were stealing 45s from the station. The request operators would write down the song names along with a dedication and put them in a pile. Then a DJ would pick up the stack and sort them alphabetically into stacks on three long tables in the studio. Songs that received the most requests with the biggest piles were most played. Soon *Open House Party* was receiving over a thousand requests every afternoon. The overflow was sorted into piles on the floor.

Listeners completely drove the music, not the program or music director, not record sales, and certainly not the *Billboard* and *Cash Box* national magazine charts. *Open House Party* made WORC into the world's first interactive radio station and it was unbeatable. The ratings soared. Nationally, WORC became a leader as the most influential predictor of American hit music and dozens of now-classic hit songs got their breakout because of WORC's request lines.

Budd explained a little of this as he walked me through the station. The whole place pulsed with energy and I was drooling at the chance to work there, but there weren't any openings. I felt so disappointed. Here was a station that did the kind of radio that was so alive, so in tune with the audience. It was the most exciting thing in radio I had ever seen, and yet I couldn't be a part of it. Budd could see my disappointment. He smiled. "You know, we might need a summer replacement," he said. "Leave your tape and I'll keep it on file."

Knowing that a station like 'ORC even existed, made it that much harder to go back to Milford. Playing boring music, confined to reading liner cards and slogans—I hated every second of it. Days became weeks and nothing changed.

Then, one late spring weekday evening I was just hanging out at the station with the night DJ when I got a call from my mother. A "nice man" named Budd from a Worcester radio station had called and was looking for me, she said. I couldn't get off the phone fast enough to call him back.

"That opening came up," Budd said. "It's for the summer. If you're interested in applying, make a new demo tape I can play for Bob Bryar and drop it off."

I had one done in a day and then drove it out to 'ORC to leave it with Lillian to hand off to Budd, who had already gone home. I waited a good week to hear back. Nothing. I thought about calling him up, but what was that going to do? He'd say he hadn't listened to it yet, or worse, had decided to go with someone else. Yeah, we'd met, but really, he didn't know who the hell I was. The best option, I told myself, was to go back to Worcester and meet with him in person again. Maybe it would backfire, or maybe it would make all the difference in the world.

That next day, a soggy May morning, I returned to 'ORC. I wanted to catch Budd just as he was getting off the air. Budd was surprised but not annoyed to see me. "Yeah, Bob and I listened to your tape," he said. "It's okay. You're still young. You need some work. And truth is, we had fifty other applicants. But we haven't made a decision yet and I'll have to get back to you."

I could have left, could have let the situation take shape in a way that was out of my control, but I'd never felt so determined to get something in my life. Then came my opening: Budd mentioned to Lillian that his wife had the car and he had to take the bus home. "Let me give you a ride home," I offered. "I'm in no rush. My car is just out front."

Budd was a bit taken aback by the offer and at first refused, but then looked out the window at the rain. It was a total downpour. "Okay," he said.

Life sometimes affords lessons in unexpected situations. For so long I'd been shy with people, afraid of intruding on them or being rejected. Standing there with Budd, sensing my one shot at working at 'ORC was slipping away, I decided to take control, to try and steer my own fate and not leave it in the hands of others or chance. If I wanted to work at 'ORC, I needed to go for it. I may have been shy but I also knew that I was likable once people spent a little time with me. By the time I'd pulled up in front of his house, Budd was laughing out loud at the ridiculousness of WMRC. "They told you couldn't laugh on the air?" he said. "Jesus! That's the problem with these little stations. The people running them have no imagination. You've gotta be willing to experiment." As rain pelted my Buick, Budd said, "Do you want to come in?"

Budd's house was this little Cape style in a tree-lined neighborhood in North Worcester. He shared it with his young wife Brenda, a hot little redhead who had worked on the request lines when he met her. She wasn't around so the two of us sat in his living room, sipped on a couple of Cokes, and I continued asking him questions about himself and radio. We chatted for a good hour, and the entire time I wanted to pump Budd for some clarity. *Why did he invite me in? Did I have the job or was he just being friendly?* But I was afraid of offending him by coming across as aggressive. I'd come this far, and now with the finish line in sight, I was about to pull up. I was getting ready to go, when Budd took a final swig of his Coke, stood up and extended his hand. "Hey, John," he said. "Let's give you a shot. Why don't you come in Sunday night and do the show. See what you can do. If Bob thinks you're reasonably good, the job is yours."

The only thing better than hearing that I'd landed a chance at WORC was giving my notice at my old station. I was out of the woods. Ready for the big time. The big city. Five thousand fucking watts and the chance to play real rock 'n' roll!

I nailed that Sunday night audition and that summer I spent more time at the station than anywhere else. 'ORC was like a big clubhouse for young people—practically everyone who worked there was between eighteen and twenty-five years old. I'd hang out in the studio while somebody was on air, and then a carload of us would go out afterward either to Leicester for a bite at Hot Dog Annie's Silver Grill or the New Yorker diner on Route 20 in Oxford.

Being on air was something else entirely. The station was alive. It wasn't this typical tightly-formatted machine where you played two songs, read a liner card, promoted something, then moved on to the next tune. The DJs picked the music based on the requests coming in during that time period. At 'ORC they encouraged you to innovate and entertain the listeners. It was electric, quick, fast—listeners kept the station on because they were afraid they might miss something. Maybe it was hearing a friend being put on the air—'ORC started airing telephone calls a decade before any other station—or it might be a hilarious slip-up, because there was no seven-second delay. If someone said "shit" or "fuck"—and invariably someone did—out it went. This being Worcester, though, nobody ever complained. Before every song, the DJ would read a stack of dedications. But whoever was on air had to pay attention or they'd read a bogus name with double-entendre meaning, like "Dick Hertz from Holden" or "Mike Hunt" would go out over the air. Budd made a point of warning me about that.

"Just be sure you're looking over the name before you say it," he said. "Our listeners will keep you on your toes."

The station's spirit, this constant push to be creative and spontaneous came straight from the top. From Bob Bryar. Bob was an unlikely looking radio revolutionary. With his standard white shirt, dark tie and blue sports coat, he looked more like the company man than out-of-the-box thinker. He was short, a bit stocky, with a sweep of dark, black hair parted in the middle. A certain anxiousness defined his personality. I'm not sure I ever saw him eat a meal. He subsisted on caffeine and nicotine. A typical day saw him down, no exaggeration, seven or eight cups of coffee and at least eight packs of King Sano cigarettes. He frequently had two butts going at the same time, one in the ashtray he'd forgotten about and a new one pinched between his pointy finger and thumb as though he was trying to sneak in a couple of drags. During *Open House Party* he'd whip through a good five or six packs easily. The studio smelled like an old ashtray.

By the time I arrived at 'ORC, the Bob and Shirley team had long broken up. Behind Bob's back, Shirley had started screwing the show's young engineer, Mel Miller. Then one day, Shirley said she had to go shopping and never came back. She and Mel ran off together and started a new life in Hawaii, working the morning show at KPOI in Honolulu. But that didn't slow down the radioman in

After co-hosts Mel Miller and Bob Bryar's cheating wife Shirley skipped town and took their secret love affair to Honolulu, Bob (left) replaced them with Dick Smith (right) and nineteen-year-old request operator Patty Drake (middle), who soon had Bob's baby.

Bob. He replaced Mel's *Open House* co-host duties with Dick Smith, who'd been doing the night show, then turned his eyes on a 19-year-old, drop-dead gorgeous redhead who'd been working the request line (and Bob).

Even at a station like 'ORC, where there were a lot of good-looking girls hanging around, Patty Drake stood out. She was tall and voluptuous with a curvy body, long red hair, and this breathy voice that was like Ginger on *Gilligan's Island*. How much real radio talent she had was up for debate. But Patty was sexy and hot and had the power to woo any man, including Bob, who began sleeping with her. Soon he named her the third co-host of *Open House Party*. Right before I arrived in the summer of 1959, she had gone off the air to have Bob's baby.

Most of what I learned about radio, I learned at 'ORC. And nearly everything I learned at 'ORC I learned from the fertile soil created and nurtured by

Bob Bryar. He was supportive and always encouraged innovation and creativity. Trying new things out meant making mistakes. If you did something new and it didn't work, or you just screwed up, Bob would pat you on the back, and say, "You're not going to put us out of business. Don't worry about it." There was such freedom in that.

Bob's own innovation was more accidental than anything. He usually did the right thing but for the wrong reason. Like playing that Bill Haley record for the first time, great ideas often found him. He liked to take chances and if he saw something succeeded, he ran with it, even if it flew in the face of convention. He was a maniac for listener participation. He didn't give a crap if it didn't follow broadcasting convention. "Put the request callers on the air," he insisted. In those days radio stations *never* put telephone calls on the air because it was not considered "professional broadcast quality." But, 'ORC did.

Every hour of the day, during any show you'd hear a DJ talking to a listener gabbing away about a song they wanted to hear or a person they wanted to send out a request to. On *Open House Party*, to keep people listening, Bob packed in contests every half hour, "forced listening" contests which made listeners stay tuned longer. The big emphasis was on "audience participation." "Rate the Record," "Album of the Hour," "Secret Sound," "Musical Math," "The Mystery Voice," and "Who Sings It?" were a few of them. He'd play a popular song and then give out a prize to the first caller who could name the singer. People ate it up and all the phone lines were constantly ringing. Most important, they kept the spirit and energy up and increased the time spent listening.

Bob also was a great mentor. The fact that so many young people liked to hang out at the station wasn't just because 'ORC played Elvis, Chuck Berry, or the Beatles. He loved the spirit they brought to the place. They gave it energy. Yeah, a good thirty years separated us, but the two of us just clicked. We never spoke about it but by the time he invested in teaching me, I knew he saw talent and potential in me. That like him, I was passionate about radio. He saw what it meant to me. That I wasn't just at 'ORC because I needed a job. I was there because I loved the culture he'd created and the programming, which had built a huge fan base and incredible ratings.

John Garabedian

It wasn't unusual for me to finish my night show at 1 a.m., and then head over to Bob's house afterwards. He was always up, smoking his King Sanos, listening to the station. He might offer some gentle critiques of my show, then we'd talk radio and programming until four in the morning. He'd tell me about his old life working in New York radio and TV, recalling stories about events and some of the famous people he'd met and worked with. He knew the better he made me, the more successful WORC would be, and his confidence in me only pushed the confidence I had in myself. I had my own stage. A place to be funny. A place to make jokes. A place to interact with listeners and create and deliver great radio. It was the summer of '59, I was seventeen, and I unleashed myself on my show.

A big change I made after arriving at WORC had to do with my last name. Those were the days where everyone in show business had a marketable, fake white, Anglo-Saxon "nom de plume," or stage name. At a little place like WMRC I hadn't paid much attention to how ethnic "Garabedian" sounded. But at a bigger station, playing to a larger audience, I worried that it might be a turnoff. It's not like anyone came to me and suggested I make the change. I just wanted to make sure I fit in and have something that sounded more glamorous and star-like.

I spent days thinking about different options and eventually landed on the name of a city in North Worcester County, Gardner. But I couldn't use John Gardner. That sounded like somebody from the 1800s, not some fun-loving Top 40 DJ. Then I thought: What about Johnny Gardner? It kind of rolled off the tongue. And that remained my on-air name for the next ten years.

The whole thing—the scene at 'ORC, the aura and life around it—felt like another planet compared to stuffy old Weston. For the first time in my life, I was out from under the routine of being a high school kid. I came home when I wanted to. Worked hard. And partied just as hard.

Which is why it felt so difficult to say goodbye to WORC. In late August I broadcast my last show. I'd promised my parents I'd give college a try. Harvard had turned me down and Emerson College felt too close to home. I wanted a change. So the University of Miami became the choice. Screw it, I thought, if my parents want me to go to college, I might as well try some place different. That Sunday night, as I prepped for my final broadcast at the station, Budd Clain came by with a couple other friends. I guess it was hard not to notice how much I didn't want to leave.

"Johnny," he said, "just remember: You've always got a family here at 'ORC."

Little did I know just how prophetic that would turn out to be. 🔇

8. Miami

Will Smith, 1997

For Thanksgiving, 1959, my mother and sister Jackie brought my car to me in Miami. They treated me to an elegant turkey dinner at the legendary Fontainebleau Hotel in Miami Beach.

never particularly wanted to leave Boston. Just felt like I had to. That I needed to try some place different. I mean, I was seventeen years old and had spent my entire life in Boston. I wanted to leave the nest and get away from home. My idea of driving to Miami so I could have my car got turned down, but they insisted it was a temporary thing.

"You take that car and you'll just be too distracted," my father said. "You're not there to have a good time. You're there to learn something. If you do well, we'll bring you your car around Thanksgiving." Not even my mother would side with me.

This being a more formal era, she insisted I wear a jacket and tie for the plane trip down. I let her have her way on this, but, boy, did I come to regret it. When we landed in Miami that September afternoon it was scorching hot, close to a hundred degrees with humidity a good ninety percent. Things were made even worse by the fact that I had on a wool jacket, white shirt, and necktie. I got off that airplane and it was like being slammed head first into a brick wall. Off came the jacket and tie, but my shirt was already soaked.

The seeds of a lifelong dislike for Florida had been planted.

Back then, before it developed any clout as an elite athletic school, the University of Miami was a smaller institution. The campus had a heavy Florida feel to it. Lots of palm trees, and the buildings were very plain with a design plagued by an obsession with stucco. My dorm building at 1237 Walsh Avenue was one of dozens of converted World War II barracks with no air conditioning. Each one of the two-story buildings contained six apartments shared by six guys, with three bedrooms.

My parents later accused me of not giving school a shot, but that's not true. I'd gone there with the intent of being excited. It was the first time I'd ever been on my

My first long-term relationship lasted three years and began on a blind date with Carol Ann Crenshaw, a descendant of President Tyler, a John Robert Powers model, and a size 36D. Then I met Joe.

own and staking out my independence felt important to me. While I didn't have my car, I still managed to have a good time. I met a beautiful sweet girl, Jackie, a blonde from Hollywood, Florida. She loved the beaches and showing me around. Every chance we got we'd go up to Fort Lauderdale or Miami Beach and enjoy the scene.

My roommates were awesome and we became great buddies. One of them, a kid from Palm Beach named Robert, owned a huge 1940 Rolls Royce convertible. We'd all pile into it and cruise up Route A1A and over the causeway to Miami Beach, attracting attention because the old beast was in desperate need of a muffler. Although I didn't enjoy alcohol and was still only seventeen, I was the tall one and looked the oldest, so they always nominated me to buy the beer. We'd head to the beach, stay up late, and lie on the sand under the palm trees as we watched the stars and surf. Jackie and I enjoyed some memorable nights under the Miami moon.

The school itself was a different matter. Besides the beach and the partying, I was there to study broadcasting. One of the broadcasting program's big claims to fame was that Frank Stanton, a retired famous old radio announcer and the voice of Lucky Strike cigarettes in the 1940s, was one of its professors.

Unfortunately Stanton and the rest of the school hadn't caught up with modern radio. While Top 40 had taken over the country during the previous five years, at Miami it was like I'd traveled back in time to 1940. We dissected radio dramas like *The Shadow* and *Lights Out*, got behind the mike to hone our announcing, and rehearsed making different sound effects. It was so obsolete!

I'd sit in the back of the classroom and think, "This is stupid. Is this what I'm going to spend four years of my life studying? Am I really going to be a total failure if I don't get my degree in *this*?" It was such bullshit. But I was clearly in the minority. All around me were plenty of students who were like penguins, just nodding their heads and accepting what was being dished out to them. If I was going to last in Miami I needed to find a job in radio.

My sister Jacqueline with her baby Phillip. He served in the U.S. Navy before attending Rutgers Law School to earn his law degree. Phillip was heading home from a dinner celebrating his new job at a law firm when he was killed on the New Jersey Turnpike. He had just turned thirty.

My mother and sister Jackie came to visit me in late November for Thanksgiving. It was nice to see them. But it was even better to see my 1954 Buick Special, which they'd driven down for me.

Having wheels again was an awesome change. Every chance I could I got off campus. We hit the beach even more, stumbling home at who knows what hour in the morning and then just barely making it to class a few hours later. Maybe my parents knew me better than I thought. But I also used that car to do a sweep of the city's radio stations, hauling in my demo tape and doing my best to charm every program director I came in contact with. I covered every station in Miami, Miami Beach, and Fort Lauderdale. The responses were all the same: *We'll be in touch if we have anything.*

A couple of weeks of hard work finally paid off when I got hired by WAFM, a brand new 20,000-watt Miami classical music FM station. It was only a year old and had very little money behind it. The studio was right in downtown Miami, in a tall art deco office building, and was run by a pair of optimistic middle-aged guys whose hopes were not dampened by the fact that they still had to pump their own money into the operation to keep it afloat.

Unfortunately, the station didn't have any money to pay me. But they did have a seven-to-midnight shift they were desperate to fill, and I was willing to

At seventeen, I took the eight hour FCC exam at the Miami field office to get my First Class Radiotelephone engineering license.

take anything that came my way. At least it would add something to my resume. I didn't know much about classical music, but they didn't care. The side benefit was that because I played long classical pieces, I could do my homework studies during my shift.

I can't pretend I was good at announcing classical music. In fact, I was pretty dreadful. The few listeners that WAFM claimed were avid classical fans, many of whom were unforgiving elitist snobs and music aficionados. Every single time I mangled the name of a composer or conductor they phoned the station to complain. And they called often: *Please tell the announcer it's pronounced "Shoss-ta-KO-vich."*

The more I worked at the station and the more I continued studying subjects which I saw no value in, the more I felt I was missing out on accomplishing something with my life. In Boston my buddies and I would hop in a car and in a few hours be in New York City, the mountains of New Hampshire, or the beaches of Cape Cod. You couldn't do that in Miami because it was hundreds of miles from anything. It was just the city and the swamps. Back then, even Palm Beach and Orlando were sparsely populated farmland.

My grades weren't helping. I was bored. English literature, history—I'd studied that stuff already in high school. Now it felt like I was in the thirteenth grade. But physics was my real downfall. I was always really good in science. During orientation I had done so well in placement tests I'd qualified for advanced junior level physics. In the class, though, the material flew right over my head. To just do okay I needed to know calculus and had never studied it.

Everything was made worse at the realization of how much I loved Boston and missed my friends and familiar haunts. During Christmas vacation I seriously started tossing around in my head the idea of quitting school. Finals loomed at the end of January and I had a choice. I was getting a D in physics and figured that the big test would sink me. I could either take it and keep the college charade going or just skip finals completely and not give my parents an excuse to pressure me back to Miami. Make a decision, move on, and deal with the consequences, whatever they might be.

God knows I certainly wasn't going to invite my parents into the debate, or even give them a hint of what I was thinking. But I did feel comfortable talking it over with my sister Doris and her husband, Jack Carlson. Home for Christmas vacation, I had dinner at their home in Weston. As I munched away at a plate of roast beef, green beans, and potatoes I explained my frustration with school. How I was restless. How I felt like I was wasting my life and just postponing my real life and career in radio.

"I don't even know what I'm doing there," I said, stabbing a piece of meat with my fork. "It's not like I'm studying to be a doctor or a lawyer. I'm studying liberal arts with a broadcasting major. I want to be a disc jockey and grow in the radio business. School is just getting in the way of me actually getting to work and building my career."

Jack patiently listened. From the time Doris started dating him in college, Jack was someone I respected. He was always calm, reasoned, and empathetic. His family owned a large construction business and a few years after graduating Harvard, Jack had taken it over from his father. He became a mentor to me.

"Are you sure you're not giving up on things a little prematurely?" Jack asked, after letting me whip through my diatribe.

I stabbed a couple more bites with my fork and then looked up at him. "But I already know what I want to do!" I said. "I'm not learning anything there that is going to help my career."

Doris stayed out of it. She watched me grow up and knew there was no use in trying to convince me to change my mind. The best course: Try and change topics. "Who'd like some apple pie?" she asked.

◀

Miami was simply gorgeous when my plane landed at Miami International airport in early January. Boston was in the middle of a deep freeze when I

John Garabedian

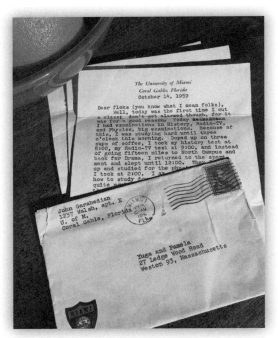

Yuga and Pam were the names of the family Pomeranian and Afghan Hound dogs. Letters to mom and dad were a sugar-coated way of getting spending money. For that reason I wrote frequently.

left—ice bound with a couple of feet of crusty snow on the ground. Compared to Miami's crystal blue sky and hot sun, the contrast couldn't have been more striking.

But the beaches and night life was about all Miami had going for it. I despised the heat. Going home at Christmas hadn't helped at all. Living in Miami did only one solid thing for me: It confirmed that I was a Boston boy, a real New Englander who liked the changing of the seasons, thrived on the personality and edginess that came with living in the northeast. Miami? It was dull, flabby, and rundown. As I returned to my dorm, my heart sank. Not a single part of me wanted to be there. It looked like something from my past.

In my dorm room I dropped my bag on the ground and sat on my bed. My roommates were out and in the silence I could hear the faint sounds of "El Paso" by Marty Robbins wafting in the open window from a radio in the apartment next door. I looked up at the calendar. Finals were coming. They hung over me the next few weeks, until finally I decided I was done. No more of Stanton's irrelevant classes. No more boring English lit. I wasn't going to stick around and waste three-and-a-half more years of my life going through the motions to satisfy my parents' well-intentioned ideals. I was going to return home to Boston and get to work in the field that I loved. Just making that decision was liberating. I felt light.

Over the next day I said goodbye to most of my friends. Then on a warm Tuesday evening I packed my car full and turned in early, about 8:30. My plan was to leave at four in the morning and barnstorm up the coast.

But friends kept streaming into my room like a parade, one right after the other, waking me up. *I heard you were leaving buddy. Sorry to hear that. Good luck with everything.* By ten that night I'd gotten sick of it. Every time I tried to go to sleep someone would come in to say goodbye. *Screw it,* I thought, *I'll just leave now.* Fifteen minutes later I was on the road, blazing up Route 1 toward Boston. About three hundred miles north in Jacksonville, just before dawn, I pulled in to a truck stop for gas and bought a big bag of fresh oranges. They were sweet and yummy, the only things I ate that entire drive home. The oranges and a scattering of Top 40 radio were my diet. I carried WQAM from Miami to Jacksonville, then picked up WKBW from Buffalo, WLS from Chicago, WABC from New York City, then finally WBZ, Boston, before the sun came up and the skywave signals went to sleep for the day.

As I hit Connecticut early Friday morning the snow was coming down pretty hard, and by Hartford the roads had become extremely icy. Visibility was tough but my old tires were the biggest problem. They were practically bald. I skidded all over the road. I should have pulled over, but I was completely exhausted after almost thirty hours driving with no sleep and I was too determined to get home.

My parents never saw it coming. At around seven that Friday morning the sun was just coming up as I pulled my Buick into our driveway. I parked right in front of the house and looked into the kitchen window to see my parents looking out in full shock at my appearance. Then they got a better sight of me. My hair was a mess. My shirt was covered with orange juice stains. I smelled and looked terrible. Mustering as much enthusiasm as I could as they opened the front door I stumbled into the house. "Good morning!" I exclaimed with a wide grin as the two stared at me.

"What are you doing here?" My father asked, his eyes growing large.

"I've decided to take some time off from school."

God, did it feel good to be back home. 🔇

John Garabedian

9. Make Your Own Kind of Music

Mamas & Papas, 1969

Lovable WORC receptionist Lillian Brown. She always reminded me of actress Marian Lorne who played Aunt Clara on "Bewitched."

If my parents were pissed about my reneging on my commitment to stick out college for a year, they didn't show it. To my mother I was still her darling son Johnny. She did my laundry, made my bed, cooked my meals. But unlike before, I had total freedom to do what I wanted. I relished being back in Boston, back in New England, back with my buddies, like Evan. We partied most nights, hanging out with our girlfriends and driving around, not getting home until 3 or 4 a.m. I'd do my best to get quietly back into the house, but the squeaky front door always awoke my father, who was a total insomniac. "That you, John?" he'd growl from his bed as I tiptoed down to my room. "No, it's the burglar," I'd usually answer.

A few hours later, at breakfast, he'd grumble something at me about how I should get home earlier. *What in the world could you possibly be doing at those hours?* Then my mother, always image-conscious, would come in from the other side. "What do you think the neighbors think, you being out so late?" she always asked.

My response was always the same. "Why do I care what the neighbors think?" I'd say through a fog of fatigue. "I'm not robbing banks or breaking into houses! Besides, what are they doing up at 3 a.m.?"

Not much had changed in Weston since I'd left for school nearly five months before. The breadwinner husbands still went into Boston to work every morning. The stay-at-home moms remained tethered to their vacuum cleaners and ironing boards. Suburbia rolled along just as content and placid as it always had.

Radio was a different story and the changes were revolutionary. That year had seen rock 'n' roll music get a clubbing. Elvis had been drafted into the U.S. Army; Jerry Lee Lewis's career ended quickly in scandal after he not-so-secretly married his thirteen-year-old-cousin; and Buddy Holly, Richie Valens, and the Big Bopper were killed in an airplane accident. It really was "Bye Bye Miss American Pie."

The most striking event was that during the previous fall, 1959, when Congress launched an investigation into "radio payola." Rock 'n' roll music was not understood or appreciated by people over thirty, just like rap and hip hop wasn't in the early 2000s. When a few congressmen learned that record companies were actually paying thousands of dollars to get deejays to have songs played over the public airwaves, the Congressional Payola Investigations were launched. The revelations in those hearings resulted in numerous firings around the country, including Alan Freed, the father of rock 'n' roll. Even Dick Clark narrowly missed conviction under the bribery statutes by selling his interest in a record company and then cooperating with the investigators.

The problem with "pay-to-play" was that of the top forty songs on the national charts, maybe ten or fifteen were truly smash hits. The rest were mostly junk but, backed by a few crisp hundred dollar bills, they received just as much airplay as the good stuff. To the conservative white-haired congressmen who were leading the investigation, the scandal also explained the popularity of all this devil music. This full-fledged witch hunt nearly obliterated Top 40 radio. When I left for college in September, 1959, Boston had ten Top 40 stations (WEEI, WTAO, WNAC, WHDH, WORL, WBZ, WILD, WCOP, WVDA, and WMEX). When I returned just a few months later, only WMEX, Arnie Ginsburg's station, had the courage to stick with the format. Every other station had gotten scared and changed formats. They turned to talk, oldies, or inoffensive "middle-of-the-road" music or as it was mockingly called, "chicken rock."

It meant that finding a job I would enjoy at a "good" radio station was tough. Being young and idealistic, I had strong opinions about what was good and what was bad. So once more I hit the road, trying to smile my way past secretaries and charm the hell out of program directors.

Ever since leaving Worcester for school and seeing how so many other stations were run, I had come to appreciate 'ORC's greatness even more. It wasn't just its sound, its vibe, its crazy energy. No. Its whole approach to music was revolutionary. It was far more than just a Top 40 station. Even though it was in

Worcester, Massachusetts, WORC had already broken out dozens of unknown singles as major national hits, launching number one songs like Elvis's "Can't Help Falling in Love" and "Blue Hawaii;" Johnny Mathis's "Wonderful Wonderful" and "It's Not for Me to Say;" Buddy Holly's "True Love Ways;" the Tokens' "Lion Sleeps Tonight;" and most of Roy Orbison and Connie Francis's popular songs. It would continue to do so for another decade.

But it didn't end there. Before Ed Sullivan introduced the Beatles to America, "She Loves You" made its American radio debut on *Open House Party* in 1963. Same thing with the Rolling Stones. Their first American concert ever was at the Worcester Auditorium, in part because their version of Buddy Holly's "Not Fade Away," the group's first American hit, was broken on WORC. They were paid $800. And on it went. The role this little Worcester radio station played in American hit music was striking.

The catalyst behind it all was the *Open House Party* request system and the music director, "Honest" Dick Smith, who spent every waking minute documenting listener requests for songs. For Bob and Dick, requests were the only way to truly measure a song's popularity. In 1965, for example, when an advance copy of the Beatles' *Rubber Soul* album was rushed to *Open House Party* the station played a cut every half hour. But by 5:30 that afternoon when the request lines shut down, "Michelle" was the number one requested song in the city. It was the same with the Beach Boys album *Party*. For its debut, we played a different cut from the album every thirty minutes on *Open House Party* and at the end of the afternoon "Barbara Ann" requests had lit up the phone lines, ending it up at number one in requests. Capitol Records future president responded by immediately releasing it as a single and it went on to become a national number one hit in the United States and in countries around the world.

WORC's approach flew in the face of normal Top 40 metrics. *Billboard*, *Variety*, *Cash Box*, they all based their numbers on record sales. It was widely understood inside the industry that those charts were corrupt, made inaccurate by aggressive record companies who literally went to record stores in major cities and handed out boxes of free records in exchange for them reporting those records as being "sold" to the influential radio stations and music publications.

John Garabedian

WORC's main studio was huge. Long tables lined the walls to accommodate the many stacks of alphabetized listener requests. Pictured above Dick Smith (left) and Bob Bryar (right).

That went on for decades. When computerization in the late eighties permitted accurate tabulations of actual unit sales to try to make the system honest, chains like Tower Records would be supplied with thousands of free cassettes for a particular song. They would then sell them for the giveaway price of forty-nine cents at the checkout counter, which would inflate the sales numbers. Then there would be the shady claim some song was a top seller. Why? Not because it was good but because it was forty-nine cents! The result was that stations relying on manipulated sales to program music were playing lots of crappy music.

WORC and Smith were above all that. WORC determined what listeners *really* wanted to hear because it ignored sales and national charts and heard from the audience directly. At the end of each week Dick Smith had eight thousand to ten thousand requests to tabulate. And what WORC tabulated went straight to Bill Gavin, publisher of the nationally trusted *Gavin Report*. That weekly paid newsletter was the bible of radio programming and everyone knew it could be trusted. *Billboard*, *Radio & Records*, and *Variety*'s charts could be bought. But not Gavin. His chart numbers were the most reliable and credible in the country, and they were based in large part on what he got from Dick Smith. Imagine; a Worcester radio station was driving popular American music. It was awesome.

A few years before, Mel Miller, the former co-host of *Open House Party* at WORC, who'd run off to Hawaii with Bob Bryar's wife, had moved back to Boston to become program director of WMEX when it launched as a Top 40 station. Mel, and Bob's former wife, Shirley, debuted on the morning show as "Melvin and the Blonde." After leaving college I applied for jobs at all the Boston and Providence stations and Mel promptly offered me a full-time job doing afternoon news for $85 a week. While thinking it over, I received a call from Budd Clain, WORC's program director. There was an opening for production director, he said, and with it a Saturday night air shift from 7 p.m. to 1 a.m.

I wasn't crazy about the production job—it mainly involved producing commercials. The pay was smaller than what WMEX offered—just $50 a week—but it returned me to the WORC I loved and my old Saturday night shift. WORC was one of a kind. There I could continue to learn more about the kind of radio I believed in, and I could make extra money deejaying parties and clubs. The decision was easy.

Back in Worcester, I returned to the station I never wanted to leave. It felt as comfortable as an old chair. I turned my Saturday night show into something that packed all the production value of an Academy Awards presentation. Throughout the week I assembled bits, stunts and jokes to use, anything to keep those request lines constantly ringing, which always made Bob Bryar happy. Groupies were also a part of the scene. It was a regular thing for horny girls to call in to try to get you to meet them.

Now making money with a full-time paycheck and weekly DJ gigs, I traded the '55 Buick Special for a robin-egg blue '58 Chevy convertible. Man, what a hot-looking car! Two weeks after I bought it, I was tapped to fill in on *Open House Party* because Bob Bryar had gone to Chicago for a radio convention. Late one afternoon as I was wrapping up the last hour of *Open House Party*, Patty Drake suddenly showed up in the studio.

"I'd love to see that new car of yours," she said, in that low, sexy voice of hers. "How about taking me for a ride?"

After struggling with my image in the '54 Buick, my second car was a fabulously hot robin-egg blue '58 Chevy convertible. Patty Drake wanted a ride, and I got the ride of my life.

We ended up parked on a dirt road by a lake in West Boylston when the next thing I knew she had her head on my lap and was blowing hot breaths into my crotch. A half hour later we ended up at her parents' house, where she still lived. They were out of town, she assured me, and invited me in. The next thing I knew we were having crazy sex in her bedroom. There I was, lying on her bed, Patty bouncing on top of me moaning and squealing. Holy shit, I kept thinking to myself. I'm fucking my boss's girlfriend. I'm going to get fired! As far as I know he never found out.

Back at the station while filling in hosting *Open House Party* for the first time, I was learning a new kind of radio. Every hour was filled with contests and games, including "Scavenger Hunt." We'd name an item on the air we were looking for, and the first listener to show up at the station with that item won a record album. We asked for expected things—a two-dollar bill, a Barbie Doll, or photo of Elvis in an Army uniform—but sometimes I liked to be outrageously entertaining and push for something ridiculous. A call for a snowman resulted in a few listeners wheeling in full size snowmen through the lobby of the Bancroft Hotel. Bob got a big laugh out of that one until the hotel complained. He was less enamored when I offered a prize to the first person to show up with a dog and two-dozen people showed up at nearly the exact same time. Big dogs, little dogs, barking the whole time, sometimes fighting—the elegant hotel suddenly morphed into a dog-riot kennel. Afterward, a very serious Budd and Bob sat me down.

"You're going to get us kicked out of here and force us to find a new home for the station," a still smiling Bob said. "The Bancroft's manager wasn't happy. So don't do it again."

If I couldn't have the kind of fun I wanted inside the hotel, I reasoned, then maybe I could try doing something outside it. Late one August on a Saturday night I asked listeners to bring their hot cars downtown for a WORC car show. Within a half-hour there were a dozen vehicles and more than a hundred people milling about on Portland Street. Engines revved and bystanders erupted in cheers when I leaned out a window and yelled live into my mike, "Let's do a drag race!" As those cars roared down the street, I hung out the window with a mike delivering a play-by-

WORC's very strict general manager, Bart Coblentz, peeking in a studio window at WORC. Bob Bryar brought him in as a partner because Bart was once the top ad salesman in Worcester. Once at WORC, he never left his office and never made many sales.

play account for listeners. Nobody was hurt, but to this day I'm still not sure how I wasn't arrested.

I guess WORC's management team wondered the same thing. That Monday I received another call to Bob's office, but instead of Budd standing by the owner's side, there was Bob's partner, Bart Coblentz, the station's always-serious general manager. Bart was everything Bob wasn't, a by-the-numbers guy who managed sales and the business affairs of the station. Bart had little appreciation for creative people and preferred the station to run like a bank.

"You know you could get the station sued," Bart snapped as I took a seat in front on Bob's desk.

"I'm sorry," I said. "It won't happen again."

This time, though, I wasn't there to be warned or simply reprimanded. Bart wanted me gone and Bob, reluctantly, signed off on it. "The station dodged a bullet," Bob said apologetically. "But we may not be as lucky the next time."

It wasn't the last time I'd work at WORC. And it wouldn't be the last time I'd be fired there.

With my second stint at WORC behind me, I was off on another job search and eventually landed at WSMN in Nashua, New Hampshire (*Weather-Sports-*

John Garabedian

Music-News). Soulless chicken rock was its music of choice. Really boring, soft, with no edges. I might as well have been back at WMRC in Milford. That's certainly what it felt like.

I did a little of everything there. I had a regular afternoon shift, produced commercials, and I even did some news. But really, how credible is a nineteen-year-old kid? On the day of the NASA Mercury launch, May 5, 1961, Ed Lecius, WSMN's news director, sent me out to interview the parents of America's first astronaut, Alan Shepard. Shepard had grown up in Derry, a little town about twelve miles northeast of Nashua, and his folks still lived in the family home in Hudson, New Hampshire. The station's mobile unit was a Volkswagen microbus that packed this weak thirty-horsepower engine that maybe hit fifty miles per hour on a flat stretch of highway with a wind behind it. Going uphill, you always had to shift into a lower gear.

Out I drove to Hudson. It wasn't until I actually pulled into town that I realized I didn't bring the slip where I wrote the address, just a foggy memory of the street name. With not even a dime in my pocket to make a call from a phone booth, I drove around for an hour before I turned back west and returned to the station. My news director was pissed and the poor Shepards lost out on their chance to be interviewed about their famous son, live, on a crappy little station.

Bored out of my mind, I bolted Nashua the first chance I could and landed at a small Top 40 station, WSAR, in Fall River, Massachusetts. They needed an afternoon deejay with a first-class engineer's license to operate their four-tower directional antenna. I needed to get as far away from chicken rock as possible. The people there were nice. The music was okay. But it wasn't WORC. Nothing was.

Redemption came in the summer of 1961, when Bob Bryar called me up at home. We'd stayed in touch intermittently over the last year and I'd certainly made it plain to him that I missed 'ORC. But openings never came around. Then without warning, he lost his nighttime guy. The night shift started following *Open House Party*, five nights a week at $85 a week. That was real money back then. Plus I'd again have my Saturday nights free to DJ dances for additional income. It was a no-brainer.

Stepping back into the 'ORC studios felt amazing. It was like I never left. Lil Brown, the front desk secretary, greeted me with a big smile. "Welcome home, Johnny," she said.

And that's what it felt like. I was back where I should be. I was also better on the air; still outrageous, still funny, but I'd tempered my personality. I didn't blow through commercial breaks like I had before. There were no more drag races on Portland Street. As Bob pointed out time and time again after my return, I had matured. I had learned that being wild, crazy, and successful are different than just being wild and crazy.

Joey Reynolds is one of the all-time great American deejays. Joey grew up in Buffalo listening to the same Dick Biondi show I'd grown up with in Boston. But in creating wild antics to build audiences, he'd gotten fired at over thirty of the best stations in the country. It was the same pattern every time: A station would put Joey on the air, the ratings would soar, and then he would pull a Dick Biondi and do something completely outrageous, getting canned. Joey actually replaced Biondi at WKBW, the same 50,000-watt Buffalo station where Biondi made his name. Joey's legend is that after being fired at WKBW he nailed his shoes to the program director's door with a sign that read "fill these."

A radio station wants you to be outrageous but they don't want the sponsors to cancel, lawyers to call, or the police to show up. Losing the FCC license doesn't hold much appeal, either. As I matured, I learned the importance of respecting limits.

Something that kept my show fun and packed with energy was the guy I had at my side answering the request lines. John Cooney was a rotund Irish kid who had a wicked sense of humor. He'd say something sarcastically funny about anything—a song, an artist, the news—and I'd use it on air. It was like having my own staff comedy writer. He had no filter. Whatever came out, came out. After the show, we'd always go out and grab something to eat.

One night in the middle of the show I got a call from Nancy Boyd, a former WORC request operator who had left the station a few months before after getting married and then becoming pregnant. She was a complete hot shit, a total straight-shooter. She was like a lot of Worcester women and packed this fearless

John Garabedian

in-your-face personality. Nancy could handle anyone and seriously didn't care what anyone thought of her. She was Jewish, white, and twenty-five when she married a forty-two-year-old black man, hardly a popular concept in 1961.

"I'm moving," she said. "And I need some help. You can crash at my house after your show on Friday night and I'll cook you breakfast in the morning. After all, a friend in need is a friend indeed."

It wasn't exactly an offer I couldn't refuse, but I agreed to it. That Friday, at around 1:30 in the morning, Cooney and I headed over to Nancy's on Garden Street in Worcester. She'd left a key for us under the floor mat but every light in the place was off. The two of us stumbled around, stepping around boxes and other stuff, and Cooney was making me laugh. On the living room floor I spotted a skinny kid about my age fast asleep on a blanket on the floor and turned around to shush Cooney. But that was impossible. No sooner had I brought my finger to my lips than he made some wise-ass remark and I busted out laughing, waking up the kid on the floor.

Joe Premo had been renting a room from Nancy. And like us, he'd been recruited as a member of the moving committee. How the hell Nancy or her husband never woke up that night I'll never know because for the next few hours the three of us ended up having a wild time. Cooney had us both rolling on the floor with laughter and then we headed into the guest room where the three of us got into a big pillow fight. I got maybe an hour of sleep that night.

Part of it was the fun we had. But another part about it was this great new friend I'd made. There was an excitement that jolted my body just being around Joe. He was tall like me, and slender with this gorgeous head of strawberry blonde hair. He also had a street-wise confidence that was hard not to admire. A couple of times we caught eyes and he gave me this sly smile, like he knew something that nobody else did. That whole night I kept thinking, *I really like this kid. How can I make sure we hang out and become friends?*

That morning, I was a sleep-deprived wreck. At about 5 a.m., Nancy began banging loudly on the door. I dragged myself from the bed, figuring I'd least get recharged with some eggs, bacon, and coffee, but what awaited us was a box of donuts and some coffee her husband Minton had picked up. With no sleep, I felt

Request operator John Cooney in the WORC production studio around 1961. Cooney had the Irish gift of humor. It was like having a great comedy writer on staff to feed me funny lines.

like complete shit that whole morning and after a couple of truckloads I turned in my resignation. I had to DJ a dance that night at St. Mary's High School and needed sleep.

That whole drive home down Route 9 from Worcester to Weston, all I thought about was that kid Joe. Would I see him again? How could I see him again? I wasn't sure why, but I'd never met anyone who'd made me feel so twisted up inside. Even if I'd had the guts to tell someone about Joe, I didn't know what I'd say.

Later that afternoon, he stayed on my brain all the way back to Worcester. Even during the dance I kept thinking about him. At around midnight, after things had wrapped up, I decided that instead of heading straight home, I'd swing by Nancy's to see how the rest of the move went. You know, be a good friend. That's the story I told myself as I drove across town. Really, I was hoping Joe would be up. Maybe we could hang out for a bit.

I buzzed down Worcester's South Main Street. The bars were just emptying out while a few big trucks rumbled past me on their way to make early morning deliveries. Then I hit Harvard Street and it was like I was the only one in the

John Garabedian

world. It added to the heaviness, the nerves I was feeling. Where the hell was I going? Why did seeing Joe again feel so important?

When I arrived at Nancy's new place I pulled into her driveway, killed the engine, and sat for a minute in my car. With the exception of a kitchen stove light, the whole house was dark. I knew there wasn't a chance anyone was awake, but I got out anyway, stepped up to the front door and knocked gently a few times. Nothing. I put my ear to the door to see if I could hear any rustling. Silence. I knocked again, and still nothing. I had just turned around to head back to my car when I heard the door unlock. On the other side of it was Joe, who'd clearly been crying.

"What's wrong?" I whispered, stepping closer to him.

Joe wiped his eyes and then stuffed his hands in his pocket. "Oh, it's my mother," he mumbled, stepping out on to the front porch. "She's just, um, been having some problems. It'll be okay." He then let a slight smile emerge.

It was only later that he admitted he was lying. Joe's mom had nothing to do with it. He'd later told me he was worried that he would never see me again. Seeing him there, looking so beautiful and vulnerable under the soft porch light, I didn't want to say goodbye. I didn't want the night to just end.

"You tired?" I asked him. "You feel like going for a ride?"

Over the next hour Joe and I buzzed around Worcester's empty streets. Joe loved my car, a slick looking 1957 Triumph TR-3 convertible that I'd traded my '58 Chevy Impala convertible for a couple of months before. It was a challenge to fold my lanky body into it but, man, was it fun to drive.

Joe was different than anyone I'd ever met. Clearly a city kid, he was cut from a different cloth than anybody in tony suburban Weston. His home life had been a mess. His dad died when he was young and his mother had married an alcoholic asshole with an immediate dislike for his outspoken new stepson. Soon after, Joe moved out. School had been another miserable experience for him and at seventeen he dropped out and joined the U.S. Marines. By eighteen, around the time I met him, he had been discharged and was living with Nancy, making ends meet by working the assembly line at a Thom McAn shoe factory on Gold Star Boulevard in Worcester.

Before dropping him off that night, we made plans to meet up again the next evening. I had Sunday off and just the thought of getting to spend more time with Joe was thrilling. The mistake I made, however, was swinging by the 'ORC studios before picking him up. Cooney was there and determined to tag along. Every part of me wanted to say no, but I just couldn't. My little Triumph car had two seats, and Cooney was huge. So there we were, the three of us trying to figure out a way to cram into my car.

As I sat in the driver's seat, I motioned to Joe. "Since you're thin and Cooney isn't, why don't you get in first," I said. My suggestion was strategic: Cooney was way too huge to sit in the middle, but subconsciously I wanted to sit next to my new friend. Joe climbed into the car and positioned his body so that instead of facing the passenger door, his body faced directly at me. That meant the only place where I could rest my arm was between his legs so my hand could reach the stick shift. I had to be very careful to keep my elbow out of his crotch.

Cooney, of course, was oblivious to all of it. We roared off and he started gabbing and singing to the radio. Non-stop. As it got dark and Cooney blabbed, my little finger bumped up against Joe's hand. He then slid his finger around mine, and almost immediately we intertwined hands. I felt a very weird excitement. I'd never done anything like this before with a guy. Sure, I'd fooled around with other boys sexually, but I'd never flirted romantically or felt this strong of a crush. It was completely different. Deeper and more powerful. We drove around for hours that night, and when WORC signed off at midnight, we pulled in more great hit music from WLS in Chicago while the cool autumn air rushed over us. All the while Joe and I held hands in the dark, outside of Cooney's view.

Around 1 a.m., we dropped Cooney off at his house. I made sure as hell his was the first stop. I wanted to just be with Joe. I wasn't ready to say goodbye to him. Joe didn't want to call it a night, either.

"What do you want to do next," Joe said, his words tinged with a slight Worcester accent. He slid over to where Cooney had been sitting, and then grabbed my hand again. "Is there some place we could go?"

I tapped my fingers on the steering wheel. My heart was racing. "How about WORC? Would you like a tour of a radio station?"

By now WORC had moved out of the Bancroft Hotel and across the street to a small high-rise at 8 Portland Street. The building was dark and empty when we arrived. I made a half-hearted attempt to show Joe the studio and record library, but neither one of us was in the mood for a real tour. Holding his hand, I led him down to the basement. We found an old American flag, spread it on the grimy floor, and got intimate.

From that point on, Joe and I spent every moment together. We made the most of the hour or so we had just after he got off his shift and before I went on air. Often he came with me to the station and just hung out. Then we'd grab a late night bite to eat when my show ended. Joe's sarcastic sense of humor never ebbed. He was fearless about throwing in a good dig, which I appreciated. But more than anything he was comfortable in his own skin, open and frank about his sexuality. He'd come out when he was just fifteen and often took the bus to Boston to hang out in some of the gay coffee shops and hangouts. He just didn't care. He didn't care what the world saw. He didn't care what the world thought of him. He knew who he was and went for it.

Me? I was a different story. Clearly I was in love, but uptight and timid about letting the world know about it. In 1961, homosexuals were generally regarded as perverts, rapists, and child molesters. Any sexual act outside of heterosexual intercourse in the missionary position was illegal in Massachusetts as a "crime against nature" and punishable with serious jail time. I still did care what the world saw and what it thought of me. But I worried about what Joe thought, too. I didn't want him thinking I was a wimp.

And yet, the mere fact that I was in love with a guy was astounding to me and a major self-revelation. Mind-blowing, in fact. Like a giant cloud had lifted and I was born again. All of a sudden, this part of me that I had repressed for so long opened up. I finally was able to reconcile those very feelings and emotions that confused me all my life and had been afraid to contend with. All the bullshit pretending and effort I'd made to just "fit in" and tell myself I was like everyone else now felt unnecessary. It was beautifully liberating.

With Joe, life changes came a million miles an hour. Two weeks after we met, we got an apartment together in Worcester. That's how quickly it all happened.

I really had no idea how my parents would react, and really didn't want to open up to them. Even later in life, when it was apparent I had relationships with guys, we never discussed it. Never had the talk. I'm guessing they just didn't want to know the details and I just got to a point where I didn't think it mattered. But to their credit, my parents never loved me any less.

Only two weeks after Joe Premo and I met, we had rented an apartment and moved in together in Worcester. Joe came out when he was fifteen, joined the U.S. Marines at seventeen, and was soon discharged for reasons I was never clear about. We met when he was eighteen.

That's not to suggest my mother liked Joe. Far from it. To her he was this gritty Worcester street kid who didn't have the class or polish of her son. Another one of those "dees, dems and dos" people she had tried so hard to differentiate me from all those years ago with that full-length camel hair coat. To me that was a big part of his charm. Those formal polite manners and social routines my mother valued were manufactured and fake, and Joe's street nature was what was real.

While we never talked about it, there's no doubt she suspected something about my relationship with Joe. Early on, right before we rented our apartment and when I was still living at home he came home with me one night after my show on 'ORC. We slept in my bedroom in my single bed, and then headed out the next morning to do some shopping. When we returned we discovered that she had stripped the bed and was washing the sheets. If she had just even casually looked at those sheets she would have seen some stains. Joe and I were totally red-faced.

Things were more tense for me at 'ORC. They'd seen Joe, had their suspicions. He was slightly effeminate, not exactly the rugged type. He wasn't a flamboyant queen by any means, but sharp people would suspect he was gay. And I guess they started to wonder about me.

One Monday morning, I got a call from Lil Brown. "Bob wants you to come in for a meeting at 2 p.m."

I thought that seemed sort of weird. Bob never asked for meetings. If he wanted to talk to me, he just called me up. He never called me into the principal's office. I shrugged my shoulders. "No problem," I said.

My concern ratcheted up when I walked in and saw Bart Coblentz sitting on the couch in the corner of the office. As I walked in, he forced a smile. It looked so forced and unnatural. All his smiles did. Bart was the kind of guy who felt much more at home looking joyless.

"Hello, John," he said.

I nodded my head. "What's going on?"

Bob, who had taken a seat behind his desk, ran his hands through his hair. "Look, Johnny, first I just wanna say you're doing a great job," he said. "There's no denying that. The ratings are great and we're happy with your work. It's just that, well, Bart has some concerns."

Bart? What the hell was Bart worried about. I looked over at him and arched my eyebrows. "Is there a problem?"

The smile had long faded from his face. "That kid you've been hanging out with," he said. "People are talking about it."

"You mean Joe?" I asked, and let out a big laugh. "What about it? Who is talking?"

"People," Bart said with some disdain. "People here, people outside of here." He leaned forward. "Advertisers."

What the hell were advertisers complaining about? My night show was pulling in a fifty share, the highest ratings on the station, even beating *Open House Party*. As if there was any doubt about my popularity, we'd recently run a promotion called "Mayor of the Air." It was around election time and we did a month-long listener poll to see who was the station's favorite DJ. I received more than ten thousand votes, double the votes of the second-place finisher. I did everything Bob wanted. I played great music, I put listeners on the air, I created buzz.

Bob tried to bring down the room's temperature. "Like I said, Johnny, we love what you're doing. It's just this Joe guy. Bart is worried about, you know, our reputation."

I cut Bob off. "What are you saying? What are you asking me to do?"

"You need to make a choice, John," Bart said. "You can either keep working here or you'll have to leave if you keep hanging out with this kid. No one would ever guess that you're *that* way. We're just worried people might begin to think that."

I let out a long breath. Then I redirected my gaze at Bob. This was all Bart's doing. He found out and brainwashed Bob into thinking that this was a crisis. I knew for a fact that Bob didn't give a shit about someone being gay. In New York, he told me countless times, there were tons of gay people in the radio business. They had to stay quiet about who they were, but they were there. He'd even told me that the big scuttlebutt in show business was that Merv Griffin was gay.

I then immediately stood up.

"Well, thanks for the opportunity of letting me work here," I said sticking out my hand toward Bob. "I guess I'll be leaving."

Bart and Bob were stunned. I was done being polite and at this moment I knew my character was at stake. Was I willing to believe in who I was and stand up for it? I'd finally begun accepting who I was and now I had to trade it all in for a job? I loved radio. I loved working at 'ORC, but I couldn't step backwards. I'd come too far.

Bob stammered and got to his feet. He looked over at Bart, who had a confused look on his face. That wasn't the reaction either of them had expected. "Well, you don't have to leave right away," Bob finally said. "Take a few weeks. Think things over."

"That's okay," I said. "I'll finish things out and go my way."

I did my show that night and then headed back to our apartment. When I got in, Joe was still up. He was fixing a sandwich for himself. I let out a big sigh and collapsed on the couch.

"How was your day?" Joe asked, taking a seat next to me.

I looked at him and then laughed. "I just got fired because of you." 🔇

10. Moon River

Henry Mancini, 1961

Having my First Class FCC license helped me get hired at WPTR, whose 50,000-watt AM transmitter blasted a powerful nighttime signal over New York, New England, Eastern Canada, and the Maritimes.

I tried to put on a good face about my decision to leave WORC. Like it wasn't something personal or even a big deal. When someone asked if I was still at the station I'd muster something up about needing a change, or wanting to take the next step in radio. "I was looking for more of a hand in calling my own shots there, but I could see that was never going to happen," became a standard line. I'd flash a quick smile and then change topics. The weather, the Red Sox, whatever. I just didn't want to linger on what had happened. Not backing down against Bob and Bart's ultimatum had been a big step for me. I felt pumped that I'd showed the strength of character in standing up for something I believed in, even though it meant sacrificing the job I loved. It's what came after that rattled my brain. The doubt. The shame. The embarrassment. The gnawing insecurity about whether I'd screwed up my career. The fear that now people may find out I was gay, and that maybe I was a weirdo. I wanted to turn my mind away from it all, but I couldn't.

The whole thing—being called into the principal's office with Bob and Bart, being made to feel like I had done something wrong. Like I was the guy who'd done something wrong. Around me was a world packed with actual problems. Wife beaters, racists, alcoholics. But following your heart? Trying to be the person you know yourself to be? If I'd gone into the station and grabbed Lillian Brown's ass I might have received a slap on the wrist but I wouldn't have lost my job. I wouldn't have been shamed like I had been, made to feel embarrassed for who I was. The hard work I poured into the station, the passion and dedication I demonstrated, and the huge ratings increases I'd piled up, didn't mean a damn thing. Bart feared losing advertisers and I had to either hide who I was or leave. For the first time in my life, when I had something major to lose, I'd stood up for who I was and look where it got me.

John Garabedian

I also played it careful with Joe. He knew exactly who he was and embraced it. He didn't give two shits about what anyone thought about him. It was one of the qualities I loved about him. And it's what I wanted for myself. But I didn't want to burden him with what was going through my mind and make him feel like he was my therapist. He'd already waged this battle with himself. Why should I put him through it again? That's what I told myself, anyway. But looking back on it now, I think I also didn't want to depend on him. I didn't want to get into a situation where I needed someone else to make me feel better. I felt I should have been strong enough to deal with this on my own, even if it was lonely and hard.

Instead I did the thing I've always been good at. I threw myself into my work. I was worried I'd have trouble finding a new job but I got lucky and a week after the "Bob and Bart meeting" a friend told me about a chief engineer opening at WESO, a small station owned by Greater Media in Southbridge, a factory town about twenty miles southwest of Worcester. While it wasn't an on-air job, I needed work and an income. It was early spring of '62, I was twenty years old, and I leapt at the chance, going at it with everything I had.

On my first day, Frank Costello, the general manager, walked me through the station. After meeting my new co-workers, we stepped inside the production studio and he let out a small sigh. "At some point we're going to need to upgrade this thing," he said, sweeping his hand across the room. Including the Scotch tape that bounded the myriad clumps of wires that plagued the place, nothing in the room looked like it had been built by a professional engineer. Looking at it all, my heart raced.

"I'll do it," I said, the words dropping out of my mouth as soon as he finished his sentence.

I came in like a tornado. Within a week or so of starting, I ripped apart the room to the bare walls. Overhauling that production studio made me feel as though I was a little kid again. It was like being back in my parents' basement, building something fresh and new, making everything work well. It also gave me a mission, allowed me to keep my head together. Like a songwriter dumping his soul into a tune he's writing, rebuilding that little studio became an outlet for all the stuff that was spinning inside my head. Clearing, cleaning, resetting. In a way, I guess, I was rebuilding myself, too. Establishing my confidence again. I had control over the outcome. The results were tangible. At the end of every day a little more of that room was put together. Work again became a place of pride, rather than shame. Within a couple of weeks after starting, the station had a gleaming new space to record programs and produce commercials.

Then, when it was finished, a funny thing happened: I realized I needed a different job. I really missed not being on the air. I missed having a show, entertaining people, finding great new songs and playing the big hits. My mind may have settled from the WORC experience, but I felt like I didn't have my voice, didn't have access to the thing that had helped me find the person inside me who wasn't so shy, who didn't like just hanging out on the sidelines of life. After four months in Southbridge I'd had enough and started looking for something new.

The search eventually landed me at WTSN, a small Top 40 station in Dover, New Hampshire, an old mill city near the New Hampshire seacoast. I didn't know where Dover was when I applied, just that it was in New Hampshire and near enough to Boston so Joe and I could get down there whenever we wanted to hang with our friends. Which turned out to be a lot. The first time we rolled through downtown Dover in my red '61 Impala convertible, Joe let out a laugh. "What a shithole," he said. I grimaced as we passed the big Cocheco Mill building, which hovered over the city like a rusted out ocean liner, saw the old farts meandering up and down Main Street, and kept my eyes peeled for any decent clubs. There were none. "Welcome home," Joe said sarcastically.

The station wasn't much better. I was hired for the afternoon shift, but the job plunged me back into the world of boring radio. It was again like being back at WMRC, where I had been yelled at for laughing on the air. All I wanted was to work somewhere like WORC again, a station with big ideas that believed in fun and entertainment, and provided fertile soil to pull it off. A few weeks after starting, I tracked down the program director before my shift and tried to politely suggest some improvements.

"You know, I used to work at WORC, which had top ratings," I said. "We took a thousand song requests a day to learn which songs listeners really wanted, and actually put listeners on the air. It was really exciting and our ratings…"

John Garabedian

A hand shot up in the air to cut me off. "We don't do that here," he said. "We're a little more professional than that." He looked at his watch. "I think you have some commercials to record before your air shift. Let me worry about the programming and you follow our format rules."

"Okay," I said, calmly and spun around and headed to the studio.

The one bright spot at the station was my afternoon newsman. He was from Arlington, Massachusetts, young like me and really dedicated to news, with a smooth, even voice that gave him the kind of gravitas of someone twice his age. Equally impressive was his gorgeous fire-engine red '57 Chevy convertible. Gary LaPierre worked in Dover for maybe two years before he was plucked away by Boston powerhouse WBZ. Over the next four decades he became the preeminent voice of morning news in Boston.

My tour of duty at the station was considerably shorter. Just three months, which was about two months more than my sanity could take. I felt out of place, out of sorts, like I was only partially following my dream. After work I'd come home to the little mobile home Joe and I rented in the outskirts of Dover with a worn look on my face, probably not unlike what my dad had when he returned from the office. The frustration of working for people who weren't as good at their job as you, or as committed, made me crazy. Every evening I'd sink into the living room couch and comb through the help wanted section of *Broadcasting* magazine. Joe didn't say a thing. He didn't have to. He wanted out of Dover as much as I did.

Then, one evening, I got a call from my mother.

"A very nice man from a station in Albany, New York, called for you today," she said.

"Are you sure he said he was from Albany?" I said, excitedly. Did he say the name of the station?

"Yes, I think it was WPRT or something."

"Do you mean WPTR?" I asked, my voice rising.

She took a drag on her cigarette. "Oh, yes, that sounds like it," she said, letting out a long exhale.

I did a dance around the room. "You're really sure about that?"

My mother let out a big laugh. "Yes," she said. "Have you been waiting to hear from them?"

I couldn't believe it. After leaving WORC I fired off my resume to any station that advertised an opening. I aimed high and low. One of the jobs had been for the night shift at WPTR 1540, a blowtorch signal that, because of its high band frequency and 50,000-watt power, at night covered all of New England, and north to Montreal, Quebec, and Canada's Maritime Provinces. When you were on that station, twenty-five million people could hear you in two countries.

Beyond its reach, however, the programming jumped out of the radio speaker. It had a huge Las Vegas vibe to it. Showy, kind of glitzy, not afraid to go over the top. The man responsible for that had been its general manager, Duncan Mounsey, former manager of the Radio City Music Hall, who brought the big tent showmanship from his old job to his new one. He was a master promoter. The deejays weren't just broadcasting from the 'PTR headquarters, they were coming live from the Golden Studios or the Crystal Studios. At one point, to create a buzz on St. Patrick's Day, he hired a group of monster women models, all 6'6" or taller, and had them spray-painted green, to walk the main streets of Albany, Troy, and Schenectady. They paraded around carrying big signs saying, "Listen to the monster, WPTR 1540."

His most legendary stunt was in 1959, about a year after the station switched over to Top 40, when Mounsey hired a new deejay, Jim Ramsburg, to do afternoons. Ramsburg came from WDGY in Minneapolis and was an unknown in the Albany-Troy-Schenectady radio market. To create excitement around his arrival, Mounsey hired a New York City advertising agency to secretly buy ad time on the four leading Albany radio stations. For a week, radio listeners kept hearing commercials about the great "Juan Fifero," the Mexican magician who was scheduled to appear at the giant nightclub at the Thruway Motor Inn. *Come see this world-renowned magician perform live this Friday night at seven! And it will be broadcast live!* the advertisements blared. As part of the ad buy each of the stations was required to broadcast the first fifteen minutes of the performance. It became this huge deal. People bought tickets; there were singers and dancers.

John Garabedian

Then the emcee took the stage and told the crowd, "And now ladies and gentlemen, the moment you've been waiting for! Here he is, the great Juan Fifero!" As Ramsburg took the stage, the emcee continued. "He starts Monday on the great 50,000-watt WPTR, Juan Fifero: one–five–four–oh!" A triumphant Ramsburg threw up his arms while Mounsey stood grinning at the side of the room as program managers from stations across the metro area tried to quickly call their station control board operators to cut the live broadcasts as fast as they could.

The station's studios were another selling point. After working at dingy, cramped radio stations, WPTR was a palace! It made its home in a massive three-story brick building on Route 5 that had once been the power generating station for the Albany-Schenectady trolley line. You walked in and immediately stepped into this towering lobby where a grand staircase led to the second floor studios and thirty-foot ceilings. Behind the building, a half-mile from the highway, stood three four hundred-foot towers, all done up with giant red neon letters that spelled out W–P–T–R, the station's call letters. It was another memorable Mounsey touch.

Even the sound of the station was huge, with a seven-person news team, four mobile units, and a stunning top-of-the-hour super produced station ID that slammed into your speakers. It came on with a flourish of music and a booming voice-over that said, "W–P–T–R, Albany, serving…" and it would name a particular city in its five-state coverage area "…plus, thirty-seven counties, five states, two countries, and *you*!" Then, *bam*, it launched into yet another great hit song. Your heart raced just listening to it. It sounded important!

While Mounsey had left about a year before I arrived in the late summer of '62, his impact was still present. The afternoon guy was this larger-than-life character named Boom-Boom Brannigan. He broadcast from the "Boom-Boom Room" and he lived the part. Boom-Boom drove to work every day in a huge '61 Lincoln Continental with a leopard-skin top. He was, to put kindly, unscripted, a loose cannon who was extremely entertaining and said exactly what popped into his brain.

The job 'PTR called me about was not glamorous. Night news during the week, plus a Saturday night air shift. I didn't care. Getting the chance to work

there felt like an important validation of my talent and a new opportunity to grow my career. That maybe I
wasn't going to be stuck in places like
Dover and Southbridge the rest of
my life. As a kid I'd dreamed of one
day landing in New York City radio.
Now, it felt like I was that much closer to reaching that goal.

WPTR's Boom-Boom Brannigan in the Golden Studio. He
was a giant entertainer and complete showboat. "Pepsi
not only hits the spot, it removes it."

But, man, it was a bit scary.
Could I do the job? Would they like
what I did? What if I failed? What
then? It brought me back to a few years before when I first landed the job at
WMRC and told only a few people about it. I didn't want to get people's ex-
pectations up and then have to deal with the inevitable explanation for why it
didn't work out.

My nerves were eased the moment I met my new boss, Don Kelly, WPTR's
program director. Don was probably forty, tall and slender with a salt-and-pep-
per crew cut and an easy-looking face that reflected his even-keel personality.
As a radio executive, he was a pro and the first guy who showed me the skills it
took to be a great manager. I saw what it meant to navigate that high-wire act of
making sure people felt invested in the operation while also making sure they understood who was calling the shots. He sought input, made you feel like you were
part of the team, but always with the understanding that he was the ultimate
decider on how things happened. Watching Don operate had a great impact on
me when I became a program director five years later, and throughout my career.

Don's smooth style was evident to me my first day on the job. It was a Monday morning and I had come in for an orientation. Don showed me around the
studios, introduced me to everyone, and then he took me out for lunch. On the
way back to the station, he received a call on his two-way radio from Perry Samuels, the general manager. Boom-Boom had gone a little too free-form with one
of the station's biggest advertisers.

"Don, we've got a big problem," said Perry Samuels over the crackly radio as we buzzed down Route 5 in Don's Thunderbird.

"What happened?" said, Don coolly.

"Boom-Boom let loose again," said Perry, anxiously. "Pepsi wants to cancel their $75,000 annual contract."

"Oh, Christ," said Don, hitting the gas pedal with a little more force.

Boom-Boom had come on right after a Pepsi commercial and told his listeners, "Pepsi not only hits the spot, it removes it!" It wasn't exactly underground knowledge that if you wanted get rid of a little bumper rust, you rubbed a little Coke or Pepsi on it and it magically disappeared. But Pepsi executives didn't share the same enthusiasm for spreading that message as Boom-Boom did. Almost as soon as the words had passed through his lips, Pepsi was on the horn with 'PTR, threatening to pull its campaign. The next call went out to Don, who never lost his head about it. Don took Boom-Boom off the air for a week and somehow Pepsi didn't pull a dollar.

At 'PTR I loved being on Saturday nights. Sure, it cramped some of what Joe and I could do socially, but it thrilled me to think that my show might be lighting up in the background of some party in New York, New England, Quebec, or the Canadian Maritime Provinces. And while we kept to a pretty strict Top 40 formula, Don Kelly encouraged me to be funny and entertaining so long as it didn't get in the way of the music and formatics.

One Saturday night while I was on the air I got a call from an old buddy of mine from Worcester. Gary Usher was a kid my age from Westborough, Massachusetts, who had dreamed of being the next great pop star. We met because he had released a record he wrote and sang on called "Lies." While his single didn't go very far, he decided to pack his things and headed west to be closer to the music world in Los Angeles. He crashed on his sister's couch and tried to make a living as a songwriter. I had lost touch with him, but apparently Gary had been keeping track of me.

"Johnny!" his voice bellowed. "It's Gary. Gary Usher. How the hell are you?"

I was shocked to hear from him. "Jesus, Gary," I said. "It's wild to hear from you. Where are you? What are you doing?"

FCC rules required a first-class engineer to operate the WPTR transmitter. At night, fellow DJ Bob Badger and I broadcast from the transmitter instead of the main studio so they could cut engineering staff. Friends would drop by and the place became a circus.

"I'm still in California," he said. "Still trying to make it in music. I've been doing a lot of writing and have recently started working with this new group," he said. "Good musicians. Cool sound. I think you'll really like them. They call themselves the Beach Boys."

Right then, Gary passed the phone over to Brian Wilson, who in his own shy way started telling me about his band and their music. He was soft-spoken, kind of quiet, but he had a real passion in his voice when it came to music, as though his very existence was wrapped up in the songs he wrote and listened to. Gary wanted to show his new friends that he had connections in radio and could help them get exposure. Eventually he collaborated with Brian Wilson to write several major hit songs, like "In My Room," "Little Honda," and "409."

The Beach Boys were just part of a music landscape that was radically changing. When I first arrived at 'PTR the rotation included hits like "Mashed Potato Time" by Dee Dee Sharp, "The Stripper" by David Rose, and "The Loco-Motion" by Little Eva. It was an amazing time for different pop music sounds to

John Garabedian

Former FCC rules required logging transmitter readings every half hour. To this day I still remember the WPTR meter readings on the huge 50,000-watt GE BTA-25A transmitter: 10.6 kilovolts, 6.3 amps, common point current 42 amps.

emerge. Introducing a great new song felt like a big event. The Ronettes' "Be My Baby" is one that's etched in my mind. Phil Spector may be a convicted murderer, but he was master of music production. His "Wall of Sound" was just something totally innovative and different. Playing that masterpiece on the big 50,000-watt WPTR AM transmitter was about as close a young white DJ could come to performing it. Dead-roll the turntable and out it went, modulating the powerful 50,000-watt AM airwaves.

Much of that pre-1964 Top 40 music like "Johnny Angel" by Shelly Fabares, "It's My Party" by Lesley Gore, and "Ramblin' Rose" by Nat King Cole sounded corny and dated even then. But mixed with big country artists like Skeeter Davis and Johnny Cash, jazz greats like Stan Getz and Dave Brubeck, and Motown hits from Stevie Wonder and Martha and the Vandellas, it provided incredible variety in the charts, from rock to country to pop.

Then in 1964 the Beatles hit America and everything changed. We played all the early songs—first "Please Please Me," then a few weeks later "She Loves You." Not long after it was "I Want to Hold Your Hand"—and the phenomenon was immediate. In order to respond to the powerful audience demand, WPTR changed the music rotations. Every other song became a Beatles tune. Some nights I played "She Loves You" four times over the course of a three-hour shift. It got old so fast and reminded me of my mom banging away on the piano as she tried to learn "Clair de Lune." Only this time there was no basement for me to hide in. I not only had to play the songs, I had to introduce them like I loved them. It gave me headaches.

Beyond the repetition, however, that early Beatles music didn't do much for me. It was bubblegum pop-rock; light silly lyrics for thirteen-year-old girls. When people said the Beatles were taking over the world, what they meant was, they were taking over the thirteen-year-old girl market. They weren't talking to people over the age of twenty-one, and that's the core demographic Top 40 radio wants to build. Those are the listeners who buy products which the advertisers want to reach.

It's why, decades later on *Open House Party*, I wouldn't play early Justin Bieber songs. His pre-pubescent soprano voice clearly had no adult appeal. I remember first meeting Justin in a hotel room in Boston. It was Justin, his manager Scooter Braun, and Erik Olsen, VP of his record label, and me. He was a really nice kid, smart and fun and surprisingly well-grounded for someone who had so much fame and adulation so early. But despite incredible pressure from the record label, I wouldn't budge on airplay. Playing seventh grade music designed for thirteen-year-old girls with no appeal to adults would drive away the eighteen-to-thirty-four-year-old core audience our radio station affiliates were trying to reach. Even worse, it would tarnish the image of *Open House Party* and make us sound like a children's show. Once Bieber grew up and his voice changed, test scores from adults told us he had achieved grown-up star power. Now he's a superstar.

As I settled into working at 'PTR I also continued to come to terms with my sexuality. I began to feel more comfortable with it, and who I was. But questions still lingered. What was "being in love?" Was it some chemical trance that takes over your brain? What did it mean to be gay in a culture where coming out meant you were a fag or a queer? Early on I'd head to the New York State Library in Albany, sit in the big reading room, and pore through books on psychiatry, psychology, and relationships; I wanted to understand what "being in love" really was, instead of the fairy tale bullshit that was popularized in movies, books, and songs. I suppose I was approaching it like an engineer. I wanted to break it down, see it how it was put together, and discover what really made it work. But love, as I soon realized, is difficult to measure or quantify. And so is sexuality.

In the end I came back to the thing I'd seen all my life: There's the pretend world where most people believe they live, and there's the real world where peo-

Standing in front of the New York State Capital in Albany.

ple really are and don't see. Understanding that, not feeling intimidated by them, was completely liberating. Up until then my biggest fear about being gay or bisexual was that somehow I'd lose my masculinity. That the person I was would actually change. I mean, in 1963 the only role models for what a gay person looked like were Liberace and drag queens. Gay people were acknowledged or portrayed in our culture as effeminate prancing fairies with lisps and limp wrists. That was bullshit. And it wasn't me. It certainly wasn't the kind of guy I was attracted to, either. Why would a person who is attracted to guys be attracted to a guy acting like a woman?

Living in the Albany-Troy-Schenectady tri-city area helped. Pretty quickly Joe and I discovered a surprisingly large and thriving gay scene. We hit the clubs, made lots of friends, and got invited to parties. In Schenectady our neighbors were two partnered guys in their mid-twenties who lived together and had a strong, committed relationship. They were like any typical heterosexual couple, only happier. They'd have us over for dinner, we'd go out for drinks together—it was all incredibly normal. Domestic and stable. It was such a 180 from where my life had been just a couple of years before.

Meanwhile, life with Joe began to get complicated. We'd been together for nearly two years and for the first time we started fighting. Like it is in nearly every love relationship after a couple of years, the bloom was off the rose and we saw each other's warts. Sometimes it's all we saw in one another. He was messy and didn't keep a job; I was career-oriented and worked too much.

Then, one Saturday night the shit really hit the fan. Often we'd hit the bars with friends after I got off the air at midnight. We'd stay out until they closed, sometimes coming back around four or five in the morning. We'd stumble back to our apartment and just crash.

The night that Joe and I fell apart we didn't get back to our place until almost five in the morning. But instead of everyone going home, a semi-drunk Joe invited them all into our apartment. I wasn't happy about it but in a relationship we all make compromises. Your life is no longer your own. It was certainly that way for me with Joe. All I wanted to do was sleep but the crew kept bugging me to stay up. "The night's still young, Johnny," they badgered. "You can sleep when you're dead."

"All right," I said, smiling but exasperated. "I'll hang."

It helped that one of the guys was this tall blond kid named Johnny Osterhout. He was seventeen, and lived at home with his parents a few houses down from our apartment building in Schenectady. He was funny and smart, and yummy eye candy—even when you were bleary-eyed. With him was another friend of ours named Bobby, who liked to brag how he hustled the archbishop at the Episcopal church. For his patronage, Bobby got a brand new convertible. Oh, the things you learn about the real world when you're on the inside.

As the night wore on and everyone kept drinking and slurring more of their words, I finally had enough. At around 5:30 a.m. I called it quits and bailed. I didn't even think any of them noticed I was gone until about a half hour later Joe stumbled into our bedroom and started shaking me to wake me.

"Get up," he said. "Get up, John. I have to ask you something."

I rolled over, not at all sure what was happening. I squinted in the light and saw Joe's drunken face staring down at me. "What are you talking about, Joe?" I said.

"I got something I have to ask you," he said.

"Jesus, can't this wait?" I muttered and rolled back over, pulling the blankets over my head.

"No," he pleaded. "It's very important. Come into the kitchen."

"Fine," I said with annoyance and snapped the blankets off me. "Let's get this over with!"

I pulled on my pants and walked into the kitchen where only Johnny Osterhout and Bobby remained from the original crew. Johnny was coolly leaning against the doorway into the kitchen. I looked back at Joe. "Well?" I said angrily.

"All right," he said, pointing to Osterhout. "I like *him*. Now, Johnny, you tell us who you like?"

I glared at Joe. "You've got to be kidding me," I said. "What are you, in seventh grade? This is ridiculous."

"Tell him," Joe insisted.

Poor Johnny was both confused and probably a little drunk. Even more than me, he didn't know why the hell this was happening. He looked down at the ground, and let a smile grow on his face, then looked up and right at me. "*Him*," he sheepishly muttered.

I smiled back at him. Damn he was cute and compared to Joe at this very moment, a lot more desirable. I was just sick of Joe, tired of his drama. The confidence and appeal that I'd first fallen in love with often morphed into high drama that could wear me down. It was sad and strange to realize that the more I came into my own, felt more comfortable with who I was, the less I needed from Joe. Early in our relationship, he'd given me the courage to discover who I was. It was one of the best things he brought to our relationship. But as I settled into my own skin, the differences between us began to emerge and started to dominate what we had together.

"There," I said, turning to Joe. "You satisfied?"

Joe lost it and started bawling. "But Johnny," he said to the kid. "I thought you'd pick me!" He then threw himself on the couch. It was completely bizarre. I had no sympathy for him. Finally, after a few minutes of wailing, Joe got back on his feet. "I want to go back to Worcester," he said, looking directly at me.

Maybe he expected I'd cower, start pleading with him to stay and try to make him feel better. But I was fed up and having none of it. "Fine," I said. "But we're leaving right now. Grab your stuff."

Like an old homeless person, Joe shuffled off to the bedroom to pack his clothes. A few minutes later he emerged with a half-unzipped suitcase overflowing with shirts and pants. "Let's go," I said. We all then piled into my car. Johnny and I sat in front, Bobby and Joe in the back.

That was one long drive. Nobody wanted to speak, so I turned the radio on to WPTR. As we pulled onto the New York State Thruway at dawn, the Frank

On the steps outside my apartment on Washington Park in Albany. That's where I lived while working the overnight shift at WPTR. It's there that on November 22, 1963, Joe Premo called, waking me up to tell me that President Kennedy had been shot.

Ifield song, "I Remember You," came on and Joe started bawling. "I'm sorry, John. I'm so sorry," he said over and over. I just continued to seethe, saying nothing to him as we blazed east. Joe was still whimpering when I dropped him off at his mother's house in Worcester and turned around to go back to Albany.

For the next few delightful weeks, Johnny Osterhout and I were inseparable. Joined at the hip, and in other ways. It was exciting to be with someone new and hot after being with only Joe for the last couple of years. But four or five intense weeks were about all Johnny and I had in us. As quickly as it started, it came to a halt.

Joe eventually moved back to Albany, and it wasn't long before we were a couple again. But the first two years we had together never cycled back for us. We broke up a couple more times over the next few years, and once even got into an ugly fist fight before I finally called it off for good. I'll forever be indebted to Joe for those first few years with him and what they meant for me—we remain

John Garabedian

in touch—but at some point I needed to cover new terrain and go to places Joe just couldn't.

For all of WPTR's big sound and feel, it was a rigidly formatted station. Hardly a WORC. Putting listeners on the air wasn't even something they'd consider. They were big on their idea of slick presentation and broadcast "quality." A lot of stations were. I would have been slammed for putting the Beach Boys on the air the night they called with Gary Usher. Not even the early acetate Gary Usher sent me of "In My Room" was good enough. They wanted whatever went out over the airwaves to sound controlled and perfect. I wasn't allowed to take any chances or have fun.

Things got more rigid and formulaic when Don Kelly left and Jim Ramsburg, old "Juan 5–4–0," got elevated to replace him as program director. Don had allowed some creativity while maintaining a tightly programmed station, but Ramsburg was a programming Nazi. After every song you had to give the time, and after every other song the weather. The call letters were the first words out of a song and the last word spoken when you went into the next element, whether a song or a commercial. Then there was the constant stream of liner cards you had to read to promote all this crap. There was no room for jokes or improvisation. You felt like a robot. And worse, I knew it was unappealing to the listener.

The exposure WPTR gave me was incredible, but I grew tired of its restrictions. I again craved to do radio that was fun, innovative, entertaining. It made me question my career path. It was one thing to be twenty-one and dealing with this stuff but even if I made it to the mighty WABC in New York City and made a quarter million dollars a year, did I really want to be putting up with "no-fun" radio when I was thirty?

On a two-week vacation in 1963, I went to New York City and had the chance to hang out at the WABC studios on West 62nd Street. I felt like a kid at a candy store. The excitement ratcheted up when I first met Dan Ingram, a superb DJ idol of mine who everyone in the business considered a pro's pro. He

After water skiing on Lake Sunapee, New Hampshire, with my friend Rob, we pulled into The Anchorage to grab a drink. We were served by this skinny fifteen-year-old kid with ass-length hair and black horn-rimmed glasses held together with tape. It was Joe Perry, and this is where he met Steven Tyler and Tom Hamilton, forming Aerosmith.

was irreverent and exciting in a way the Top 40 format demanded. He knew how to make you laugh and howl with just five words. That is an art.

It was a thrill to see him live but also eye-opening. He, too, was constrained with formatics like the rest of us in conventional Top 40 radio. Everything he was supposed to do was formatted in, including WABC's big bell, which rang at the end of every song as he announced the "WABC chime time." It helped with WABC branding, no doubt. There was no mistaking what station you were listening to. Friends of mine who grew up in New York City told me they automatically turned their radios down at the end of every tune just so they wouldn't hear that damn bell.

That kind of stuff drove me insane. What did it matter if I made a ton of money if I hated going to work? For the first time in my radio career I started thinking about where I really wanted to take things. Not just what kind of work I wanted to do, but what I wanted that work to look like and mean for my life.

John Garabedian

Making money was one thing, but enjoying your work and having freedom to do what you believed was the right thing was more important.

Finally it came to me. I wasn't going to get artistic freedom or control as a mere deejay. It wouldn't come as a program director, either, since they're controlled by the general manager. And being a general manager wasn't any different. I'd still have to answer to an owner who may have stupid ideas of how to

The studio setup in the WPTR transmitter room. On a remote back road a mile away from station headquarters on Central Avenue, management never came by, so lots of friends would stop in and party.

program a station. No, to create the kind of great radio I loved, I had to be the one calling the shots. All of them. I had to be the owner.

What did that mean? How would I pull that off? How could I end up owning my own radio station? I was just twenty-one years old, and it wasn't like I had some trust fund to tap into. But working hard in radio to me was not like working at all. With my radio engineering knowledge and abilities, if I performed an allocation study and could successfully find a new frequency which met FCC regulations, I could apply for my own radio station license. All I needed beyond that was some investors. It made sense. In fact, it made too much sense not to try. As it turned into 1964, my brain churned through this idea. Man, I thought to myself, even if I play it conservatively, I bet I could get a new station on the air in two years, three at the most.

I couldn't have been more wrong.

John Garabedian

11. Cast Your Fate to the Wind

Sounds Orchestral, 1962

Selfie with Joe Premo.

As I think back on it now, the role WORC played in the first decade of my radio career is striking. It influenced everything I thought about radio. How it should operate. How it should sound. How the experience should feel to the listener. I ended up working there five different times during those ten years. A huge chunk of my early life was spent at that little station in Worcester.

Even when I wasn't drawing a paycheck from WORC, it was there in the background, playing some kind of role. When I decided to pursue building my own radio station, I knew immediately that I wanted it to be in Boston. Living in Albany reminded me of what it had felt like going to school in Miami. I was out of my element. I missed my close friends, missed the social scene, missed the much bigger Boston life I had once taken for granted. I was more of a hometown boy than I cared to admit.

As I started poking around for jobs, I learned there might be something at WMEX, the Boston Top 40 station I'd listened to growing up and by now the home to Arnie Ginsburg and his "Night Train" show. Its program director was still Mel Miller, who'd offered me a job at the station a few years before. In April of 1964, I gave him a call.

"John!" he boomed. "How are things? I hear you every so often on WPTR. You're sounding great. How's life been treating you since you left Worcester?"

"Excellent," I said, trying to sound cool. I wanted desperately to talk about work but was trying not to sound eager. "It's been a good couple of years."

Mel was impressed with the WPTR stint. "That's a big station," he said. "But I gotta say I was surprised you left 'ORC. I liked your work, thought you were a great fit for them. What happened?"

Oh, Jesus, I thought. That's all I needed. To explain why I'd left. I stumbled around a bit, trying to find my ground again. "Just felt like it was time,"

Backstage at Blinstrub's Village in 1964 with WMEX program director Mel Miller.

I said. "Was ready for a change and you know how things operate there." A sudden panic came over me. Did he think I was gay? Did he think I was making some vague reference to him and Shirley? *How things operate there?* How would he read that? I felt all tangled up. I quickly tried to change topics. "I'm, uh, thinking about making another change," I said. "I'm putting together an application for a new radio station in Framingham and need to move back to Boston. Do you have any openings?"

"Actually, yeah," he said, kindly. "As it turns out, I'm looking for an overnight guy. Nothing glamorous. Far from it, actually. You'd be following Jerry Williams, the talk show host, which means you wouldn't go on the air until one in the morning."

I was ecstatic, but tried to not sound it. "How can we make that happen?" I said, sounding much more forward than I would have liked.

Mel paused again and he shuffled more papers. "Send me an air-check I can play for Mac, the owner, and I'll get back to you in a few days."

🔊

What had always driven my parents crazy about my approach to school was that they knew I was smart and could do the work. I knew it, too. But it was the sitting still, hunkering down for a few straight hours and memorizing Latin vocabulary, world history, or some English poem, that drove me crazy. Whether it was ADD or just complete boredom, I couldn't do it.

A funny thing happened in 1964, however, as I dug into Part 73 of United States Code, the FCC's rules and regulations governing radio station engineering that outlined procedures for applying for a new station. I found I could spend hours at a time poring over this government publication. I found the rules fascinating! All the technical details that could drive most people to sleep, I devoured and memorized every rule and table. I came in early to the station to read the rule books 'PTR had on file and then wrote to the U.S. Government Printing Office to secure my own copy. It was a three-inch thick, four-pound volume, and in my off-hours I made myself comfortable and studied them. Taking notes, drawing up to-do lists—I became the student my mother had hoped she could send to Harvard.

I got lucky, too. The FCC didn't fool around when it came to allocating a frequency for a new station. They had just adopted new "go-no go" rules that said that if the application was incomplete or defective in any way, it was permanently rejected. The engineering part of the application required a detailed frequency allocation study that showed the proposed new station wouldn't cause interference with any existing stations on the same or adjacent frequencies. You had to prepare and present all these insane charts and graphs that showed, for example, the ground wave coverage of both the protected coverage area of the proposed station and the potential interference curves to any adjacent channel stations.

I understood a lot of it, but there was plenty that went right over my head. Fortunately, I had become tight with WPTR's chief engineer, a mellow older guy named Russ David whose engineering knowledge was outstanding. With his starched shirts, pleated pants, and a mop of white hair, he gave off all the appearances of someone who spent most of his life thinking about numbers. I'd kept quiet about my plans to build the station, but I knew I could trust Russ with my idea. Outside of making sure the station ran well, he had no allegiances. I'd stroll into his office toward the end of the day and open up a couple of manuals or a book and ask what something meant. Russ would drop his glasses to the end of his nose, look over the info for a few minutes, then explain it all to me in actual English.

When I wasn't at the station, or in the library, I was in my red '61 Impala convertible heading back to Boston. Sometimes I'd leave after work and then wheel right around the next afternoon to get back in time for my night show. There'd be nights I wouldn't get more than a couple hours of sleep. I didn't care. I was powered by the project. Never had I felt so clear about my focus, what I was

John Garabedian

aiming for. The whole thing—the engineering, the program planning—brought together everything I loved—the technical and the creative.

The biggest challenge was finding a frequency that would meet the FCC rules. Russ had warned me, "Everyone's tried for years to squeeze in another station within a hundred miles of Boston, but no one's ever succeeded."

The AM dial was certainly tight. But the center of the AM dial looked promising, though nearly all the available frequencies ran the potential of bumping against some powerhouse signal: WBZ's 1030. WHN/New York's 1050, WTIC/Hartford's 1080, KYW/Philadelphia's 1060; even CBA 1070 from New Brunswick, Canada, posed a problem. But if I moved the proposed transmitter site a few miles west of Boston to Framingham, a thriving Boston suburb, a whole new opportunity opened up. There was a frequency I found which might work there, 1060 kHz, which, if the antenna was well-placed and engineered correctly, wouldn't bump into any existing station. It would be a definite squeeze and wouldn't technically be a "Boston station," but that now seemed like an advantage. I'd be at the center of all those rich suburbanites and huge shopping malls in the exploding MetroWest area.

There was just one issue—the money. Squaring up all those engineering docs didn't mean a thing if I couldn't finance the station. The FCC required all applicants to present a detailed financial plan that demonstrated that applicants not only have the means to build the station but the ability to sustain it for three months of operation without income. I understood the reasoning. It served no one any good for the government to hand out frequencies to people whose stations would quickly go out of business. For a guy like me who was making $600 a month, it meant I had to find an investor. So a lot of my trips back to Boston cast me as the salesman, selling my idea to banks and business leads that friends passed on to me.

Once again, I was forced to step away from the sidelines. To put myself out there, to lay who I was on the line and risk the chance of being rejected. I thought it would be daunting, even a little scary, but instead I discovered that because I believed so much in my idea, I didn't have to fake anything. I didn't have to pretend to be someone I wasn't.

The Meadows supper club in Framingham. I took my girlfriend Carol Ann there for New Year's Eve, 1959, returning five years later to meet a potential investor, owner Norman Farley. His son became my investor.

That came in handy one early March day when I found myself sitting down with Norman Farley, a Framingham businessman whom the Framingham Chamber of Commerce had introduced me to. He was a bald, heavy-set man who had just turned sixty, and was never without a cigar. Farley's world revolved around Framingham. It was where he'd made his fortune in real estate and restaurants. By the time I met him, his most famous operation was The Meadows, a big dine-and-dance nightclub he bought from Vaughn Monroe, a baritone singer who'd made his name in big band music in the 1940s and '50s. Farley bought the Route 9 place for a quarter million dollars sometime around 1960 along with twenty-six acres of prime commercial land. Two years later, he sold ten acres of the land for $600,000 to Caldor, a chain of discount department stores.

Farley packed a presence that filled a room. You could just feel him churning through his thoughts as he chewed on his stogie. When he finally did speak, what he had to say was trimmed of all fat. He was direct and didn't dance around what he was saying. Like his business approach, he spoke with ruthless efficiency.

"Sit down and tell me your radio station idea," Farley demanded when I walked into the club's empty barroom one afternoon to meet him. He didn't bother standing up to shake my hand. He just pointed to the chair. I took a seat and went right into my presentation.

Because I knew Farley was a man who liked making money, that's where I put my emphasis. I had looked at enough stations, how they worked, what they

John Garabedian

made, and felt certain that within a couple of years my new station would be turning a good profit. "As you know, this area's exploding, and the only radio station serving it now is WKOX. You'll get your money back in two years," I told him.

Farley looked straight at me, chomping his cigar as I spoke. It didn't change when, after five minutes, I'd wrapped up my pitch. I slid a couple of pieces of paper across his desk—budget forecasts and timetables—which he studied for a few minutes in silence. Finally, he looked up from the papers. The old man wasn't interested.

"Not my thing, kid," he said. "I'm sixty and no Farley male has ever lived past sixty-one." My heart sank. But then the old man's voice picked up. "But I think I know someone who might be interested in it," he said. "My son, Norman, Jr." Then he reached for the phone and called up his secretary. "Lucy," he said. "Get my kid on the line."

The younger Farley ended up committing $38,000 to the venture, about a quarter million dollars in 2016 currency. For a young guy like me who made less than ten grand a year it sounded like a fortune, but when you factored in what it would take to get a new station going—the real estate, the equipment, the payroll—the number was pretty modest. When the dust settled from working out all the particulars, Norman Jr. got two-thirds of the company, I got one-third and was elected its president. With everything in place, I was ready to put in my resignation at WPTR and return to Boston to put together the FCC application for the proposed new station.

After two years away, being back in Boston felt fantastic. I was back in a place that had energy, a real nightlife, and a thriving radio community. The payola scandal that had decimated Boston's Top 40 scene a few years before was in the rearview mirror and with the Beatles dominating the charts, Top 40 music was soaring with the British invasion.

Joe and I were back together, too, and we got an apartment in Boston's South End, a newly renovated two-bedroom place on the second floor of an old townhouse at 34 Lawrence Street. Being on the air at WMEX, the Top 40 station I'd listened to as a kid, felt even better. Mel had liked my style, and with a little coaxing, got the station's mercurial owner, Maxwell E. "Mac" Richmond, to sign off on my hire.

Mac was a legendary asshole. Everybody had a bad thing to say about him. He was tough and ruthless and didn't suffer fools gladly. He couldn't care less about team building. If somebody screwed up,

New Year's Eve, 1964. I didn't start drinking alcohol until my late twenties when Mateus Rose, Blue Nun Liebfraumilch, and Boone's Farm Apple Wine became popular accompaniments to smoking weed.

he let them have it. He didn't spend any time worrying about hurting someone's feelings. His demeanor was backed by an intimidating presence. He was tall—about 6'2"—in his late forties with a bit of a belly and this thick black hair that he left long on the top so that it moved around like a bowl of Jell-O whenever he got animated, which was often. He was always in the same suit and I don't think the man owned an iron. His clothes were constantly wrinkled, like he'd slept in them.

Mac was a workaholic and WMEX was the most important thing in his life. That was a little tough to decipher considering the condition of the 70 Brookline Avenue studios, which adjoined Fenway Park. Filthy is a good description of it—dust, dirt, and papers everywhere. But Mac lived and breathed the radio business. Over time, he became one of the great mentors in my life. He'd bought WMEX sometime in 1957 and eventually took its 5,000-watt signal and cranked it up to 50,000 watts. It was Mac who, in the face of the payola scandal, was the only Top 40 station owner in Boston with the courage not to cower and change formats. He just didn't have it in him to back down.

It all emanated from his background. His Philadelphia upbringing gave him his toughness while his Wharton Business School education at the University of Pennsylvania honed his natural business sense. It really wasn't until my second

John Garabedian

Maxwell E. "Mac" Richmond (right) was easily the most detested boss in radio who boldly rolled over everyone, except Arnie Ginsburg and me. I think he respected us because we were authentic and always stood up to him honestly when we disagreed.

go-around at WMEX from 1969–'72 that he and I became close. I discovered that if you got past the gruff exterior and dealt with him openly and directly, he would get into a conversation. He had a lot of knowledge and experience to offer. Mac once told me one of the most important things he learned at Wharton is that every part of the business has to make money. You can't have one part of the station dragging down everything else.

That's one of the reasons he hated doing news. *People don't listen to us for the news*, he often barked. *They come to WMEX for the music. The hits!* But the FCC required radio stations do news, so Mac being Mac adhered to the letter of the law as little as he could. Eventually he ordered the station to only do the headlines in the morning when people were truly interested in finding out about the world, like who won the game, who got shot, or where the big car crash was.

Mac couldn't resist micro-managing everything. He was an insomniac and listened to the station at all hours. Even during my overnight show it wasn't unusual to get a call from him at three in the morning and hear him start barking orders. No hello. No hi. Instead, it was "Write this down!" That was a famous line of his. Sometimes he'd have you write down a joke and tell you to read it on the air. It was ridiculous. His big fetish with deejays was that he wanted them to make the music louder under them when they talked over the beginning of a song. Many announcers are tone deaf, or they just don't understand that when a song ends and a new one comes on, they need to be talking *in* the music. They shouldn't bury it with their voices. Mac made sure every DJ at the station understood this.

Other times, his calls involved less helpful advice. He'd demand the newsman play up a story a certain way or stop reporting something altogether. "I don't care if he's got a minute left," he'd holler. "Just end it!" One night he called

Arnie Ginsburg and told him to start announcing WMEX was going to give away a pony to one lucky listener. Then, the next day when some poor announcer was still promoting the giveaway, Mac called up again and ordered, *Forget the pony! We're not doing that.* It was loony seat-of-the-pants radio and I relished it.

One of the better known Mac stories was about a deejay he'd hired to do middays. The guy had come up from Oklahoma, hauling his house trailer as a place to live for him and his family. He got Mac's permission to park the thing at the station transmitter site until he found a more permanent place for it. Mac gave him a hearty welcome when he came through the door, but as soon as the guy went on air the boss gave him the cold treatment. Hardly a word was said to him. The next day, he was on the air for maybe twenty minutes when Mac stormed into the studio. "You're not the guy who was on that demo tape!" he blasted. "That was somebody else! You're fired!"

He was stunned. "I'm fired?" he said. "What do I do?"

Mac just stared him down. "Not my problem, Jack." That's what he called you if he didn't like you. Jack. And because he was Mac, he ordered his now ex-employee to get his trailer off the transmitter site. "I want that thing gone by sundown," he barked. "You got that?"

Dejected, Mac's suddenly new former midday guy shuffled out of the station and went back to Quincy to tell his wife and kid he needed another job. But he thought no one would bother him if he stayed for the night. Mac didn't mess around. When Mac had the transmitter engineer check the transmitter site around midnight and found the family still there, Mac called the Quincy police, who ordered them to vacate immediately.

Even with those who did well for him, Mac could be ruthless. In 1959, Mac lured Arnie Ginsburg away from WBOS to replace departing Joe Smith and made the "Night Train" show the most popular Top 40 program in the city. But in 1968, frustrated with Mac, Arnie left to join a brand new Top 40 station in Boston, WRKO.

Mac went berserk. Arnie had been on the air at 'RKO for just a few weeks when suddenly, his former boss produced an alleged contract with Arnie that included a non-compete clause that stated if Arnie ever left WMEX he could not be on the air in Boston for two years. Arnie fought it, insisting Mac had forged his signature. The battle went to court but in the end, Mac won. Did Mac forge Arnie's signature to that contract? Probably. Did Arnie hate him for putting him through the ringer? For a while, yes. But Mac was impossible not to respect in some way and when he died in 1971, Arnie joined me as one of Mac's pallbearers.

At night, WMEX switched gears. Mac had recognized that in the evening, television offered stiff competition. To keep listeners tuned into the station, Mac created a new radio format and created what is commonly known today as two-way talk radio. This was in the late 1950s, when nobody else was really thinking about this stuff. He realized that listenership at night drops precipitously, so to attract a large audience and advertisers, he decided to put on a controversial talk show to follow Arnie's "Night Train" show.

The guy he hired to anchor the format was an up-and-coming radio host named Jerry Williams. It was at WMEX where Williams helped pioneer the whole concept of the telephone talk show format. He could be absolutely ruthless, unafraid to put listeners on the air and was even less scared to hang up on them if he didn't agree with what they had to say. "I don't care," he'd yell, then slam the receiver down. One time a woman called up and because the screener didn't take the call, Williams picked up the phone himself and put her on the air. The caller was so nervous she didn't know what to say.

"Hello?" Williams shouted. "Hello?"

Finally the woman muttered a meekly sounding "How are you?"

Williams had no time for her. "I'm not going to answer that!" he screamed and hung up.

For eight years, Williams dominated the Boston nighttime airwaves on WMEX. Arnie Ginsburg had a thirty-share, but Jerry Williams regularly pulled in a fifty. Part of it was his energy, but he also attracted high-profile guests to his program. A-listers like Malcolm X, Tony Bennett, Jack Kennedy, and Ted Williams. It's not like today where people appear on talk shows to plug something. Jerry had real conversations with them, and gave his listeners a better sense of who his guests were.

In the dressing room after a 1964 show with Diana Ross and the Supremes at the legendary Blinstrubs Village in South Boston. The 850-seat nightclub presented the biggest superstars. It burned down in 1968 and never reopened.

My show followed Williams, which, although it was 1 a.m., was a thrill. Unfortunately, it didn't last long. In true Mac Richmond fashion, in late August of 1964, I got a call at home from Mel Miller.

"Johnny," he said, taking a deep breath. "I've got some bad news for you. We're going to let you go."

I was floored. "Are you serious?" I asked. "What did I do?"

Mel took another deep breath. "It's Mac," he said. "You know how it goes around here."

There wasn't any use fighting it. Even if Mel had thought it was a bad move, sticking up for me would have been useless. But I'm not entirely sure Mel disagreed with his boss, because the guy Mac brought in to replace me was Larry Glick, another future talk show titan who went on to have a legendary career at WMEX and WBZ. Mac had discovered him while on a trip to Miami, where Glick was working. He stumbled across his show on Miami radio one night and got it into his brain that he just had to have him at WMEX. "He's just what we need," he told Mel. "He'll hold the Jerry Williams audience and keep them listening." That's how Larry Glick ended up in Boston. Mac certainly made the right call, but it left me out of a job.

◀

John Garabedian

As I navigated the combustible work environment that Mac Richmond had created at WMEX, life with Joe was also proving complex. Some of that early excitement from the early days of our relationship returned after we got back together in Albany. But it didn't last. And then the wheels came off in Boston.

In early July of '64, about a month before Mel Miller called to fire me, I made my way home after doing my usual overnight show and then the 6–8 a.m. stretch of morning headlines. It was a little after nine and the morning rush hour traffic had been a bear. It didn't help that I was beat and the weather was muggy as hell. All I wanted was to crawl into bed and lose myself in a good seven or eight hours of sleep. When I finally got to the South End and parked my car in front of our building, it felt like I had just crossed the finish line at the Boston Marathon.

I trudged upstairs and opened the door to our apartment and immediately sensed that something was off. Normally the window shades in our apartment were wide open but on this morning they were all closed. It was pitch black. I walked into the bedroom and flipped on the light, and there was Joe, naked, lying next to the guy from the apartment next door, who was also naked. I went insane.

"What the fuck are you doing?" I said, glaring at Joe. I marched closer to the bed to let my 6'4" frame tower over the two. Then I came at both of them with fists flying. I picked up Joe's friend, threw him against the wall, grabbed his face and shoved him back to the ground. "Get the fuck out of here," I screamed as he scrambled to find his clothes.

Joe was another story. I wanted to kill him and he knew it. He looked at me like I was this raging animal. While his "friend" threw his pants on and ran for the door, I grabbed Joe and tossed him out of the bedroom like a rag doll. "Get your fucking ass out of here," I yelled as I marched toward him. Joe stumbled to his feet.

"John, wait," he said, raising his right hand. "Please, just give me a second to talk to you or at least get dressed."

"You want your fucking clothes?" I screamed, tossing a pile of stuff at him. "Maybe you should have kept them on in the first place."

I wanted to beat the hell out of Joe. I probably would have, too, if he hadn't left right away. But Joe was nothing if not street-smart, and he knew when to bolt a losing scene. He ran down the stairs and into the humid morning air. My mind raced with anger and after several long minutes I pulled open the window blinds and let the new morning light flood the apartment. A sense of calm started to take over me. Then I sunk into the couch and let my head roll back and I stared at the ceiling.

I wasn't just angry or exhausted. I felt resigned. More so than I had ever felt in Albany, I realized that Joe and I didn't have a future. I'm not sure what I had expected when we first got together in Worcester. I guess I was just blinded by the thrill of being in love. But I was older now. Knew myself better. Understood who I was and had a clearer idea of what I wanted out of life.

For the rest of the summer of '64, I let loose. At twenty-two years old I was a hot-looking boy who knew how to be charming and I played both for all they were worth. Even after all I'd been through with Joe—coming out with him, moving in together, making a life together—I still felt the shackles of my parents' conservative influence. They'd put such an emphasis on being proper that it felt strange to feel like I didn't have to worry about what people thought or how they wanted me to act. I was less afraid to make a mistake, to do the wrong thing. It's no coincidence that about the time I was coming into my own as a person, I took the ambitious step to start my own radio station. The two were connected. Without a doubt. I was learning to say screw it, I'm going to do this. I don't care what anyone says. I want to be happy and not conform to what anyone else thinks I should do or be like.

That summer became a wild time for me. And a lot of that wildness began with nights at the Punch Bowl, a club that was for several decades the epicenter of Boston's underground gay nightlife. Located in Park Square, it had opened in the 1930s and by the mid-1960s was one of the oldest gay bars in America. The hilarious part about it was that it sat directly across the street from the elegant Park Plaza Hotel. It made for an interesting contrast. On one side of the street were all these stiff society types coming and going, on the other side something quite the opposite.

The electricity of the place hit you as soon as you walked through its doors. The "PB" had two levels and on a good night six or seven hundred guys would pack inside it, drinking, dancing, and cruising. In a city with so many college kids, a number of whom were away from home and coming out for the first time, it was like a buffet. For Boston's gay community it was the place where the under-thirty crowd hung out. Older guys and the younger guys who liked them tended to prefer The Napoleon Club two blocks away.

In the pre-Stonewall riots age, gay clubs had to put up with a lot of shit. Mostly raids. The Punch Bowl was no exception. When employees saw the police coming, the ones on the upper level would flash a light to the crew on the basement floor and within seconds people would stop dancing, something which could actually get you arrested. *No gay scene here, officers!* The place had cornered the market on being resilient.

The characters who worked there were legendary. One very ugly, loudmouthed waiter named Sidney Sushman became a drag queen star using the name Sylvia Sidney. Another was this busty waitress simply known as Tex. She was an ex-stripper, probably in her fifties, with big blonde hair and even bigger tits. She was what is termed a "fag hag" in every sense of the term and loved working at a gay bar because she didn't have to put up with a bunch of straight guys staring at her chest. Tex was a great waitress and her unfiltered personality fit in perfectly with the Punch Bowl's atmosphere. One night I noticed she had changed her hairstyle.

"I like your new hairdo," I remarked.

She casually flipped one side of her hair back, as though she was giving a little performance. "Yeah," she said. "It gives me that just-fucked look."

How could you not love a woman like that?

Of course, I wasn't there to chat with Tex. I was there to meet guys. And that's just what I did. Almost every single night for the rest of the summer, I stopped in there and invariably would leave with someone. *I've enjoyed talking with you, but how about you come over to my place to check out my "etchings?"* It felt so incredible. I was free. For the first time in my life I didn't have a single care about what anyone thought of how I was living.

In the midst of all the craziness surrounding Joe and WMEX, I continued to push forward with my station. My new business partner, Norman Farley Jr., suggested we build it in Natick. "Why be the second station in Framingham when we can be the first radio station in Natick," he said. He was right. It covered the same Boston MetroWest area, had a decent downtown, but its real asset was the soon-to-open Natick Mall, which would end up turning the Framingham-Natick metro into the single largest retail trading zone in New England, surpassing even downtown Boston.

One of the challenges was trying to find a site for the tower. I hadn't budgeted much for any real estate purchase but if you work at it, opportunity presents itself. At Natick Town Hall, I studied the zoning maps for open land. At 1 Speen Street, Natick, on the Sherborn town line, I discovered a five-acre parcel next to a chicken farm. Its owner, a jovial older guy with a curly steel gray hair, fit the scene perfectly. He was an old time Yankee who packed a certain warmth around his standoffishness. We needed all five acres of land for the ground system that would surround the tower. I explained what we needed, and he eventually agreed to give me an option to lease the five acres for $150 a month plus the taxes.

Tapping my brother-in-law, Jack Carlson, I got access to his corporate lawyer to set up our corporation. I gave it the mundane-but-FCC-friendly name of Home Service Broadcasting Corporation, something I hoped the feds would regard as a community-minded company.

Finally, on September 4, 1964, just weeks after Mel Miller fired me, I filed our application with the FCC, along with the required statements of citizenship, engineering studies, community leader survey, business projections, and the tower plans. Packed inside a folder, the documents were more than an inch thick and bound together with big brass staples. I put the required legal ads in the local papers announcing our application and then mailed it off, three copies in all. Several weeks later, I received a letter from the FCC announcing it had received the application. It had been deemed "accepted for filing" and the letter established May 10, 1965, as the cut-off date for any mutually exclusive competing applications for the 1060 frequency. Now it just became a waiting game.

Little did I know that the real effort to get WGTR going hadn't even started.

John Garabedian

12. Mr. Tambourine Man

Bob Dylan, 1965

Late spring afternoon at Rob Seely's South End attic flat, Boston.

No Boston radio station wanted to touch me. The radio community is like a small town. Everyone knows everyone, and no move goes unnoticed. The fact that I had filed an FCC application to get my own station started hadn't flown under the radar. As soon as it appeared in *Broadcasting* magazine, every station manager and program director in Massachusetts knew what I was up to. The thought that I would not only be a potential competitor but a short-term employee made it almost impossible to land a new job. Dozens of tapes and resumes went out. I heard nothing.

Every day, it seemed, my geographical scope widened when it came to my job search. From Eastern Massachusetts it became the entire state. Then most of New England. After that it became anything interesting advertised in the Help Wanted section of *Broadcasting* magazine. That's how a job in Mocksville, North Carolina, eventually caught my eye. It was a position as chief engineer at WDSL, a brand new station that had recently gone on the air. The location didn't exactly make my heart leap—a tiny Southern town twenty-five miles south of Winston-Salem in the middle of tobacco country—but the position did.

It was more than just playing records. It was working at a brand new radio station where I could learn the challenges of what I would be facing in building and launching my new station in Natick. So I sent them my resume and tape and a week later nailed the phone interview with the owner, a guy named Roland Potter.

As it had been with Miami and then Albany, I wasn't excited about leaving Boston. But I needed a job and I needed to be doing something to build my experience and skills. I couldn't stay in Boston waiting for job callbacks and waiting out the FCC deadline. I would have gone crazy. I needed something to do, even if that something was a thousand miles from home.

John Garabedian

I didn't move alone. Somehow, Joe wandered back into my life. We had started talking again. He apologized over and over about what had happened. I didn't want to think about it. I was done feeling bad, being hurt. Talking turned to hanging out and the next thing I knew he was in the passenger seat of the red '61 Impala convertible as I drove south with all my things packed in the back. I was genuinely happy to be back with him, but that incident at our place a few months before hadn't changed what I thought about him or us. We weren't going to be together for the long haul. I knew that, maybe Joe did, too, and in a way that felt okay. The future was the future. Who knew what it would look like? For now, we were friends and got along well and all we had was right in front of us. It felt pretty good.

We found a place in a trailer park on the outskirts of Winston-Salem and while Joe played househusband, I went off to work. Being at WDSL was actually refreshing. Roland Potter, the station's owner, was a real southern gentleman. He had a slow, confident way of talking while he looked you in the eye. Maybe it was because the pressure was off him to make this new venture an immediate money-maker. At the time I was there, WDSL was a sideline project. His real money-maker was another, bigger AM station in North Wilkesboro, North Carolina, which he owned with his wife.

Being new also gave it another distinction for me. Unlike so many of the places I worked at, WDSL was actually clean. The place got vacuumed. You didn't walk out of the studios feeling like you needed to take a shower. But its real prize was its transmitter, a brand new Collins 21E, the exact same transmitter WORC used. It had a magical way of making music actually sound better. That's not just some anecdotal observation. Years later, an engineer friend and I traced what caused it by performing some extensive audio tests on the WORC Collins 21E unit during an overnight. We discovered that it somehow actually enhanced the audio waveform—similar to what an Aphex synthesizer does—by inserting even harmonics above a certain part of the midrange. It made the music sound crisper, more alive, and the bass firmer, more solid. I didn't know it then, but that was one of the things that had blown me away when I first tuned in WORC in my car on that spring morning back in 1959. It was the same sound at WDSL.

As for the music itself, the station wasn't a trailblazer. The focus was a cross section of styles. There would be smooth hits like a Dean Martin tune in the morning, then country music from 10 to 2, and finally Top 40 until sunset when the station had to sign off the air to protect clear channel stations WKBW in Buffalo and KOMA in Oklahoma City. Unlike other places I worked at, it was all over the place, musically. Johnny Cash, Roy Acuff, Eddy Arnold, Roy

The Collins 21E transmitter at both WORC and WDSL transformed the audio to somehow make it crisper, more FM-like. Years later, Bob Lund and I spent an overnight shift measuring what it did and how it did it.

Orbison, Elvis Presley, the Beatles, Perry Como, Ray Charles, The Supremes. But it was quite listenable and served the needs of the rural farming area south of Winston-Salem. Potter gave me the 10 a.m.-2 p.m. country show, and surprisingly, I actually got to know and enjoy the country music.

For me, though, the thing it had that most stations didn't was total freedom. I didn't have the owner or general manager hovering over me. I came in and was allowed to simply do my job. One early afternoon in February, the transmitter suddenly went off the air. Total silence. I was working on something at my desk when the speakers just cut out. "What happened?" I shouted out. I shot a look into the studio across the hall where the afternoon guy was working the transmitter remote control, looking bewildered. "I'm pushing 'plates on' but nothing happens," he said.

I grabbed my jacket, hopped in my car and roared out to the transmitter site, which was five miles away in the middle of a big tobacco field. When I got there I found the main overload breakers would trip every time I tried to activate the high voltage. After spending a couple of hours probing around with a multi-meter, trying to isolate the problem, I found that the heart of the transmitter, the three hundred-pound iron-core modulation transformer, was short-circuited to its case. I immediately called Collins Radio Company in Cedar Rapids, Iowa, to order an

John Garabedian

emergency replacement, but there was no shot of getting one flown in to Charlotte for at least two days. In the meantime I had to get the station back on the air.

After thinking about it for a couple of minutes I had an idea: I looked around the transmitter building and spotted a broom. That was it! I grabbed it, broke it in two over my knee and stuck both pieces under the transformer to insulate its case from the grounded metal transmitter cabinet. With six thousand volts running through the transformer, I wasn't sure the wooden broomsticks wouldn't arc over, causing another failure, and maybe even a fire. My heart raced with excitement. I pressed the high-voltage "on" button. Up came the carrier and the station went back on the air! I loved the rush and satisfaction of coming up with an emergency fix.

Yet life in Winston-Salem, North Carolina, got to me. It was beautiful. The rolling North Carolina hills, the forested landscape—it actually reminded me a lot of New England. And the people who lived there were warm and extremely hospitable. But my appreciation for the place only went so far. Winter was ugly. When it snowed, the stuff was slushy and only stuck around for a few hours. Back home, a big winter at least looked like a beautiful painting. North Carolina winters were just mushy and gray. You were convinced it was never going to be sunny again. I hated it.

The conservative religious people didn't help. You had to practically beat the Southern Baptists back like black flies. They were nice enough, of course, but they were relentless. Joe and I would be lying in bed on Sunday morning and like clockwork there would be a knock at the door. Good morning. We're going to church and just wondered if you'd like to join us. That's when I'd pull out my mother's well-worn line. "Thank you," I'd say graciously. "But we have our own religion." And then politely say goodbye, making sure not to give them a chance to extend the invitation.

By early '65, I was ready to get back to New England. I was done with the Southern Baptists, done with the wishy-washy winters, done with living in a little place with no excitement, away from my friends and family. The tapes and resumes I had sent out to stations the previous fall were still out there and then a mid-February afternoon I got a call from my mother.

"Johnny," she said. "A nice man from a radio station in Manchester, New Hampshire, called for you."

Two weeks later, Joe and I had my '61 Impala packed up again and headed north. My new employer, WFEA, was a Manchester Top 40 station that made its home in Reeds Ferry right off the Everett Turnpike. It had first gone on the air right in the teeth of the Depression in 1932 and by the late '50s it began airing Top 40 hits. It was what I expected. Not too daring, not too fun. Really, its best feature was its tower, a four hundred-foot diamond-shaped Blaw-Knox. First built in the 1930s, they're

WFEA, Manchester, New Hampshire, has one of five surviving Blaw-Knox "diamond" towers in the United States. Built in 1932 when WFEA signed on as New Hampshires's first radio station, it survived the Hurricane of 1938 and is still in use today.

beautiful structures and with only a handful of them still standing, a few have even been placed on the U.S. National Register of Historic Places.

In Manchester, I was really happy to return to programming as music director and midday deejay. Being back in New England, close to my friends, the social scene in Boston, and within an hour of Natick where I hoped to start the heavy lifting of getting the new station off the ground, were important to me.

Like any Top 40 station, new records were coming in all the time. Record companies were always sending out their newest tunes, often three 45s at a time in brown paper envelopes. You knew what they were as soon as they landed on your desk. Often times what you received were duds, but sometimes it was like winning the lottery. One morning I was doing my show when the station secretary, Arlene, came in while the mike was off and dropped off a package with a bunch of new 45 record releases. Arlene barked when she talked to you. She was always bitchy, complaining or annoyed. "I'm not your mailman, Johnny," she snapped at me. "Next time pick up your stuff at the front desk."

John Garabedian

"Got it," I said, flashing her the biggest fake smile I could muster.

I picked up the package and tore it open. I gave the first two records a quick sampling. I don't even remember what they were. Nothing special. But then, as "Help" by the Beatles played out over the air, I put on the third record. From the very first few notes, the song blew me away. This is absolutely a number one song, I said out loud to nobody in particular. This is a smash.

As soon as that Beatles tune was done, I popped on that new record and New Hampshire got its first taste of Sonny and Cher's "I Got You Babe." Everything about that song was perfect. Still is, even fifty years later—the arrangement, the production, the singing, the hook, the pledge of love. The message was, I don't care about anything going on in my life because I have you. It captured everything a great Top 40 song should. Unearthing this stuff, recognizing greatness and sharing it with listeners was a rush like a drug, and one of the reasons why I was in the radio business. It still is.

What Sonny and Cher were crooning about, however, was nothing that described my own life. From the moment we arrived in Manchester, Joe started complaining about everything. We bickered all the time. I found myself coming up with excuses to not come home. I worked late. I had to run errands. Anything to stay away from the black cloud that had become my home life. We weren't a couple. Hell, we were barely roommates. Finally, one evening, I came home from work and Joe announced he was moving back to Worcester. He didn't even say hello or how was your day. He just blurted it out hoping, I think, he'd catch me off guard and get some kind of reaction.

He didn't. "Oh," I said, shrugging my shoulders. "When are you leaving?"

Joe took in a long breath. "Tomorrow," he said. "I have some friends picking me up. I can't do this anymore."

"I know," I said, coolly. "I feel the same way." Then I left the room and headed to the kitchen to get something to eat. There was nothing left to say.

After Joe moved out, I returned to Boston every chance I could. I wanted to see my buddies, and when time allowed for it, go "shopping" at clubs like the Punch Bowl, which never got roaring until after 11 p.m. Getting out of work and going home to an empty apartment was no fun, and I only had a few friends

My 1965 Corvette Stingray convertible, which cost $5,000.05 brand new. Today that car is a collector's dream and would be worth over $200,000 if I still owned it.

in Manchester, so I was always trying to plan something to do during weeknights. I wanted to stay busy, and I guess, distracted.

Those distractions included finding a new car. I'd grown bored with my red '61 Impala convertible, and I had become obsessed with the new Chevy Corvette Stingray convertible. I started wondering if maybe I could trade my old car in for a used Corvette. After work one warm summer night, I headed to Dobles Chevrolet in Manchester to see what they had in stock. There was nothing on the lot. More determined, I headed south and stopped at Chevy dealers in Nashua, Lowell, and then right around 9 p.m. I pulled up at the Chevy place on Huntington Avenue in Boston. The door was locked but through the glass door I saw a salesman sitting at his desk. I rapped a couple of times and the guy looked at his watch and then lumbered over to the door.

"We're closed," he said. "But can I help you?"

"I know," I said, trying to sound apologetic. "I've been looking for a used Corvette and wondered if you had any in stock?"

He opened the door. "No," he said. "But we do have a brand new one that just came in today. Would you like to see it?" He smiled. "It doesn't cost anything to look."

"New?" I said. I thought back to my $135 a week paycheck. "I doubt I can afford it."

John Garabedian

"Come in," he said, welcoming me into the building.

The next thing I knew we were in the upstairs maintenance shop. As he turned on the big overhead lights, tucked away in a corner I spotted a gleaming, straight-from-the-factory, silver, 1965 Stingray convertible. The thing was gorgeous. I slid into the driver seat and as that new car smell hit my nostrils a shot of adrenalin ran up my body. A wide smile stretched across my face. The salesman, who leaned up against the car near the driver's side door smiled, too.

"Nice car, huh?" he said.

The sticker price was $5,000.05, but with my trade-in my monthly payment was $85 a month, almost identical to what I previously paid. It couldn't have worked out any more perfectly. While the radio in that Corvette sucked—the AM part sounded all right, but the FM sounded muddy and got poor reception—everything else about that car was a dream. Its low, wide body. The curves. The 327 cubic inch V8 engine. I felt awesome in it. On my visits to Boston I was quite popular.

The big brown envelope that arrived in the mail looked ominous. It was from a law firm in Washington, D.C., I'd never heard of and was a good inch thick. It arrived at my parents' place in Weston, whose address I'd used for everything to do with the radio station. It was May 12, 1965, and that week I'd been on pins and needles. The FCC's May 10th cut-off date had come and gone and I was hoping, praying, that we'd quietly passed by it without another competing application.

I waited until I got inside before I tore open the package. When I did, I stared in disbelief at what I was holding. It was a competing application for the same 1060 frequency by a company called Natick Broadcast Associates, Inc. I had no idea who the hell they were but they'd waited until May 10—the very last day you could file—to submit their application. I skimmed through it quickly.

"Dammit!" I yelled as loud as I could inside the empty house. I sank back into the living room couch. How the hell did this happen? On the last goddamn day to file? A competitor! That meant more bureaucratic holdups. More waiting.

It could even mean that after all my hard work and time someone else could win the FCC construction permit for the 1060 frequency I had worked hard to discover. It certainly meant a comparative hearing in Washington, D.C., and that meant lots more money and time.

When my head had cooled I picked up the application and studied it carefully. Natick Broadcast Associates hadn't screwed around. They'd done everything perfectly, it seemed. They'd hired a professional consulting engineering firm to do the engineering and had the whole application prepared by an impressive, expensive sounding D.C. law firm. Ours had been handled by Garabedian law and engineering. At that moment, I felt so small and insignificant. What had I been thinking? Had I really thought I could have pulled this off? I mean, as a twenty-three-year-old kid, other than being a pretty good deejay and a decent young engineer, who the hell was I? Maybe it was just ridiculous to even think that I could have pulled something like this off. With a competing applicant, we were going to be forced to go before the FCC and make the case that our company was better qualified to get the license. That meant lawyers and cash. My heart sank. How was I going to pull this off?

From there, things only got worse. Next came the call to my partner, Farley Jr. Like me, he was pissed at first. Then, when the news settled in, he realized he just wasn't up for the fight. "I've gotta back out, John," he said a couple of weeks later. "I'm sorry. This could cost a lot of money. I'm not wealthy enough to go up against those guys."

I wasn't sure what to do next. I was twenty-three years old with no money to my name. Worse than that, though, my whole future felt uncertain. The jobs in Mocksville and Manchester, working overnights at WMEX in Boston and then getting fired, the long sleepless days and nights prepping my application— everything I'd done over the last year had been in preparation for the station I dreamed of building. There had been a clear goal in front of me. A finish line to aim for. And now everything ahead of me looked blurry and out of focus. What the hell was I going to do?

Making things worse was the group I was up against. Natick Broadcast Associates, Inc. was made up of eight people. Four of them were young guys like

With my dad at our home in Weston. Don't know why I was wearing a tie.

me who worked in radio and television. The other four were major corporate titans, older guys with deep pockets. Stanley and Sumner Feldman were the president and treasurer respectively of the Zayre Corporation (now TJX), Richard Smith was president of General Cinema Corporation, and Newell Kurson headed another movie theater chain. They were beyond rich. It was a real David versus Goliath story. That's assuming David could even afford plane fare to D.C. to make it to the fight.

I did have one asset in my corner and that was my lawyer. James M. Langan was a Massachusetts judge and the corporate counsel to Carlson Corporation,

the construction company owned by my brother-in-law Jack Carlson and his family. Langan was a crusty old guy, well-connected and part of what was called the Boston "Irish Mafia," high-powered politicians who knew how to "get things done." Nothing surprised him or caught him off guard. Langan lived in Wellesley but his law firm was in downtown Boston. Watching him, I learned many lessons about the real world. "Perception is everything," he once told me. "It would be a lot easier commute if my office was in Wellesley, but then I'd be a Wellesley lawyer. A Boston address makes me a Boston lawyer. That's a big difference."

A few days after Farley backed out, I met with Langan at his 84 State Street office to discuss what my next move should be. "No guts, no glory, but of course to get that glory it always helps to have a little cash," I said. I looked over at Langan, who sat across from me at his desk, sifting through the FCC correspondence and the application he'd helped me put together. He thumbed it a couple of times, then rested his hands atop the documents and leaned back.

"Don't sweat this," he said. "This license is obviously worth something if they want it."

"I know," I said. "That's the frustrating part about this whole thing. It will make money. If we could get this license we could sell it in a couple of years, make the investment back and then some."

John Garabedian

Langan nodded his head in agreement. "You know, John, what would you think about finding a few different investors?" he said. "What if I talked to Jack? Maybe the two of us could step in. Maybe we could even get your dad to pitch in something, too."

"My father?" I said. Man, this guy really was an optimist. "You can try, but I don't know what he's going to say."

Frankly, I wasn't sure what the hell to think of any of them being a part of it. I had intentionally avoided turning to my family to help me out. I wanted to do this on my own, make the achievement completely my accomplishment. Call it male pride or whatever, but I didn't want people thinking I'd only gotten my start because my family had lifted me up. That I was somehow a part of the "lucky sperm club." But the truth is, at this point I was desperate. If someone didn't step up I wouldn't have the investment money. A year's work would be down the drain. No money meant no radio station.

Langan talked to Jack and then the two of them spoke to my father. He didn't bat an eye and agreed to cough up $10,000 to put into the radio station. "That was the money I'd put aside for your college education," he said. Another $40,000 came from Langan and Jack. The deal gave my new investors forty-three percent of the company equity, leaving me with fifty-seven percent and the title of president. But to keep ultimate control over the corporation and protect their investment, Langan, Jack, and my dad put fifteen percent of my voting shares into a trust to give them voting control over the company and be assured that their twenty-three-year-old president didn't do anything foolish.

"It's just while we get things going," Jack explained. "Once it's up and running, and going smoothly, you'll get it back." But that never happened. That's how, fifteen years later, when things started to fall apart at the station, Jack leveraged those voting shares to push me out as president and replace me with his unemployed son. But I've gotten ahead of myself.

About a month after the meeting with Langan, I got together with Jack, my father, and the judge in his office and we officially inked the deal. I'd come a little early and went over things with Langan as I waited for the other two to arrive. When they did, both pulled out checks and placed them on the judge's desk. Langan smiled and waited for everyone to get comfortable. "I guess it's time to come up with my share," he said, and reached under his desk and pulled out two shoeboxes, both of them neatly filled with stacks of cash. "Here you go," he said, without even so much as cracking a smile. The three of us looked at the judge, stunned, and then we all burst out laughing as he counted out $20,000. Langan didn't explain where all that cash had come from and I didn't dare ask.

That little moment broke some of the nervousness I felt about forming our partnership. As we signed the papers and then chatted afterwards, there was an excitement about the project. Even my dad allowed himself to not be skeptical.

"Well," he said, in his deadpan way. "Hopefully we won't lose our shirts." 🔇

13. Elusive Butterfly

Bob Lind, 1966

Back in Worcester at WORC and co-hosting *Open House Party* with creator and station owner Bob Bryar, I learned most of everything I know about radio programming and how to build giant ratings by attracting loyal "fans," not just "listeners."

"**J**ack!" I yelled into the phone, trying to catch my breath. "You're never going to believe it!"

It was an early February morning in 1966 and as fast as I could, I'd dialed up my brother-in-law at his Wayland headquarters. He had just wrapped up a small meeting and was trying to head out the door to lunch when I caught him. "I'm assuming this is good news, right?"

"Good news," I bellowed. "It's unbelievable news. The FCC has rejected the Natick group's application. Said the engineering is faulty. That what they've proposed will interfere with a station on the same frequency in Philadelphia. Can you imagine? Those professionals with all their fancy titles screwed up on the engineering study. Me, John Garabedian, college dropout, got it right."

I could hear Jack sit down in his chair. "Wow!" He said, "You mean we've been approved?"

I would have liked to have said yes, but I knew better. "Not quite," I said calmly. Even my limited experience with the FCC told me that nothing was ever a done deal until you had the actual document stating that, but things were looking up. Langan had been a little less optimistic. "They're going to appeal it," he had said in a matter-of-fact tone. "They have a lot of money. Which brings clout. And with clout comes the chance that they'll hope the court of appeals can be swayed."

The truth is Natick Broadcast Associates did have a case, although a longshot. The FCC's theoretical calculations of their signal using the Commission's conductivity charts had shown it would interfere with co-channel station KYW in Philly, but subsequent to their dismissal, their consulting engineer had gone out and taken field measurements of actual ground conductivity to show that their proposed antenna in reality wouldn't cause an issue. With the measurements in hand, Natick moved to amend and resubmit its application with a

Petition for Reconsideration in late summer of '65, but the Commission refused to accept it. The FCC's "go-no go" rules had been put in place to prevent endless filings when applicants came in with defective applications. A deadline was the deadline, it argued, and if you filed a defective application on the last possible day, and it was found to have errors, there would be no reconsideration.

Once that decision was handed down, Natick hustled its appeal together and submitted it to the D.C. Circuit of the U.S. Court of Appeals. "Just as I expected," Langan told me in late fall of '66. I was sitting in his office—the place had come to seem like my second home these past few months—going over our next steps. Langan, whose long legal career had given him the wisdom to be patient with this kind of stuff, looked across his desk at me. "You probably don't want to quit your day job just yet."

I was feeling good about things, but I wasn't crazy. I knew I still needed to work. But through much of '65 and into '66, as I sorted through the ups and downs of trying to get the Natick station launched and toiled away at WFEA in Manchester, New Hampshire, I felt the pangs to be excited about where I worked. I wanted the thrill of that old WORC feeling again. So back on the job hunt I went, looking for something that would bring me closer to Natick—and closer to my long-term goal of getting my station off the ground.

As luck would have it, my search didn't take that long. A small Top 40 station in Lowell, Massachusetts, WLLH, needed a program director. I'd known the station since I was a kid. It was founded in the 1920s by Gerry Harrison, the father of one of the neighborhood kids I went to elementary school with in Belmont. By the time I filed my FCC application in 1964, WLLH was owned by Arnold Lerner, a cool young guy who wasn't fazed at all by my plans to start my own station. "Come in here and do a good job," he told me. "That's all I ask." But life is good at throwing curveballs. I accepted Lerner's offer to become WLLH program director and gave my two-week notice to WFEA. One week before starting at WLLH, Bob Bryar called me up out of the blue.

"Hi, Bob," I said. "It's great to hear from you. What's going on?"

I could hear Bob take a long drag from his cigarette. "We've changed some things," he said. "I've moved Dick Smith to mornings. Which means I need somebody to co-host *Open House Party* with me in the afternoons. You are a great talent and I've always felt very badly about how you left. But Bart was pressuring me because he was afraid of what advertisers might think."

I was torn. Flattered and confused. I wanted desperately to go back to 'ORC but I had to think of the long game, about what would make me a better station owner. Choosing *Open House Party* was a real honor, but even if it meant working with Bob again it wasn't going to cut it. "Arnold Lerner has hired me as program director," I told him. "I can't give that up."

Bob took another drag. "Hold your horses, John," he said. "I haven't finished yet. You wouldn't just be the afternoon guy. I also need an operations manager. You'd be in charge of everything but sales. Basically, you'd be my number two man and report directly to me."

I swallowed hard. He wasn't going to make this easy. Then a face flashed through my mind. "What about Bart?" I said in a serious tone. "Does he know you want to bring me back?"

Bob let out a laugh. "Don't worry about Bart," he said. "I'll take care of him. You just figure out a way to get back here. I need you at the station."

I was excited by Bob's proposal, but tortured at having to tell Arnold Lerner I was breaking my word to become his PD. "Let me think about it," I said. "I'll have an answer for you tomorrow."

When I hung up the phone, I felt this knot forming in my stomach. I knew what I wanted to do, but I also knew what I'd be doing to Arnold if I did it. He was a really good guy and I would be putting him in a spot. That whole night, I barely slept. I just kept rehearsing what I wanted to say, how I wanted to say it.

That next day I called Arnold and stumbled through my explanation of why I couldn't turn down the WORC opportunity. "It's just a chance I can't pass up," I kept saying in some form or another, nervously. Arnold was pissed. I offered him two weeks to help him find my replacement but he wanted nothing of it. "We'll survive without you," he snapped.

The guilt I felt for backing out of my commitment to Arnold receded a bit as soon I walked through the doors of WORC again. Good old Lillian Brown at the front desk gave me a big hug when I returned, and between his King Sano

Davy Jones of the Monkees. In fall, 1965, before the launch of the TV show and release of "Last Train to Clarksville," there was a lovely private party in a suite at the Sheraton Boston Hotel to meet the Monkees.

cigarettes Bob went on about how thrilled he was that I was back. "It's going to be great, John," he gushed. "You're just what the station needs."

It's funny, but in some ways I didn't really appreciate Bob's talents and style until I actually worked on the air with him. I loved *Open House Party*, the energy of it, its frenetic pace. But I looked at Bob and saw a guy in his fifties who was always hyping up a contest, or the request lines, as someone who didn't have much to teach me as an announcer. I couldn't have been more wrong. Until then, my idea of what radio announcing should sound like was warm and friendly. Maybe a little crazy at times, but also easy-going. Bob's style was the complete opposite. The old pitchman in Bob—he'd made a fortune in the early days of New York City television hawking products like Ginsu knives, no-leak pens, blenders, Florida real estate—never left him. In fact, that go-go pace framed his entire approach to radio. Everything had to be exciting.

The WORC main studio.

I saw that immediately. I'd get on the air and say something about the phones being open and we'd get a few calls. Then Bob would grab the mike and bellow into it like the room was on fire. And in a way it was, because Bob had those damn cigarettes going nonstop. You could barely see your hand right in front of you, there'd be so much smoke. But wouldn't you know it; those phones would light up and stay ringing for the next twenty minutes.

With the Animals. Bass player Chas Chandler left shortly after to manage a young guitar player he'd discovered named Jimi Hendrix; both are now dead. Animals lead singer Eric Burden (third from left) is still kicking it.

Open House Party was also alive because of the music we were playing. The pop sound had changed so much in the last few years. The Beatles were way past their bubble gum hits and had moved on to *Rubber Soul* and *Revolver*, albums with deeper stuff like "Day Tripper" and "Nowhere Man." You had the Stones exuding some early darkness with a song like "Paint It, Black," while Donovan pushed his own form of emerging psychedelia with "Sunshine Superman." Young baby boomers weren't just looking for a song they could dance to, they wanted something that packed social statements they could listen to and connect with. For us, the world looked radically different, felt different, than anything our parents had grown up with. And it was important that our music reflected that. The WORC request lines kept us intimately and immediately in touch with this trend.

I never got a real handle on how Bob Bryar felt about the changes he was seeing in Top 40 music. He probably didn't care for a lot of the stuff we played. It might have even gone over his head, but he loved the response the right kind of hits elicited from his listeners. All those tens of thousands of phone calls each week, the letters, the sense that WORC was *the* radio station for twelve-to-forty-four-year-olds in Worcester, that was huge for Bob. It never got old for him.

To his credit, Bob let me share control of the show. I always ran the control board and was in charge of most music selection and all its production—Bob was a mess when it came to that stuff—and I made major changes in the way we played the music. Bob was not musical at all. He only cared about playing what the listeners were calling and didn't worry if those songs were played in random order. This could create a situation where we'd play three burned-out hits in a row, followed by two newer, unfamiliar songs. That was an approach that ran the risk of alienating listeners and pushing them to change the dial. Addictive radio programming requires control of music flow. You play a hit, then something fresh, then something recurrent, then another hit, then a throwback, and so on. You work it to appeal to all members of the target audience so that no matter what song is playing, it sets up the very next song to sound like something they like. So I instituted formatic structure, which worked with the request format, leaving artistic control to the deejays while assuring smooth music flow. Bob agreed with the logic and supported the changes, but left me to enforce them. Within a year, *Open House Party* boosted its Arbitron ratings from a twenty share to a thirty among all listeners twelve and over in Worcester. At night, we jumped to a fifty share in total audience. It really did become a party.

In early 1967 more changes came to WORC when Dick Smith left the station to become program director of WCOP, a Boston station. His departure opened up the critical morning slot and Bob felt I was the guy to replace him. A year working alongside Bob had certainly helped evolve what I sounded like on the air—I was slicker sounding, more amped up—and Bob thought my radio personality suited the 5:30-noon slot perfectly.

A part of me was nervous about leaving *Open House Party*. It felt like we had fallen into this great groove—the ratings had improved, the music sounded awesome— and now suddenly I was being asked to leave it for something that needed to be more family oriented, less hip. And yet, I was intrigued by the challenge. The morning show is important to every station, because the audience it builds there often doesn't change the dial for the rest of the day.

But while Bob gave me carte blanche to do what I wanted in the morning, he didn't give me any additional resources to make the show better. I pleaded with him to let me hire a sidekick, another personality to keep the show moving and funny. But he blamed Bart, like he always did when he wanted to deflect an

The Beach Boys 1966 hit was "Wouldn't It Be Nice." I happened to check out the B side and it immediately reminded me of my big summer romance with Brian McIlwaine (above left). Playing it heavily on *Open House Party*, suddenly "God Only Knows" became our number one request. Boston stations WMEX and WBZ soon began playing it and finally the Gavin Report spread the news and it became a national hit.

unpopular decision. "Bart won't spend the money for it," he said over and over. That forced me to innovate. I developed characters, invented their voices and pretended I had someone else in the studio with me. The most popular was probably Clara Clout, whom I made out to be this gushing, older lady who came in every morning to read the school lunch menu, which was really fodder for jokes. If she said they were serving meatloaf, I'd mutter something about "Don't let your meat loaf," which caused her to get all flustered. "Ooooh, Johnny," she'd say.

It was a drag and waking up at 4 a.m. was miserable, but I liked being the first radio voice people heard when they woke up, the one who energized the city and got things going for the station each day. When the spring Arbitron ratings were released, everyone was shocked that we had become number one in total audience in the morning. It was the first time in the station's forty-year history that had ever happened.

Even better, every high school and college kid in Worcester listened to the station. They'd see me on the street and yell out my name. They'd call the station. A few even came down for a visit. One of them was this gangly seventeen-year-old high school kid named Mark Parenteau. He was a Worcester kid through-and-

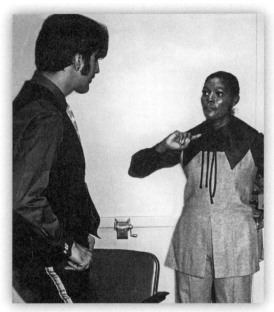

With a young Dionne Warwick for an interview backstage at a Framingham concert in the late sixties. With her beauty and magnificent singing elegance, I was surprised that she was as chatty as someone you'd sit next to at Bingo.

through. Sharp-tongued, with a wickedly sarcastic sense of humor, and street-smart. His father, Paul, was head swimming coach at Holy Cross College.

I was in the middle of my morning shift one spring morning when I turned around and saw him standing behind me in the studio. "How did you get in here?" I exclaimed.

Mark smiled. "Oh, I just told the receptionist that I was a friend of yours."

I chuckled. It was hard not to appreciate his gall. "Well, you're here," I said. "What do you want?"

"I love your show," he gushed. "I listen to you every morning. I want to be in radio and you do the kind of radio I want to be doing."

It seemed downright mean to send him away now. He seemed harmless. "Here, sit over there and don't talk," I said, motioning to a chair. It was probably the only time in his life Mark had been told to shut up, and he actually followed orders. I didn't know it then, of course, but Mark and I would go on to become lifetime friends. He and I were similar in many ways. We both felt like outsiders in our community, insecure about our place in the world, and driven to overcome that. Like me, Mark was tall—he was 6'4" —and like me he had to deal with the shame from others when they saw he couldn't put that size to any use on a ball field or basketball court.

We also shared another thing in common: From an early age, a passion for radio had been burned inside him. It had started with his mother, Lorraine, who spent most of her working life as a personal assistant to one of Worcester's wealthiest women, Vera Green. Lorraine did everything for her boss, and that included playing second-fiddle on a talk show Green hosted on Worcester's WAAB. When the two women occasionally couldn't find guests for the program, they brought in young Mark, who by age six showed he had a natural gift behind the microphone by waxing on about whatever came into his mind, whether it was the train set he'd set up or the tree house he'd started to build. Mark didn't just grow up with radio, he grew up *in* it.

Mark Parenteau at age 18.

His mother's connection to WAAB also had one other side benefit for her son. Every week record companies sent the station packages of 45s. But because WAAB wasn't a music station at the time, all those records were given to Mark. By the age of ten he had one of the most impressive Top 40 collections in the city, one that rivaled many small radio stations. By age fifteen Mark put those records to good use by deejaying local church dances. On a good Saturday night he'd have Bethany Congregational Church hopping to the sounds of "Satisfaction," "Wooly Bully," and "Louie, Louie."

Mark's interest in radio—and connection with me—eventually landed him a weekend shift at WORC at age eighteen. But it was the FM revolution that made him a national name in the business. In the 1970s he became a virtual cult hero on the Detroit airwaves. His ear for music led him to discover Bob Seger and bring him to the masses. He then returned to Boston and eventually held down the afternoon show on WBCN, the groundbreaking FM rock station where his program became a regular stopping point for some of the biggest comedians and musicians. Steven Tyler, Jerry Seinfeld, David Bowie, Sting, Alice Cooper, Tom Petty, Bono, even old school types like President Jimmy Carter and Little Richard.

For comics especially, Mark's show was an important stopping point. They loved him because he was one of them. Self-loathing, plagued by personal demons, and funny as hell, he spoke their language, knew their pain. For Mark, being funny was a tool, a way to overcome his own social anxieties. He could drop a few bombs, get everyone laughing, and then leave as quickly as possible

John Garabedian

In front of my little house in East Natick, sitting on my brand new 1969 Toyota Corona.

without having to weather a bunch of small talk. To this day, he's one of the funniest people I've ever met. From that first 'ORC visit, Mark eventually became a fixture in my life. I introduced him to the Boston night life and later, he became part of the regular Vermont crew, piling into my blue GMC van with a bunch of friends for the trek to the mountains. Between the drugs and the drinks, he became even funnier. Some weekends it felt we were all attending the Mark Parenteau comedy fest. It was nonstop.

Mark was also a part of the scene at my house. In 1967 I bought my first home, a small four-room cottage in East Natick. My father was more excited about the purchase than I was. "Guess that means you can stop freeloading off us now," he said, trying his best to pretend it wasn't a joke. I couldn't wait to leave. After moving out to go to college at age seventeen, living back at home with my parents meant conflicts with my father and his "rules."

Having my own place also gave me some stability. It allowed me to have friends over to hang out, for getting high, for partying, for "other things."

One of the people I had come to know in Worcester was an older guy named Joel. He was probably in his mid-forties and packed a stocky build and a constant five o'clock shadow. Joel was entertaining and fun, but I always kept a careful distance from him, even though boundaries weren't exactly things he respected. It was like he never entered adulthood. He worked as manager of a supermarket in Worcester, a job he landed because his family owned the store, and even though he was in his forties he still lived with his parents.

On the side, however, he kept a small apartment on Park Avenue near Webster Square in Worcester that he called his "party pad." Joel was gay, and lots of good-looking young guys were always hanging around his place. He was an open book that way.

When he wasn't working, he often spent weeknights cruising downtown Worcester in his big Chrysler. If he spotted someone attractive, he'd pull over to the side of the road, roll down his window and call him over. "Have you ever thought about modeling?" he'd ask. He'd then launch into a story about how he was a modeling agent and with a few quick phone calls could probably get the guy some good paying work. His game was to get them in the car and then actually get them to sign some bogus contract as their manager—he always had a folder of those fake contracts with him. After that he'd whisk him back to his place for a photo shoot. Eventually he'd have the kid strip for the camera and then begin hitting on him. Sometimes it worked, sometimes it didn't. Joel didn't need to bat a thousand to feel successful.

"Hey, when do I get to see your new house," Joel asked me one afternoon on the phone. "Any Monday night" was my answer. I always made a point of staying home Monday nights to recuperate from partying every other night.

Joel didn't wait long to take me up on the invitation. About a week later, on a warm July night, I was sitting in my living room when I heard what sounded like a big car and a motorcycle roar into my front yard. When I jumped up and looked out the window I saw Joel's Chrysler parked right on my lawn. Next to it was a motorcycle ridden by two of Joel's buddies, Jesse Johansen and Jamie Marciano. Then the car doors swung open and a small army of people tumbled out, including Joel and his sidekick, a short, fat, effeminate Italian guy everyone called "Mother Bob." I don't know who gave him that nickname but it fit, and he was always with Joel. I never especially liked him. Joel was at least entertaining. Mother Bob just took up space.

"Johnny Gardner!" Joel bellowed as I opened the front door. "I thought you wouldn't mind if I brought a few friends over."

A bit stunned, I nervously laughed and moved out of the doorway. "I guess I don't have a choice."

We sat around talking that night and then at around nine Joel went out to his car and returned with a movie projector. "Who's up for a movie?" he hollered out.

We set up the screen but I should have known better. Joel had brought along a film of a couple of naked guys wrestling. I mean, it was just totally dumb and pointless. It wasn't even porn, just two guys groping around, trying to pin one another to the floor. It was boring and I was embarrassed to even have it playing in my house, but Joel loved it. He hooted and elbowed me in the ribs when one of the wrestlers bent over in front of the camera. A couple of the guys giggled but nobody seemed to actually like it. After a good ten minutes I'd had enough. "Jesus, Joel," I said, turning off the projector. "This is stupid."

Joel laughed hard. "It's just a little entertainment," he said, packing up the film, completely unphased by the rejection. The guy was incapable of being embarrassed. By around 11, Joel collected most of the crew, packed them back in the Chrysler, and headed back to Worcester. But the two visitors who'd arrived by motorcycle, Jesse, who I'd become friends with and enjoyed "private" time with a few times before, and Jamie, the kid with the motorcycle, stuck around. Over the next hour or so the three of us got to further enjoy each other's company in the privacy of my bedroom. The whole time Jamie kept softly moaning his girlfriend's name. *Oh, Debbie. I love it, Debbie.* I'd lean over and say, "Debbie? No, it's John. Remember? John." Jesse laughed. It was hilarious and sort of sad. But that's what repression does to people. It makes them live in this kind of pretend world.

At around three in the morning, the guys got dressed and hopped back on the bike. Jamie was nervous about hitting the road because he only had his junior driver's license. Like Jesse, he was only seventeen and wasn't supposed to be driving after midnight, but Jesse didn't care. "Relax," he kept telling Jamie. "Everything will be cool."

Of course it wasn't. A few miles down Route 9 in Framingham the Massachusetts State Police nabbed them and immediately began questioning the two. *Where have you boys been? Have you been drinking? What have you been up to?* Jesse played it smart, knew the deal, and kept his mouth shut. Jamie, however, was a different story. He had been drinking and couldn't shut up. He opened his mouth and out it all came, and then some. *We were at this DJ Johnny Gardner's house. We just hung out, had a couple of beers and watched some porn.* Jesse was just shaking his head, trying to quietly signal to Jamie to shut the fuck up.

A month or so later at around 6 a.m., I was awakened by a loud knock on the front door. And then a second one on the back door. It was hard-fisted pounding, like they wanted to knock my house down. "Hold on, hold on," I said, still groggy, and stumbling around to put on a pair of pants. I opened the front door and there was this linebacker-sized cop holding a piece of paper, which he shoved in my face.

"Corporal Smith from the State Police," he said. "This is a search warrant for your house for pornography."

I didn't know what the hell was going on. Meanwhile the knocking on the back door continued. "Wait a second," I said. "I have to get the back door."

"That would be Sergeant Connolly from the Natick police department," Smith snapped, and then stepped inside my house with two detectives. Sure enough, Connolly was back there, too, and came in as well. Over the next hour the police combed through the house, turning stuff everywhere, leaving my place a complete mess. There was nothing I could do. I just stood there and watched as the cops tore everything apart.

"You're not going to find anything," I said, as calmly as I could a few times. "I don't have any dirty pictures."

There was no convincing them, however, not even as they stood like an invading army over my upturned house, finally leaving completely empty-handed.

"That's that," I said, closing the door after the last cop had left my house. But it wasn't. Far from it. In ways that I never would have imagined, that incident eventually came back to haunt me and nearly kill my dream of building my radio station in Natick.

In April, 1967, I received an envelope in the mail. It was from the FCC. Things had been frustratingly quiet over the last few months. There'd been no news from either Natick Broadcast Associates or the FCC. The case still seemed to be before the U.S. Court of Appeals and as far as I could tell was never going to leave its hands. "What do you think is going on?" I kept asking Judge Langan.

The antenna base of the WGTR antenna tower in Natick. The 2" copper straps connected to 120 radial wires of #10 copper, each 250' long totaling nearly six miles.

He'd shrug his shoulders. "These things take time, John," he'd say, doing his best to keep me from walking off the ledge. "The question is: Will they uphold the FCC rules? I think it is likely, but you never know in court."

Patience, though, was not a currency I had huge quantities of. When that letter arrived I looked at it nervously. I went back in the house, sat down at the kitchen table, placed it down in front of me, and finally tore it open.

I couldn't believe what I saw. It was an FCC grant of the construction permit to build my station. We had the license! We could start building the radio station! "Holy crap!" I yelled out, jumping up from the table.

I was on the phone immediately. Calling Jack. Calling Judge Langan. Calling my father. I had work to do. With the security of the license in hand, I eventually quit WORC. I had a mission to build the station and just didn't have the time to hold down a full-time job.

Over the next few months we cleared the five acres of land we leased from the chicken farmer and put up a utility building to house the transmitter equipment. We poured a foundation and erected the 150-foot tower. By that fall we had plowed in five and a half miles of number ten copper ground radials around the structure, 120 of them, each 250 feet long. By Christmas I'd flown to Dallas where we recorded a batch of jingles for the new station with PAMs, the leading radio station jingle company in broadcasting, and we were about to sign a lease for studio space.

We also needed to select the right call letters for the new station. That wasn't easy. I wanted it to sound memorable, crisp and important. I pored over different combinations and examined the call letters of successful stations. The one I liked best was my old place of employment, WPTR. I liked how its three-letter short name, 'PTR, rolled off the tongue. What if I changed the "P" to a "G," I wondered. A check with the FCC Call Sign Desk revealed that the call letters "WGTR" were available for assignment. They also had a real history behind them, having previously been used for the first commercial FM station in America. They were first issued in 1941 to the General Tire & Rubber Company ("G.T.R." for short) for a commercial FM station in Worcester. It didn't hurt that my last name began with "G" ("Garabedian's Terrific Radio?"). After getting a blessing from my partners, I quickly applied for letters and WGTR became the name of the new Natick station.

In early '67 everything was coming together. It seemed like a foregone conclusion that WGTR would be up and running by the spring.

And then lightning struck.

It was an early November day in '67 when Langan called me up. "Come into my office," he said somberly. "We need to go over some things."

I had no idea what the hell he was talking about. "What do you need to discuss?" I meekly asked.

"Come in here," he said and hung up the phone.

Langan was sifting through some papers when I walked in.

"I don't have a good feeling about this," I said, sitting down and letting out a nervous laugh.

Langan looked at me and pursed his lips. "I know you've put a lot of work into the station," he said. "I know things are close, but we're going to have to suspend operations." He then slid an envelope across the desk.

I could feel my whole body tighten. I looked at him and opened the letter up.

The notice was from the U.S. Court of Appeals D.C. Circuit. They had called the FCC rejection of Natick Broadcast Associates application "hyper technical and arbitrary" and remanded Natick's application back to the FCC for "further proceedings." The court stated that the FCC should have given Natick a break on the deadline and allowed them to cure the engineering violation by submitting real-world ground conductivity measurements.

I got up out of my chair and began pacing around Langan's office. Outside, a light snow had started to fall onto the Boston streets, giving everything a beautiful fresh white covering. The peaceful scene outside was such a contrast to what was roiling around inside me. After doing a couple of silent circles around the room I stopped in front of the judge's desk. "What does this mean?" I said. "Is there anything we can do?"

Langan took in a deep breath and locked his arms behind his head. "What it means," he said, matter of factly, "is that the FCC is going to set aside the Construction Permit for WGTR and designate both applications for a comparative hearing in Washington, D.C. I have no idea how it's all going to shake out, but I can tell you it is going to take a long time and cost a lot of money, and," he paused, "and we may lose."

The disaster wasn't just that I suddenly couldn't finish building WGTR. I was also out of a job. My bank account was getting low and I needed to find work. I called up Bob Bryar, hoping he might have something for me, but he was fully staffed. In fact, when I left the year before he had replaced me with two people. I good-naturedly made sure to give Bob a hard time about that.

Truthfully, I was back to the same spot I was a few years before when I'd been let go by WMEX. No radio station in Boston wanted to touch me. Back to *Broadcasting* magazine and the help-wanted section I went. There, I stumbled across an opening for a chief engineer for a pair of stations owned by Merv Griffin in Waterbury, Connecticut. The AM side of the operation was Top 40, and the FM side was a 50,000-watt country station. I was desperate enough to take it when it was offered to me, and honored but not desperate enough when they later asked if I wanted to become director of engineering for all the Merv Griffin stations across the country. Waterbury was a dump. The thought of jetting around the nation to all these other stations was even less enticing.

For several months I held that job. Driving down to Waterbury on Monday morning and crashing on a cot at the AM transmitter for the work week before returning home Friday for the weekend.

Then one day, out of the blue, once again I received a call from Bob Bryar. One of the two guys he'd hired to replace me had resigned, and Ron Frizzel, the other, was good at commercial production but not so hot as a DJ. Once again Bob needed an operations manager and someone to co-host *Open House Party*.

It was almost comical to be back. When I stepped out of the elevator and into the WORC lobby Lillian smiled and shook her head. "Have you been on vacation?" she asked.

"I know, I know," I said, letting out a laugh. "I'm like gum on your shoe. You just can't get rid of me."

The summer of '67 in America saw the launch of a major social revolution. WORC responded with a series of "Happenings," mini-concert/dances at outdoor parks that would attract over 10,000 people. Note my cigarette (yuck).

I settled back into life at 'ORC pretty quickly, running the station and working with Bob on the afternoon show. But for all the familiarity that came with being back at my old stomping grounds, the place just felt a little different. Some of that old energy seemed to be missing. The circus atmosphere was a little more subdued. It was less electric. A lot of it, I think, stemmed from Bob. He seemed less engaged with the station. He didn't put in the hours like he had before and the long talks we had always enjoyed about radio didn't materialize.

All of it had to do with his personal life. He had remarried since I'd left and was caught up in his "in love" state, which meant he spent all of his time with his voluptuous new bride, Marilyn. He had even made her the music director of the station. They were like John and Yoko, inseparable 24/7. Then, on a cold, windy March morning in 1969 Bob called me into his office and shut the door.

"Have a seat," he said, motioning to a chair. Bob remained standing, leaning against his desk and folding his arms. "I've got some news that's going to affect you, and I wanted to let you in on it before we made an announcement."

"Okay," I said nervously. "What's going on?"

Bob looked around the room for a quick moment and then locked his eyes back on me. "We've sold the station," he said in a near-whisper. "We've been quietly shopping it for a while and have finally found a buyer."

Len Talbot, my news director at WORC, who through expert ass-kissing and back-stabbing, was promoted and promptly fired me. To my great satisfaction, the station did so badly under his incompetent leadership it had to be sold and ultimately changed to a country format.

I was completely dumbfounded. "You serious?" I asked.

"I am," he said, shifting his eyes to the ground.

This was my last stint working for Bob, and the last time I worked for WORC. It was all so odd. I'd certainly had lots of practice leaving the station, but working there, being at the station without Bob, was strange. Meeting the new owner weirded me out. Bob's buyer was a man named Roger Knowles, a conservative Amsterdam, New York, businessman who wore skinny neckties and had made a fortune in the plastics industry. Bob had assured me that my job was safe, but it was obvious from the moment I met Sam Slade, an ancient has-been CBS executive Knowles brought in to run the station, that being gay and having long hair wasn't going to sit well with him.

Slade was a piece of work. Rotund with slicked-back hair, tattered shirt collars, worn-looking suits, and a personality that never deviated from grumpy, he instantly turned the station into a library. Overnight, the place went quiet. Music no longer pumped into Lillian's reception room. Everyone was suddenly required to wear a necktie. Even the mood of the on-air talent changed. I did my best to keep doing what I'd always done there. I still fooled around and had fun with my listeners, but the writing was on the wall.

Almost immediately Slade named Len Talbot, my news director, as program manager. The shock was when he told me I'd be reporting to him. Talbot didn't have a lick of programming experience but he was an obedient two-faced ass-kisser and good at taking directives from Slade. Then, in early May of '69 Talbot stopped me in the hall as I got off the air and asked me to come into the music room.

"We're letting you go," he said matter of factly.

"What?" I asked incredulously.

"We're changing things here," he said, going through the stupid formality of pretending he actually had a legitimate reason for letting me go. "You've done a good job but we're going in a different direction."

I stared at him for a long couple of seconds. "Okay," I said coolly. "I'll collect my things." I grabbed my FCC license from the wall, headphones, and a few papers, hopped on my motorcycle and took off down Route 9 to my little house in East Natick. Spring had hit and as I rode along through the warm sunshine I actually felt liberated, like a giant load had lifted. It reminded me that WORC was only a small part of who I was, that life was still really good and that maybe this was the best thing that could have happened.

I guess I should have been more nostalgic about leaving 'ORC, felt sadder about how it all ended. But the truth is the station I'd loved, the one that had taught me so much about programming and the radio business actually died the moment Bob Bryar stepped away from it. A whole chapter of my life had come to an end. It had been exhausting at times, a bitter finish to my time there. I was twenty-seven years old, and in saying goodbye to WORC, I was also saying goodbye to my youth and the first episode of my career in radio. But it was time to let go.

The future was where I was going and I was ready for a change. 🔇

14. Born to be Wild

Steppenwolf, 1968

Bruce Brody.

I don't know. I guess I could have let my sudden state of uncertainty really get to me. I was out of work with absolutely no job prospects. The station I'd been tethered to in some kind of fashion over the last decade—the magical place that literally taught me everything I loved about great entertaining radio—was now gone forever. And I also had no clue what was going to happen to WGTR. The FCC, Natick Broadcast Associates—the whole thing was a mess that showed no signs of easing.

So I did something I'm not always good at. I said "fuck it" and took it easy. Disillusioned from the grind of the last few years, I was prepared to completely say goodbye to radio. There were a million things I'm really good at, I reasoned. I'll figure out a way to make a living. So, with a weekly unemployment check from the Massachusetts Department of Employment Security and a little savings in my bank account, I spent the summer in pleasure heaven, hanging out with friends, getting high, getting laid, shooting some weddings for a little income, and selling a little THC, MDMA, and acid. Here and there, I deejayed at some Boston clubs. It was the summer of '69 and I was doing what a lot of young people in my generation were doing. I was checking out of the "machine" and checking into life.

It was a strange time in Star-Spangled America, hopeful and scary. The country was in turmoil. The race riots, political assassinations, and the Vietnam War. I mean, you weren't sure what would happen next. Suddenly, we learned that the government was corrupt, that our democracy was a sham manipulated by paid-off politicians, and we had a military-industrial machine that was fueling war for profits and seemingly couldn't be stopped. On the other side of the world, American kids were being killed in Vietnam, a country we didn't care about. And for what? Some stupid geopolitical victory? It was ridiculous and depressing, and there was a feeling that the America we'd been brought up to blindly trust was out of control.

As the world weathered turmoil, my own personal liberation continued. Drugs were a big part of that. Well into my mid-twenties, I was not a drinker. Alcohol was never my thing. Pot or LSD? They weren't even on my radar. I'd never even been around those kinds of drugs. I mean, I wasn't even sure what weed smelled like.

That had all changed back in 1967.

One of the places in Boston I liked to hang out at was a restaurant on the corner of Charles and Chestnut streets on Beacon Hill called Sharifs. It was a popular spot for under-twenty-one gay kids who couldn't get into the clubs. You'd go there, get a Coke or a coffee, hang out with some friends, and maybe meet a good-looking boy. It was like a clubhouse and an easy place to make new buddies. One day I was sitting there with three of them: Bruce Brody, a handsome 6'2" model from Newton, along with Kenny Richards from Portland, Maine, and his boyfriend, Wally Rouleou from Marlborough. Bored, we were trying to figure out something fun to do, and out of the blue someone blurted, "Hey let's go to New York City for the night!" That was it! Five minutes later we piled into my brand new '67 Pontiac GTO and blasted west down the Mass Turnpike to the city.

Two hours into the ride, somewhere in Connecticut, Kenny and Wally started to bicker. It was annoying, and they sounded like two crabby old ladies. On and on it went. Bruce and I were ready to kill them. I kept turning up the radio, but I couldn't drown them out. It was around 4 p.m. when we finally got to New York and Bruce thankfully suggested we split up and meet them the next day. It was brilliant.

"Yeah," I snickered. "We don't want to hold you guys back."

The rest of that afternoon, Bruce and I hoofed it around lower Manhattan on our own, eventually making our way into Greenwich Village. It was while we waited for the light to change at Christopher Street near Sheridan Square that we found ourselves next to these two guys around our age. They were both good-looking, wearing jeans and white T-shirts, and had a cool look about them.

Wally Rouleou (center) and Kenny Richards (right). Wally succumbed to complications from AIDS at age twenty-seven.

"Where are you guys from?" one of them finally asked us.

"Boston," Bruce replied, sounding a bit taken aback. Back home strangers didn't just speak to each other on the street. We weren't used to this. "Are you guys from here?"

"We live a few blocks away," said one of them, sticking out a hand. "I'm Stephen and this is James."

We exchanged a few other pleasantries and after a minute or so of small talk, James, who hadn't done much talking, leaned in toward us and in a low voice said, "Would you guys like to smoke some *marijuana*?"

I blinked hard a couple of times, unsure what I should say. But Bruce immediately jumped right in. "Yeaaaah!" he exclaimed. A few minutes later we were climbing the stairs to a fifth-floor apartment where our new friends lived. It was a small place, sparsely furnished, kind of dimly lit, and it smelled like patchouli incense. Bruce and I sat on the floor while our hosts brought out a couple of Budweisers. I didn't care for beer but to be polite I took a couple of sips, pretending like I didn't mind the stuff. As I knocked back a small swig, Stephen pulled out a small leather pouch and proceeded to roll a joint. When he was done he fired

John Garabedian

it up and took a long, slow drag from it before passing it on to Bruce. Then it went to me.

I held it between my finger and thumb for a second and looked at it. For a guy who'd spent his whole life scared as hell about standing out, looking different, I sure wasn't going to admit I hadn't smoked pot before. But there was no fooling the fact that I looked like a rookie.

I nervously brought the joint to my lips and took a big drag off the thing. "Hold it in," James said. I nodded my head and did my best to follow the advice, but coughed out a small cloud of smoke. Bruce chuckled.

Washington Square Park, New York City, with Bruce Brody and some kid from Brooklyn I'd picked up the night before at Stonewall, the legendary gay club. It was the morning after I smoked my first joint.

I smiled and leaned back against the couch, passed the joint to Bruce and then waited my turn for another round. We finished that one, then Stephen rolled another. By the second joint I'd not only gotten a handle on how to smoke weed, I was also pretty fucked up. It was then that I took notice of the music our hosts had playing on the radio. It was WLIB, an urban station that had this fabulous black announcer with a voice that sounded like God. His voice was slow, sensual and warm, a deep voice that filled the room and my head. As I let the R&B music wash over me, I relished how I felt. I loved how mellow weed made me feel, how it slowed things down. It was nothing like what I'd been told as a kid.

The scene, however, ended rather quickly when Stephen and James tried to put some moves on us. We played it politely and thanked the two for the buzz, then stumbled out the door and eventually found our way to the Stonewall Inn, the coolest dance club in New York and the biggest gay bar in America. Like most weekend nights, the place roared with excitement. Probably a good thousand people were jammed inside the place. This was still two years before the historic riots that would launch the gay rights revolution, but the scene was unforgettable. From the street we went down the stairs to this huge subterranean room packed with guys. Motown blasted out of these big speakers and all around us guys threw back beers and danced, many with their shirts off. It was tribal energy and felt electric and liberating. There was solidarity in that, a feeling of connection. Two years later when those riots erupted at Stonewall in June of 1969, I wasn't surprised at all. If any place was going to launch a new era for gay liberation, it was that club.

Sometime around four in the morning, Bruce and I left the Stonewall. Each of us had hooked up with someone and we all headed to Brooklyn where the guy Bruce was with had an apartment. Unfortunately, it was a one-room studio, and so while Bruce and his new buddy spent the next couple of hours in the privacy of the bathroom, my friend and I made the best of a futon.

When we returned to Boston, the next night I went to Logan Airport to pick up my parents who were returning from a California vacation. "Guess what I did this weekend?" I said excitedly as they settled into my car. My father turned to me, shaking his head.

"Do I really want to know?" he said.

I laughed. I'd always been honest with my parents and didn't feel like I needed to be any different in this case. "I smoked marijuana for the first time," I said.

My father just stared at the road. "You'll probably end up doing heroin next," he said. My mother frowned. She either didn't care or have a clue. "Well, I hope you don't get in any trouble," she said.

From that point on drugs were in my life. Not in some crazy way, but if they were there and somebody was offering, I participated. That included acid. I dropped my first tab about a year after my introduction to pot. It was a friend of mine, Peter Gowan, the chief engineer of WROL, a religious radio station in Boston, who turned me on to it. With his big square glasses and a mop of curly hair, Peter had this mad professor look about him. Smart but fun and wacky. In addition to his work at the radio station he was, unbelievably, also the minister of music at a church in Natick. Peter was bisexual and enjoyed fine wine and high quality drugs, earning the nickname "Doctor Go" from his friends. In addition to simply doing them, he was a drug connoisseur and loved talking about them, like he was spreading some kind of psychedelic gospel.

His parties were legendary. Not because they were huge or wild, but because of the cool people who showed up and their location, the WROL transmitter building that sat adjacent to a huge radio tower on the Lynn Marsh Road in Saugus. It was located halfway between Revere and Lynn, in a salt marsh, miles from any other buildings. Every few weekends a bunch of select cool people would head out there to smoke and trip.

The first time I attended one of these gatherings, we all tripped our brains out, smoking weed from a hookah, drinking wine, and listening to music as we sat around a huge round table. People started hooking up, and eventually everyone passed out.

The sun was just cresting over the horizon when my eyes peeled open. I felt awful, sweaty, dry-mouthed, and dirty, with this dull hangover headache. The aroma of weed was in the air, and I could barely remember where I was. Right then, a booming voice came over the transmitter. It was 6 a.m. and WROL had just signed on the air with a church broadcast. Through the speakers a Bible-thumping preacher boomed, raving about how Jesus was going to save our souls. I looked around the site of naked bodies passed out all around me. The contrast was absurd and hysterical.

One Friday in late October, 1969, Peter called me up at my house in Natick. "John," he said in his typical cheerful tone. "I've been invited to Hartford this Sunday to a party for the Moody Blues' new album, which won't be released for a few weeks. My friend Randy Mayer is the general manager at WHCN, and he's getting an advanced copy. He and his girlfriend live in a big old house in Windsor with a bunch of people. It's like a little commune. You interested in coming down?"

"He's getting their new album?" I said excitedly. "Wow!" As a huge fan of the Moody Blues, I'd been eagerly waiting for its new record. The band was unlike anything previously released in the world of music, delivering this powerful spirituality through their lyrics and music, which at that time artfully epitomized the hopes and dreams of the new generation. The band had launched with the album, *Days of Future Past*, which featured great songs like "Tuesday Afternoon" and "Nights in White Satin." Their second album, *In Search of the Lost Chord*, took their music into the world of psychedelic vision and transcendental thought. They were a major influence on the later sound of Pink Floyd. It

John Garabedian

became *the* soundtrack for LSD-tripping kids and was written after the group's inspiring acid experiences with Dr. Timothy Leary of Harvard University. He's the guy who coined "tune in, turn on, drop out." The album Peter's friend had gotten his hands on was *To Our Children's Children's Children*.

"I'd love to go," I said, knowing full well that Peter's invitation came with the expectation that I would drive. "But I'll be hanging out with my friend, Andy, and he has to be home before his parents wake up."

That evening, ten of us sprawled out in the big living room of this huge gothic-looking home in Windsor, which reminded me exactly of *The Munsters*. Black lights gave the room a trippy glow and big speakers sat in every corner of every room. The sweet aroma of incense filled the air. When Peter's friend Randy turned on the stereo system the room mystically came alive, like a magic space ship. We all lay out on the floor and our hosts cranked up the record. I rode along with it, magically rising and falling as it ascended and then tumbled back down again. As it played, Peter rolled out some fat joints, then passed out a round of chocolates.

The drugs completely enhanced the atmosphere. After the first side of the album finished, Randy's girlfriend went into the kitchen and returned with loaves of freshly baked homemade bread. The warm smell was delightful, and it was enhanced with a stuffing of flavored cream cheese. Each bite was like an explosive sensual experience, which radiated rushes of pleasure. We attacked that bread like we hadn't eaten in days, tearing off huge chunks and cramming them into our mouths. "Oh my God," I said. "My mouth is exploding with orgasms of pleasure. I could die right now and be happy."

I looked around the room and could tell everybody felt the same way.

Drugs offered a marvelous escape from the craziness in my life and the world. It was like taking a fabulous vacation without the inconvenience of leaving home. And God knows I needed a break. I loved the city, being in Boston, but between the social strife in America, Vietnam, and the nuke threat, nobody had any idea how the next few years were going to play out, or if we'd even all be alive. At times it could be that scary.

Thankfully, I had met Angus McPherson and he introduced me to Vermont. That single event dramatically changed my life. Spending time up north, hanging out and intimately bonding with my closest friends, I discovered more about who I really was, getting closer to life's reality as I became more capable of evolving my philosophical beliefs, figuring out answers to questions about what's important and how the world should be. It was an intellectual explosion for a John Garabedian awakening.

Like Bob Bryar and Jack Carlson, Angus McPherson became a mentor of sorts. He was in his early fifties in 1969 but to me then he looked like an old guy. Probably it was the way he dressed—buttoned down shirt,

Angus McPherson introduced me to Vermont and was a friend of Massachusetts' closeted governor, Paul Dever. Angus was classy, but also the first alcoholic I ever met. One sip of vodka and he'd be off on a two-week long bender until he was shipped off to rehab.

tight at the belly, wrinkled tie, and sport jacket. But he was welcoming and always positive. He was always telling stories and was tough to shut up once he was on a roll. The problem was he had a propensity to tell the same stories over and over again. You'd be like, *Angus, you told me that story already.* He'd pause for a second, then despite what you'd just said, launch back into his tale. *"Right, but anyway…"* and off he'd go. It was fruitless to interrupt him.

Meeting him was pure accident. Back in 1962, Joe and I had gone out for a Sunday ride into Boston. It was early summer and we decided to cruise up to Boston's North Shore around Revere Beach and hit a fried clam shack. We were slowly cruising along Revere Beach Boulevard, checking out the beach, arcades, and rides when we noticed this good-looking kid walking on the sidewalk. Joe blurted out, "He's gay. Pull over."

"What? How can you tell that?" I said, in disbelief of whatever the hell kind of intuition he had.

"I just can, John," he said. "Park and we'll see where he goes."

I found a parking spot and we followed the kid into an arcade where we found him playing pinball. Joe just started chatting with him and the next thing I knew we were driving him back to Berkeley Street in Boston to meet his roommates. It turned out Joe had a better sixth sense for this stuff than I knew possible. Not only was our new friend gay, but all of his buddies were, too, and soon we were all regularly hanging out at their apartments. We'd get together on the weekends, hit the clubs, whatever. It was through them I first met Angus. He'd liked to throw cookouts at his farm in Holliston, and eventually Joe and I just became part of the scene.

Angus had grown up working on a chicken farm in Medfield, Massachusetts, and later earned a very nice living in the livestock business by running cattle auctions every other Monday at his farm. He traveled all over New England and Quebec, buying cows from farmers and then shipping them by rail to his farm for auction. He had this unusual ability to recognize any cow just by its face. You could put him in a field with a hundred cattle and he could tell you immediately who was who.

Angus had "been around the block" a few times and had seen plenty of real life. He understood human nature and wasn't afraid to see things as they were. He was totally practical in his view of life, saw through people's charades, and had a hell of a time telling everyone about it. One of his buddies in the early fifties was Massachusetts governor Paul Dever, a tough-looking son of a bitch with a round face and a scally cap that gave him this sort of Al Capone appearance. But beneath that gruff exterior was a secret.

One of the stories Angus told me was about a Christmas Eve party he'd thrown in the '50s. One of Angus's farm boys was a favorite of the governor's and on the night of the party Governor Dever dropped by for the festivities. The governor had a few drinks and after a trip upstairs to a private bedroom, the boy was sitting on his lap. Nobody said a word. As they watched a live television broadcast of the Midnight Mass at Holy Cross Cathedral in Boston, the announcer said "...and we're still expecting the arrival of the governor," which, of course, wasn't going to happen because the governor was currently cuddled up with a twenty-year-old boy. Everyone all laughed at that. After slurping down another cocktail, the governor made it to his car, where his State Police driver had been patiently waiting. Angus let out a good laugh when he recounted that one. "The church was waiting for the guy to get that kid off his lap," he howled. "You can't make this stuff up."

That's how life is for closeted men. They've got their life and follow the script everyone expects them to follow, but secretly, silently they have this whole other thing burning on their inside that they are unable to confront. It's like that for many guys. It doesn't matter how much power they've accumulated. There's a line they are wary about crossing.

Angus knew this better than anyone and yet all his clarity about how life really was, Angus packed his demons. He was the first alcoholic I ever knew. Not a drunk, but an alcoholic who lived life mostly sober, could put deals together, talk business, but every few months would carelessly take one sip of vodka and then go off on a two-week drunken binge.

The other thing about him was that he was sometimes the "victim" of mysterious fires. Every few years when he received his annual tax bills for the golf course he owned in Holliston or his property in Vermont, some building of his would mysteriously burn to the ground and he'd collect the insurance. He was never fingered or arrested, but it happened enough times while I knew him that it seemed to be more than just a coincidence. You just knew that if things started to fall apart around him, some barn or home of his was going to go up in flames.

It was his cattle auction business that first brought Angus to Vermont. He knew every square inch of the state and over time most of its farmers. Angus liked to make a buck, but he also had a heart. He knew the struggles some farmers faced and let them buy cows on margin for half down with the balance due in payments. That's how he ended up with nearly a thousand acres on a mountaintop in Cabot. An old farmer named Angus Beaton to whom he used to sell cows ran into hardship after the 1953 cattle crash, and to square things up with Angus McPherson he signed over his grazing property.

John Garabedian

To me, Vermont seemed like it would be nothing more than chickens, trees, and cows. Once there, I discovered a new dimension of life which transformed me.

Angus loved it up there. By the time I met him, he talked regularly about his plans to build a house and big pond. It was June, 1969, when I got a call from Angus one morning. "I'm going up to Vermont for a few days to cut trees for the power line to my new house," he said. "Would you like to come along?"

Vermont? To me it sounded ridiculous. I was a Boston club kid. I'd never been to Vermont, and I envisioned cows and chickens and just being bored to death. It brought to mind trying to get through the days visiting my parents' place on Lake Sunapee in New Hampshire which was like *On Golden Pond*. It was pretty, but after one night, I was like, *Okay, I get it. When can I leave?* My father sat by the water gazing and whistling, my mother was inside picking up the house. Where was the fun?

Angus, though, was persistent and convinced me to come along. The following Friday morning, he and Wayne Morris, one of his farm boys, swung by in Angus's black Bonneville convertible. Angus got out of the car and threw me the keys.

"Take the wheel, John," he said. "You're driving."

We drove and drove for hours, and then drove some more. It felt like we were heading to the end of the earth. The interstate highways weren't finished yet, so we had to follow all these back roads. The farther north we got, the back roads turned to dirt roads and the worse they became. Finally, just southeast of Barre, we arrived at this old farmhouse deep in the Vermont woods with a beat-up washing machine and rusted out truck with no hood decorating the front yard. Angus hopped out, disappeared inside the house for a few minutes, then reemerged with three brothers, all handsome, strapping farm boys, each of whom carried a chainsaw.

I don't how we all managed to fit. The three brothers squeezed into the back of the Bonneville, with Wayne in the middle and Angus riding shotgun. Between the six guys, the logging equipment, the bumpy dirt road, and all the crap in the trunk, the ass end of the car was constantly scraping the ground. Of course, the roads didn't improve, either. From one dirt road, we turned off to another. And then another. There was maybe a house every two miles. Then we started climbing. It had been over six hours since we left Natick. The sun was getting low in the sky when we turned down a dirt road at an old farm, which came to an end in front of a chicken wire fence, behind which was fresh un-mowed hay about three feet high. "Okay, John," said Angus. "Better let me drive, I know where the road is."

I looked at the field and then back at Angus, "What road?"

"Watch," he said with a laugh and bounded out of the car to move a gate. He got into the driver's seat and we pushed onward, the rear end of the overloaded Bonneville banging and scraping the ground all the way as we then climbed up this long steep trail to the top of a cleared hilltop where there was an old, run-down camping trailer.

"Okay, boys," said Angus. "Let's unload the car." Out came the chainsaws, a case of warm beer, and a big cardboard box filled with junk food: Twinkies, Ring Dings, Hostess cupcakes, all stuff he had bought at the Wonder Bread "day-old" store in Natick. Then back into the car went Angus to head to a motel in nearby Lyndonville to spend the night. "OK, boys," he said, waving goodbye.

"Have a good night. I'll be back in the morning with breakfast and we can get to work."

I felt about as far away from civilization as I ever had. We were completely stranded on top of a mountain in the middle of nowhere with no electricity, no telephone, no water, and no way to leave. But after watching the sunset, which filled the sky with a flaming display of deep oranges and purples, I saw the beauty that captured me for a lifelong love of that mountaintop and Vermont. Amid 360-degree views of the nearby mountains and valleys, it was almost overwhelming.

It didn't hurt that I was up here with a crew of cool guys who were friendly, fun, and good-looking. That helped any situation, even if Angus hadn't exactly played the part of the perfect host. "Let's build a fire," someone said, and for the next few hours we sat around the flames, got to know a bit about each other, talked about life, and soaked up the spectacularly starlit sky.

By the end of the second day, I felt like I was tripping on acid. Everything was just so beautiful and peaceful. It was like there was this big glow to life and the universe. More noticeable, though, was that for the first time in a long time I felt a wash of real serenity. I had talked about needing to let things go, of not feeling like I had to keep pushing my life a thousand miles per hour, of pulling back from being such an energy junkie. It was one of those things you think about but never get to. But up there, completely disconnected from civilization, there was no choice and it just came naturally, and all that peacefulness settled down on me like a soft rain. It was a new sensory experience. I had no idea the role Vermont would play in my future, I just knew I needed more of it.

We returned to Boston and I started raving to my friends about how wonderful the place was. I immediately realized this was a perfect place to share with my closest friends, a place where we could disconnect from the pressure of life and bond, sharing experiences, and enjoy nature and each other. We went up there every chance we could. In the beginning we slept on blankets under the stars, then in tents, and as the weather got cool that fall I bought a big white Ford F300 van that I outfitted as a camper. Up there, chilling with nature and sharing experiences with my closest friends, the pleasure meter was off the scale. Every pilgrimage was an escape to freedom from the worry about stupid things.

Often times the party started in that van long before we even hit Vermont. The trips up there were crazy. Today it's a three-and-a-half-hour drive from Boston, but back then before I-93 was finished, it took nearly five hours. One summer night in 1974 a crew of us—my niece Laura Carlson, three of my close buddies, Jimmy Harrison, Gary Blease, Mark Parenteau, and another friend, Stuart Soroca, then the TV weatherman for Channel 7 in Boston—piled into my van and we headed north, smoking our brains out and tripping our way north through New Hampshire on Route 3, the Everett Turnpike. We had passed through Manchester alongside the mighty Merrimack River and were slowing for the Hooksett tolls, when I suddenly caught sight of a friend, Bob Brooks, a few lanes away, heading in the same direction.

"Hang on everyone," I said as we pulled out of the toll lane. I bombed sideways across three lanes toward the lane next to Bob's car to try and catch up with him, cutting in front of a few cars pulling into the toll booths, but never really endangering anyone. In the back, people were astonished at my gall, howling with laughter and doing their best to hold on.

"Jesus!" Mark yelled. "Where are you going?"

While I managed to get in the toll lane adjacent to Bob, a state cop I didn't notice who'd watched the whole thing, turned on his siren and blue light and pulled us over. "Shit," I said, pulling the van over to the side of the road. I then wheeled around to face my friends. "Quick, open the roof vent to let out the smoke," I said frantically.

There was no secret of what we had going on. The van reeked of weed. I knew if that cop got within just a few steps of the van, he'd pick up on the scent, there'd be a search, and we'd be under arrest. This was conservative, uptight New Hampshire.

I looked in my rear view mirror and saw the cop, a skinny young guy, emerge from his cruiser. I took a breath. I had to distract him to keep him away from the van. Impulsively, I fired open my door, hopped out of the vehicle and made my way toward him behind the van, apologizing the whole time.

John Garabedian

Cabot, Vermont, sitting on the dam in the summer sun. (Left to right) Mark Parenteau, Jimmy Harrison, niece Laura Carlson, and Gary Blease.

"Whoa, whoa," the cop said. "Where exactly do you think you are going?"

I dropped to my knees, and got into a praying position. "I'm sorry, officer, I didn't mean to do it. I saw two friends of mine in the next lane and was so excited I did the wrong thing." Then with great drama I added, "Please, please forgive me!" And with that I bowed my head.

The cop started laughing. "All right, all right," he said. "You know what you did could have caused an accident, don't you?"

I nodded my head, and let my eyes get big. "Yes, I know, Your Excellency," I said. "It was a stupid thing to do. Thank you for the wonderment of your kind grace."

"Yeah, thanks," he said, continuing to laugh. "Don't do it again, and drive safely." I rose to my feet, dusted myself off and made my way back to the van. When I sat back down, I was sweating profusely from the stress.

"I don't believe you got away with that!" shouted Mark.

I took a deep breath and let my hands rest on the steering wheel. Then I let out a big laugh and turned back to face my friends. As we paid our toll and pulled away I looked at my friends again and said, "Somebody give me a hit on that joint!" Everybody laughed.

It took Angus years to get his house built. He planned on raising enough money to finish it by selling off dozens of ten-acre lots on his massive property. For years he toiled away at trying to comply with the strict requirements of Vermont's recently passed Act 250 law, which restricted land use in order to prevent land speculation and over-development.

One day, Angus showed me the new plot plan for subdividing his property, which would allow him to keep a twenty-one-acre chunk where he'd already begun construction of his new house. Behind it was a piece of land I knew well, probably better than Angus. It was the same spot where I first camped with my friends under the stars, and where I'd laid out a few years before contemplating what I wanted to do with my life. It was sacred ground for several of us, the place we all migrated to watch killer sunsets, trip, bond, and get a little taste of heaven.

"Angus," I said, sort of wishfully. "You've got this back land here. What if we redrew the lot lines and you kept the entire road frontage, but sold me the back land and a right of way to put a driveway through?"

I badly wanted a piece of land there to build a cabin, but I didn't have much money to buy the property and build something. But since it was back land, I hoped he'd sell it to me for half the price he was seeking on the rest of the lots. Angus peered more closely at the rough sketch I'd drawn, pushing his glasses to the top of his head.

"That's an interesting idea, John," he said, sounding agreeable. "You'd be a good neighbor. I don't see why we can't make it work."

I ended up buying twenty-one acres from Angus for $5,000. We closed on the land on July 6, 1976, two days after America's bicentennial. Leading up to the close I bought a publication called *Wood Frame House Construction* published by the U.S. Department of Agriculture, a comprehensive manual for building a house. It was an inch thick and cost three dollars. Absolutely everything was there, from calculating roof and floor spans, loads, and nailing schedules, to plumbing and electrical standards. It even walked you through electric windmills and how to build wells. After I bought the land, nearly every weekend, a gang of us would head north in my van, loaded with tools and building supplies from Plywood Ranch, a discount building supply store on Route 9 in Southborough. Every one of the boards that went into the place was cut by hand by me, and my friends and I nailed every nail. By mid-October of 1976, we had the cabin framed, sheathed, roofed, and insulated. It was small but warm and dry with a big wood Franklin stove and some of the best views in Vermont.

Since then, the little cabin evolved. It tripled in size and now has electricity, Internet, satellite uplink, and a complete radio studio. It also has a private grass runway and two airplane hangars. But the feel of the place, its importance in my life, what it represents, endures. When I need to get out of my head, I still go to Vermont.

◀

In the winter of '78, another one of Angus's houses burned down. Only this time he was in it. A bunch of us were in Cabot for the weekend when it happened. We'd gone grocery shopping Saturday morning and had been hiking in the last half mile through the snow with bags of groceries when the logger who rented Angus's house for the winter saw us and yelled out the window.

"John, your father called a minute ago," he said. "He's says it's important."

"My father?" I said. He never called me up here. "You know what he wanted?"

He shrugged his shoulders. "No idea," he said.

When I got my father on the line, he sounded somber. "I've got some bad news for you," he said. "I just heard on the news that your friend Angus died."

I felt like I'd been hit in the gut. I pressed my father for details but he didn't know a thing, except that there had been a fire.

The funeral was held the following week in Holliston, where Angus had lived. In trying to figure out what had caused the fire, I called Henry Holbrook, the Holliston police chief to ask what he knew. He said it was ruled a careless disposal of smoking materials. "No," I said. "Absolutely not. Angus quit smoking on Pearl Harbor Day, 1941. He told me that story at least five times."

Even stranger was the fact that his body had been found in his bedroom closet with a chunk of his skull missing. There were other details, too, which were hard to explain. Like the fact that the house got so hot that the telephone melted off the wall. Finally, on my urging, Chief Holbrook called in the State Fire Marshall's office, and it was officially determined that the fire had been set with an accelerant.

To me, it just seemed oddly suspicious, especially in the context of what had been taking place in Angus's life. Angus had recently told me that his nephew had been taking advantage of his wealth and generosity, and that he was in the process of changing his will so he could take him out of it.

But even after the determination of arson, there was never an arrest. As Chief Holbrook later told me, arson is one of the most difficult crimes to prove. "You almost have to catch the arsonist with the match in his hand," he said.

The problems didn't end there. As soon as he was buried, Angus's brother and sister suddenly showed up on the scene. Neither had spoken to Angus in years. They had disowned him because they disapproved of him being gay. Angus had told me they were intentionally left out of his will, but the moment he died they fought to get a piece of his estate. The legal battle went on for years and in the end it was the lawyers who got everything. The golf course, the farm, all the Vermont land, everything got liquidated to cover the cost of the lawyers. Like Jack Carlson had once warned me, "Always best to stay out of court...the only ones who win are the lawyers." 🔇

15. Stairway to Heaven

Led Zeppelin, 1968

Me on my high horse.

When I came down from that Vermont mountaintop for the first time in July 1969 and settled back into everyday life, I realized that I'd found a new clarity under that starlit sky which had opened a new vision of the world and my future. I was twenty-seven years old, getting restless, running low on money, and wanted to get back to work. The summer of freedom had been great, but for a guy who got high off building things, taking on projects, and being on the radio, I felt ready to sink my teeth into something. There was just that one problem.

Who was going to hire me?

I mean, it wasn't like my dream of winning the license for the new radio station had faded any. But the truth is there had been no real developments. It was back in the FCC's hands, and the comparative hearing between Natick Broadcast Associates and our company hadn't even really ramped up. Just as Judge Langan had predicted, it would be years before anything was settled.

"I keep telling you this because it's true," he said. "It's going to be a marathon."

I started doing the math and knew I needed to get hustling. I could end up thirty years old with no job, no license, no career, and no money. When I left 'ORC that last time I swore that was it in terms of working at somebody else's radio station. But after three months of being unemployed, I needed work. Shooting weddings was not a good long-term idea. Back home in Natick, maybe a day after returning from Vermont, it occurred to me that perhaps maybe I should try to get some part-time work at a Boston radio station. I called up my friend, Ron Robin, a deejay at WMEX in Boston, to see if the station might be looking for someone to do some fill-in or weekend work.

"Not sure, John," he said. "But give our program director, Dick Summer, a call. He knows who you are. He might have something for you."

Since that first short stint at WMEX five years before, the place had fallen on hard times and it had dropped to number fifteen in the ratings. Most of the damage had been caused by Top 40 WRKO, which by the late 1960s became the ruling radio station in Boston. Its rise had been meteoric. Up until early '67 it had been known as WNAC, a muddling, middle-of-the-road talk station that catered to seniors. But on March 16, 1967, it switched call letters from WNAC to WRKO—for the name of the parent company, RKO General—and changed formats.

It wasn't just a Top 40 station, however, it was a Bill Drake-formatted Top 40 station. In just a few short years, Drake had become a legend in the business, turning weak stations in cities like San Diego, San Francisco, Los Angeles, New York, and Memphis into dominant ratings powerhouses. He did it by implementing a specific, streamlined formula of programming he'd developed. Only the very big hits of the day made it on the air, deejays packed recognizable personalities, but on-air chatter was kept to absolute minimum. In fact, outside of the music, everything was stripped to the essentials. It was tight, forward-moving, and energetic.

Drake also wasn't afraid to go big. He pushed to produce a fifty-two-hour documentary called *The History of Rock & Roll* in '69. It was a monumental undertaking, with hundreds of interviews, but a winning one. It was broadcast over a three-day weekend on stations across the country and was lauded by critics and listeners.

WRKO switched to Top 40 in September '67 and even nabbed WMEX's biggest star, Arnie Ginsburg, to take over nights. By 1968, 'RKO had ended WMEX's nine-year run as Boston's number one Top 40 station and owned twenty percent of the radio audience.

Infrastructure was another thing Drake had in his favor. Both WMEX and WRKO were 50,000-watt stations, but WRKO's transmitter was west of Boston and had a massive signal that blanketed New England. You could hear it beyond Worcester to the west, plus all of New Hampshire, Rhode Island, and Cape Cod. The WMEX transmitter was in Quincy by the ocean, which meant most of the signal got pushed out to sea. Mac's station may have been number one with Gloucester fishermen, but it was barely listenable in Boston's highly-populated western suburbs.

With 'RKO ruling the airwaves, everyone else was fighting for number two. At WMEX, especially, the morale was down. Mac was always crabby and in Dick Summer they had a guy who was super nice—mellow and smart—but not the kind of programmer you wanted to lead the charge against a Drake run station. Dick, whom Mac had turned the keys over to after Arnie left, was the program director you wanted if your main competition had a format that was all poetry. He was big into New Age material. Before coming to WMEX he'd hosted an overnight show on WBZ called *The Loving Touch* where he'd go on air and say things like, *Okay, close your eyes and touch your nose. Now touch an orange. How does that make you feel?*

He brought that same sensitivity to Top 40 radio. He called his approach "The Human Thing" and it was about as soft and mushy as the name implied. Instead of the Bill Drake formula of high-energy deejays, he wanted more sensitive on-air personalities. Every other song the station played was a Top 40 hit, followed by an album cut chosen by the DJ, which often was something listeners had never even heard of. And if in-between the DJs wanted to talk about the Maharishi Mahesh Yogi or some kind of New Age philosophy, well, that was okay in Dick Summer's book. It wasn't exactly the kind of radio I loved, but I needed a job.

I got in touch with Dick immediately, as soon as I could put together a demo tape for him. He called me back right after he listened to it. "I like your style, John," he said. "You're good. Might want you to slow down a bit, talk a bit more intimately, but I think we can find a way to work together. We've got some weekend work available, vacation time fill-in, and probably some overnights."

I met with Dick in his second-floor office at the WMEX studios on Broadway in Boston's Bay Village, an artsy neighborhood in downtown Boston. Across the street was The Other Side, Boston's biggest gay dance club, and next door was Jacques, the dingy home to drag queens and drug dealers. Although Dick seemed to move easily in the counter-culture environment, he looked about as establishment as Richard Nixon. Always in a suit, his hair carefully combed with a neat part on the left side. But he was a genuinely nice person and definitely a cool guy. I felt completely relaxed around him.

Dick Summer, one of the most creative, talented, and genial people in radio I've ever met.

As we sat talking in his office I told him that in this emerging age of reality I'd become uncomfortable with my nom de plume of "Johnny Gardner." I hated anything fake and wanted to be pure and authentic. By now, I had near-shoulder length hair and a stubble beard. I looked more like George Harrison than some candy-ass Top 40 deejay.

Dick tapped his fingers on his desk. "Have you ever thought about just using your own name?"

I looked at him with surprise. "You mean *Garabedian?*" I asked laughing. "You don't think that sounds a little, you know, ethnic?"

Dick shook his head. "Not at all," he said. "I think it's got a nice rhythm to it. Sounds very authentic."

He couldn't have been more right. If you boiled the sixties down to its base element, what it represented was a movement to just be honest, less like a plastic TV show and more like reality. Grounded, even a little gritty. I said my name out loud to myself a few times. "Hmmm, I dunno."

"What's your middle name?" Dick asked.

"Hood," I replied.

"Huh," he said.

"That was my Scottish grandmother's maiden name," I mumbled.

"Johnny Hood sounds made up. In fact, anything with Johnny doesn't sound right. Sounds too kiddie. The name needs something else." Dick looked up again and then back at me. "What about John H. Garabedian?"

For years after, I went on air with that name, which for most listeners just got shortened to "John H." It was a small thing but an important one. For a young guy who had struggled so much with his identity—my height, my sexuality, my intellectual gawkiness, and my ethnicity—it was another liberating step toward proudly claiming my true identity and further validating myself.

Despite how my previous 1964 experience at WMEX had ended, I was excited about working at the station again. The station had moved out of the Fenway Park studios on Brookline Avenue and into an impressive new building off Park Square in downtown Boston. While Dick Summer may not have had a ratings-winning radio format, he knew how to assemble and motivate a fun and talented staff. A trippy blond California goofball who called himself "Cousin Duffy" hosted the afternoon drive-time slot. He often showed up for work in "creative" clothing. It might be clown pants or some kind of garishly colored shirt, with a Greek fisherman's cap, or he might just be in a wife beater and purple trousers. There was no predicting what he'd wear, or what kind of condition he might be in. Duffy thought nothing of dropping acid before going on air and then spending the first ten minutes of his show going on about AC powered light bulbs and how they can't be good for you because they pulsate and give off radiation. Then he'd play a song and spend another ten minutes talking about concepts like "puffy clouds," how beautiful the sun was. If you were lucky the next song might be a hit, but there was no guarantee. It was eclectic and unbearably boring all at the same time.

At 10 every night, the station was turned over to a three-hour talk show hosted by Steve Fredericks, which he had taken over from the legendary Jerry Williams. Fredericks hosted politicians and celebrities and listeners called in to debate the issues of the day. Should we get out of Vietnam? Why can't we legalize pot? How do you fix the Boston schools? Why won't the city fix the potholes? Things like that. Fredericks was a good-looking guy in his thirties with close-cropped hair that projected this strict and serious personality. But away from the mike, however, he was a different story.

One of his best friends was Bob Hite, the lead singer for Canned Heat, which explained why Steve had access to one of the best collections of weed in the city. We'd go over to his apartment after his show and sample his treats, which he kept in large Ball jars neatly lined up in a kitchen cabinet, labeled and dated. It was like a well-organized library. He'd pull something out then proceed to describe its taste and what it might do to you.

The timing couldn't have been any better for my start at WMEX. My first day of work was Monday, August 18, 1969—the day after Woodstock. Despite having two pairs of tickets to the historic three-day festival, I'd made the dumb decision to skip the thing. It would have been a long trek to get there, I told myself, and sounded like it could be a nightmare finding a place to sleep and eat. Besides, a friend of mine was moving to London and had asked me to help him move some furniture that weekend from his Boston apartment to his sister's place in New York City.

But as reports from the festival started to trickle out—the music, the crowds, the nudity, the drugs—I regretted my decision. What made it bearable was that the next day I was starting work at WMEX. When I arrived that following Monday morning, Dick sauntered up to me. "We've got to do something on Woodstock," he said. "Let's see if we can pull together a whole show about it. Music, interviews, whatever we can dig up. Is that something you can take on?"

There wasn't much vision beyond what Dick had laid out, but I loved the idea and the pressure of trying to pull a thing like that off in such a short amount of time. "Of course," I said. "I'll start right now and have something ready by tonight."

We didn't have live recordings from the concert to broadcast, but I had the records from every major band that played at Woodstock. Jimi Hendrix, Santana, The Who, Joe Cocker, Crosby, Stills & Nash, and so many others. We made announcements on the air all day asking for people who'd actually been there to call in or come into the studio. I wanted stories about the festival. How did the music sound? What was it like getting in and out? Did that brown acid really make you want to tear your head off? The response was good, and we got enough people on tape to give us first-person accounts and make the show compelling to listen to.

A little luck didn't hurt either. As it happened, the drummer from Sha Na Na, Jocko Marcellino, just happened to swing by the studios. The Boston band had just gotten together that year and somehow had finagled its way into the

Woodstock lineup, coming on stage just before Jimi Hendrix on the final day of the festival. It was a short performance but a memorable one and their inclusion in the Woodstock movie catapulted them to stardom and helped ignite a revival in 1950s Doo-Wop music. I sat Jocko down in the production studio and he gave us original accounts of what it was like to play in front of such a big, muddy mass of hippies, to watch Jimi take the stage, and see all those other stars—Janice, Santana, Creedence Clearwater Revival, The Who, Grateful Dead—live and up close.

The next day Dick was beaming. "That was amazing," he gushed. "I felt like I was at the festival. I loved what you did."

I appreciated Dick's praise and the freedom he gave me with my show. But sticking to his music-playing formula was at the same time liberating and frustrating. After ten years observing listener request reactions to music at WORC, I had a fairly accurate idea of what attracted and held audiences. You didn't play "Honky Tonk Woman" by the Rolling Stones, and then go to something esoteric like Jackie Gleason's "To a Sleeping Beauty." No matter how many drugs you thought your listeners might be on, you just knew that if they heard that kind of music flow they'd change the station to WRKO.

In late spring, 1970, Cousin Duffy got a job offer to move to Los Angeles and program the underground station KMET, which then opened up the 2-6 p.m. afternoon show at WMEX. Dick and Mac Richmond tapped me to fill the shift while they looked for a replacement. That replacement never came. With the musical freedom Dick Summer gave the DJs, I was at last able to start playing lots of real Top 40 hits. The results were startling. When the ratings came in, my afternoon show suddenly became the highest-rated time slot on WMEX, and Mac actually congratulated me. In a few short weeks I had managed to create the kind of buzz usually reserved for up-and-coming album rock FM stations like WBCN.

I enjoyed working for Dick. He is a great air talent and had many strengths, but having a good ear for broad appeal music wasn't one of them. I remember going to his office sometime in 1970 and raving about the song "Question" by the Moody Blues. I'd heard it for the first time in Vermont that weekend when it

John Garabedian

It was at the Strawberry Fields Rock Festival outside Toronto, Ontario, Canada, in 1970 that I got into a deep philosophical conversation in the men's room with a guy urinating next to me. It turned out to be Jessie Colin Young of the Youngbloods. (Left to right) Brad Stoic, my nephew Kris Carlson, and Mark Parenteau.

debuted on Montreal station CHOM-FM. The song was powerful, magnificent, with a timely social message and huge musical intensity. It was unlike anything on radio. I played it for him and he just looked at me with a blank expression.

"John," he said. "Take it home and play it until you're sick of it because it's never going to be a hit."

Two months later, it was number one on *Billboard* magazine's chart.

That lack of understanding of mass tastes finally caught up to him. Dick was a superbly talented performer and sensitive poet, a creative soul who believed there was a large untapped audience for sensitivity and the esoteric. But the world didn't want "The Human Touch." Every three months the ratings books came out and WMEX kept nibbling at the bottom. As Timothy Crouse later put it in his *Rolling Stone* article about the WMEX-WRKO ratings war, "Dick played album cuts. But unfortunately he played the wrong cuts."

At the end of 1970, Dick's contract expired and the poor ratings brought an end to his time at the station and "The Human Touch." For the next few months we drifted aimlessly until Mac brought in a programming consultant to try to juice up the programming. But the consultant's formula for success was the complete opposite of Dick's: Play the same seven songs every hour and five minutes, over and over. In a four-hour show I could end up airing the same song four times. When the ratings didn't budge under his watch, the consultant disappeared. That was Mac's style. No announcement. No

The "club kid" transforms into a "Green Mountain Boy."

explanation. None of us asked any questions; we just kept working.

It was total chaos. No one was running things. The DJs started improvising whatever they wanted. The music was wrong, the announcers talked way too much, and we had no clear identity or image. The radio station I'd grown up listening to, the one that had owned the "hit music" brand in Boston, was now completely irrelevant.

Working for a loser radio station made me miserable, especially when I could clearly see what was wrong and what steps needed to be implemented. The frustration finally got to me and one night after getting off the air I decided I should say something to Mac about the obvious issues I believed were holding us back. I headed up to the second floor mezzanine and through the doorway into Mac's office. You never knew what might happen when you met with him one-on-one. It was like playing Russian roulette. Sometimes you lived. Other times your head was blown off.

Everyone had gone home for the day. Mac was reading the *Boston Globe* when I dropped in, griping about some headline. He looked up and squinted his eyes, nodded his head, signaling for me to take a seat. I decided to just be as frank as possible.

"There are some key things we are doing wrong that are killing us," I said. "I want us to be the top station in Boston, and yet there's no rhyme or reason behind anything we're putting out over the air. People want to hear the hits and we're not playing them." Mac put down the paper and leaned back in his chair. Then he nodded his head, indicating he wanted to hear more. "We have no public image. The audience doesn't know what we stand for or what we do. The deejays talk too much. Everything has to be crisp, bam-bam-bam. No fat. No meandering. Get in, get out. Don't bore us, get to the chorus."

Mac leaned forward and folded his arms across his desk. "Sounds good, John," he said. "Do it."

"Do what?" I asked.

"Make those changes," he said.

I laughed. "I can't do that," I said. "I'm in the announcer's union and just a deejay. I have no authority to order people around."

Mac nodded his head. "Write a memo," he said. "Put all of it down and I'll sign it."

So I did. That night I composed a two-page memo of directives. The very stuff I'd gone over with Mac about how the deejays needed to talk less, what they needed to promote, how and when they needed to say the call letters, how the music flow would work—I laid out in that memo and then got Mac's signature. When it landed in the hands of the staff the next day the grumbling was palpable. "More orders from the king," a few said. I stayed quiet, nodding my head in agreement, but said nothing.

For the next few weeks I continued my secret meetings with Mac. More memos followed about being positive on the air, scheduling longer stretches of commercial free music, and promoting local concerts. Almost immediately WMEX began to once again sound like an exciting Top 40 station and not some social poetry experiment. It had a harmony, a pulse, some flow.

It also gave me a shot of confidence. In the wake of everything that happened over the last couple of years—my struggle to get the radio license, the abrupt end at WORC, the frustrations I'd had working for mediocre managers at other stations—now being allowed to put into place my ideas for programming and seeing them work in a great city like Boston was a shot in the arm. It reminded me of why I loved radio, and the positive turn for WMEX proved to me why I was good at it.

Mac saw that, too, and in March 1971, he named me program director and gave me a huge raise, with a salary of $25,000 ($150,000 in 2015 dollars). I was thrilled. The competitor in me wanted to go right at WRKO and Drake. Although Drake was unmistakably the best, I could see the cracks in their presentation. Even with our inferior signal, I really thought it was possible to beat them. "They play too many loser songs and

Carly Simon was one of the most beautiful women I ever met. After her performance in which she opened for Cat Stevens, we drank Mateus wine in her dressing room and ended up making out. She has a large mouth and kisses great.

keep burned out songs in rotation for too long," I kept telling Mac, who liked my confidence. "And in this era of authenticity, WRKO is fake and plastic. I think we can beat their programming and project a much cooler, funner, hipper image."

In order to fine-tune the music to the Boston audience, I immediately installed listener request lines, and then hired full-time request operators to answer the calls and tabulate the results. We couldn't afford to rely on bad information from sales or corrupt national charts, or be guessing which songs listeners might like. We had to absolutely know which big hits people wanted to hear, which new songs they loved, and which songs they were sick of.

Next, I had to hire a music director. I needed someone who could beat back the twenty-odd record label promotion reps who'd march into the station every week, pushing whatever priority singles their company wanted put into rotation. Dealing with them, fending them off, could be a full-time job. Meeting with them took hours each week and was a total waste of my time, time which needed to be spent coaching the air talent and creating great programming. But I knew just the right person for the job.

Overnight shows tend to attract a dedicated group of listeners who call the station. It was much the same at WMEX and with the late show Dick Summer originally put me on. One of the regulars was a young woman named Wendy Furiga, a husky, nineteen-year-old woman who worked at Dunkin' Donuts in

Wendy Furiga. Standing 6' tall, weighing 300 pounds, with pink eyes and white hair in a perm, Mark Parenteau remarked that she looked like a polar bear on acid.

Medford Square. She called up almost every night between 1 and 3 a.m., complimenting me about my voice or something I said or the music I played. At the end of every call she'd tell me she'd love to get together with me. "I've just got to meet in person the great John H.," she'd say.

I held her off as long as I could before Wendy finally told me she had made a big batch of chocolate chip cookies and wanted to know if I'd be at the station the next afternoon. "Fine," I said. "Come down tomorrow afternoon. I'll give you a tour of the station."

At 4:30 p.m. sharp, Wendy rolled up on her bicycle to the WMEX studios. As she got closer I gasped. She stood over six feet tall with a three-hundred-pound frame that teetered on top of the old Schwinn girls' bike she was peddling. She was an albino, with this crazy mess of big white permed hair and pink eyes that fluttered, and who walked with a waddle. I stuffed my hands in my pocket and watched with some shock through the station's glass doors as she got closer. She looked like a polar bear on LSD.

"John H.!" she grunted, raising her right hand to wave hello as she approached. In her hands she held a large plastic container of freshly-baked cookies. I opened the door for her. "For my favorite deejay," she said, handing them to me.

"It's great to meet you," I said, looking down at the cookies and then looking back up at her. I stared at her for several long seconds. "Shall we start the tour?"

It wasn't long before Wendy became a fixture at the WMEX studios. She still regularly called, but after her morning shift at Dunkin' Donuts she often dropped in at the station to hang out in the lobby, standing there for hours watching me do my show through the big double glass studio window.

As a radio station music director, it's easy to develop an oversized ego. Label reps know exactly how to kiss the music director's ass. In order to get their songs played, they introduce them to rock stars, take them to the finest restaurants, and stroke them about their supposed musical "genius." Like a drug, many programmers get addicted to the adulation. It is very easy to get lured into doing the wrong thing for your audience. To survive and do your job well requires a personality that can't be easily wined and dined.

Everyone else thought I was nuts, but my instincts told me Wendy could be the perfect WMEX music director. Her job was simple: Keep all the record reps away from me, I instructed. That was her job. I didn't want to see them. But make them feel important. Listen to everything they tell you about the songs they're pushing, and then listen to the cuts. Any song she thought I should hear she should put in one pile, the rest went into another. Every week the two of us then sat down for an hour and selected what got "added" to our playlist and chose what got dropped.

With Wendy on board as music director, I could turn my focus on the bigger picture issues. Chief among those was that we had no identity. Either we were the Woo-Woo Ginsburg station, an outdated has-been Top 40 station, or the weird poetry station that played strange music with DJs who talked too much. Some people who saw the WMEX name for the first time asked if it had something to do with Mexico. If people wanted to hear hit music in Boston they turned to WRKO, and if they wanted to feel they were cool and on the cutting edge, they claimed to listen to WBCN. WMEX was considered the "dead horse" of Boston radio.

You didn't have to pay that close attention to the rock scene to know tons of great music was being pumped out during this period. Pink Floyd, Led Zeppelin, Cream, Santana, The Guess Who, The Who, Kinks, Doors, AC/DC—some of the greatest music in rock history was being made. And it was hip. But only a fraction of it made its way to Top 40 stations like WRKO, which was happy to play sugary kiddie stuff like "Sugar, Sugar" by The Archies or "One Bad Apple" by the Osmonds. Meanwhile, album rock stations like WBCN played both obscure and iconic artists, but usually obscure cuts by the iconic artists that nev-

The Boston Garden dressing room, 1971, with John Fogarty and Creedence Clearwater Revival just before introducing them onstage to a sold-out house.

er would become anyone's favorites. That left a big opening space where I believed WMEX could come in strong. We needed to feed better hit music to differentiate ourselves from WRKO, songs they weren't playing, yet songs for which our target audience had a proven passion for.

Then the station needed to present a powerful position statement to image this format, and it needed to be on constantly. Having learned that one of the most powerful words in advertising is "new," it just made sense to position the station around the great emerging music people were calling for on our request lines. We rebranded the station with a massive new top-of-the-hour legal ID production built around "The New Music" using Strauss's "Also Sprach Zarathustra," the opening theme from the movie, *2001, A Space Odyssey*.

The heralding horns would come in like God had just arrived, "Dah Dahhhh," and then in a whisper of a voice I recorded over it, "Changes, and you've found the *new* music." Then our signature jingle, "15-10, WMEX, Boston!" and *wham!* We'd blast into some huge hit, like The Who's "Won't Get Fooled Again" or Free's "All Right Now." It sounded magnificent and impressive. The great music flow would continue, and thanks to the interactive request lines we could see quickly which songs were generating excitement and which songs were duds. Within weeks the Human Touch and Woo-Woo Ginsburg images long associated with WMEX evaporated. We sounded hip, fun, and hot, but absolutely targeted at the mainstream audience.

Throughout the day the phones rang constantly and every hour people told us exactly which songs they wanted to hear. The listeners became invested in the station because they had input, and the music they heard reflected their exact tastes.

As we pushed deeper into 1971, the radio rivalry between WMEX and 'RKO intensified. In the *Boston Phoenix*, music critic Jon Landau, who later went on to manage Bruce Springsteen, wrote about Boston's rivalry and coined the term "Radio War." He followed Boston radio closely and pointed out that we were doing something almost unheard of, keeping WMEX cutting edge and mainstream at the same time. All the while we were gaining on the competition.

"[John H.] has probably forced more record companies to release singles off of albums than any disk jockey in the country and has made more singles into hits than anyone this year," Landau wrote in October of 1971.

He wasn't kidding. Twenty-two of the top hundred singles that year—Jonathan Edwards' "Sunshine" and J. Geils Band's "Looking For A Love," The Who's "Won't Get Fooled Again" and "Baba O'Riley," Free's "All Right Now," Paul McCartney's "Uncle Albert," Joan Baez and "The Night They Drove Old Dixie Down" for example—were broken out and became national hits directly from airplay on WMEX. If we thought a song might be a hit, we tried it. It didn't matter where the song came from. While record companies pushed what they released on 45s, we weren't afraid to go deep into an album to find a great tune. Or even into the past. Our priority was to continuously play the most exciting, appealing flow of great songs we could find to deliver to our audience and then closely monitor listener interest and response.

"Nights in White Satin" was a cut from the Moody Blues cutting-edge 1967 *Days of Future Past* album and was one of the most magnificent orchestrations of the previous four years. It laid the progressive rock foundation for bands like Pink Floyd. Yet the cut had received very limited airplay, only on album rock stations, and the mass audience had never been exposed to it. Although it was nearly eight minutes long, I felt strongly it had the potential to be a major hit. Playing the Moody Blues on WMEX would definitely add to our "cool factor."

London Records vice-president Brian Interland told me that the band had been asked before about releasing it as a single, but refused, fearing Top 40 airplay would "cheapen" their musical reputation. I didn't care about their reputation,

With the J. Geils Band after a sellout concert at the Wang Center with Fleetwood Mac and The Stylistics. (Left to right) Magic Dick, myself, J. Geils, Danny Klein, Peter Wolf, Stephen Jo Bladd, Atlantic Records' Paul Ahern, manager Fred Lewis, and Seth Justman. *©Ron Pownall/RockRollPhoto.com*

only ours. They couldn't stop us from playing it, so on the air it went in heavy rotation. Within two weeks, "Nights in White Satin" was our most requested song. By this time, WRKO had become nervous about the effect we were having on record sales with the ream of exclusive hits we were playing showing up in their research. We were shocked when they added it to their rotation.

With retail reaction and airplay spreading nationally as a result, London Records released "Nights in White Satin" as a single and national Top 40 airplay took off. Interland confided to me that London Records had to keep it a complete secret from the band for fear of major repercussions. It ended up becoming the number one song in the United States, and when I heard Casey Kasem introduce it at the top of the chart on American Top 40, a tear came to my eye. It was clear we were on to something huge.

I found an obscure French song, "Je t'Aime," from Serge Gainsbourg and his then girlfriend, Jane Birkin, which Wendy played for me as a joke, telling me it sounded like porn set to music. She was right. And I immediately put it on the air. It was an incredibly sensual love song with a good hook and a pair of orchestrated orgasms. I had initial trepidation about FCC issues when we first played it, but Mac gave me the green light and within a week it was our most requested song.

"Good job on capturing the pervert demographic," Mac needled me.

It was a similar story with singles like "Signs" by the Canadian group, The Five Man Electric Band, and Lee Michaels' "Do You Know What I Mean?," both of which I heard while in Vermont on the mountaintop while listening to Montreal's CHOM-FM. We took calculated chances on new songs, but could quickly gauge from the request lines which new songs to keep in the rotation and which ones we needed to ditch quickly.

One of the exceptional record reps who managed to pass the Wendy test was a skinny kid from West Roxbury named Paul Ahern, who worked for Atlantic Records. Over the course of just a few months we'd helped Paul become a legend at the label, first by making Jonathan Edwards's "Sunshine" take off, and then by launching the career of Yes with "Your Move (I've Seen All Good People)."

Late in the summer of '71, he called to tell me he'd just gotten off the plane from London at Boston's Logan Airport with an exclusive acetate copy of the new Led Zeppelin album, *Led Zeppelin IV*. Nobody else had it.

"Atlantic Records wants you to pick the first single," he said, handing me the record. We were in the WMEX main studio, it was just after 4 p.m. and I was in the middle of my afternoon show. Paul stood nervously as I took the acetate from him and plopped it on the turntable. I listened to a good twenty seconds of each track and took notes but gave no reaction, occasionally stealing glances at Paul, who looked at the spinning album with heightened anticipation. Finally, I put the needle back on the fourth cut of side one. It began with an instrumental opening with acoustic guitar, followed by some reeds, and then a mellow Robert Plant line that went, "There's a lady who's sure, all that glitters is gold, and she's climbing a stairway to heaven." It was a song unlike anything I'd heard before, and certainly nothing like Led Zeppelin had done before, much less ever heard on Top 40 radio.

"This is it!" I said eagerly, raising my hands in the air. After Uncle Albert finished over the air, "Stairway" debuted on the radio for the first time anywhere. I cranked up the studio speakers to experience the depth of the evolving eight minute progression. I couldn't believe how great it was and loved what it rep-

wmex 1510

the new music authority

Busy week for John H. Garabedian - Top, Andy Kulberg of Seatrain brings WMMEX first tape of their new album, "Marblehead Messenger". Bottom, Robert Plante of Led Zepplin after sellout Boston Garden concert Tues. nite.

Rebuilding WMEX's image required promoting the station hard, especially to music lovers. To do so, I rebranded the station "The New Music Authority." Weekly music charts were distributed through all key Boston music outlets.

resented for WMEX and our "new music" sound.

Paul looked elated as the song blasted away in the studio and made its American debut over WMEX's 50,000 watts. "They are going to be playing this in thirty years," I confidently said to him.

That day was forty-five years ago and I obviously underestimated its endurance. When the lists of the greatest rock songs of all time get churned out, "Stairway" is always near the top. For fifteen years after that 1971 afternoon, it became the closing song I used nightly to sign off my show.

Paul Ahern went on to discover and become manager of the rock band Boston, which turned him into a multi-millionaire.

All this incredible fresh new music, all these powerful hits that WRKO wasn't playing, meant there was big talk on the street about WMEX. Critics, listeners, and especially everyone at the station were excited about us. The station pulsed with energy.

Record executives and concert promoters noticed it, too. One of the major efforts I made was to increase the station's presence in Boston's pop culture scene. At any major rock concert at the Boston Garden there were eighteen thousand music fans who were potential core WMEX radio listeners. I wanted us to be in front of them, hooked into their scene, connected to the music they loved and were listening to.

One of the people I'd become friends with the year before was a young, ambitious concert promoter named Don Law. Law was originally from Westport, Connecticut, and had grown up in the music business. His father, Don Law, Sr., was a legendary producer at Columbia Records who made his first fame by capturing a field recording of the legendary bluesman Robert Johnson in a hotel room in San Antonio in 1936. Later, he worked with stars

The classy and sensual Roberta Flack had just had her first megahit, "The First Time Ever I Saw Your Face" when I first met her.

like Johnny Cash, Marty Robbins, Ray Price, Johnny Horton, Jimmy Dean and Carl Perkins, producing a lineup of number one songs. The younger Law went a different direction—concert promotion.

When I first met him in 1968 Don was still an undergrad at Boston University but already a significant player in the Boston music landscape. As manager of the Boston Tea Party, a now-legendary psychedelic rock club with no alcohol (but plenty of LSD and pot), he booked groups and solo artists like the Grateful Dead and Jimi Hendrix just as they were breaking into the American rock scene. Out of loyalty, they stayed with him even after they blew up and started doing big arena shows. I suppose they saw what I saw. In a business filled with scoundrels and cheats, Law was savvy, a real gentleman, and honest. Aerosmith manager Tim Collins once called Don Law "a gentleman in a jungle."

In late winter of '71, Don came to me as he was preparing to present a Boston Garden show for the band Ten Years After. The group had recently signed with Columbia Records, and on their new album, *A Space in Time*, I discovered a cut, "I'd Love to Change the World," that I felt could be a huge hit. It was beautifully produced and the lyrics, along with Alvin Lee's sweet, biting, flash guitar sound, captured the revolutionary spirit of the time. I immediately added it to the WMEX rotation. The only issue I had with the song was the screaming guitar solo right in the middle of it. I loved it, thought Lee was brilliant, but I worried many of female listeners would find the aggressive solo annoying and change the station. In radio we call it a "programming irritant." I spliced it out. The song subsequently became a top ten hit on WMEX. Columbia Records released it as a single using my edit with Lee's guitar solo deleted.

As Don geared up for his first major Boston Garden show with Ten Years After, we struck a deal. WMEX would run his ads and double his schedule in exchange for promoting the concert as "WMEX Presents Ten Years After." In addition, for a price I agreed to, I would be the emcee of every Garden show and supervise production of all his radio commercials. Our call letters were splashed everywhere, on the tickets, in print, on the TV, and posters. When the concert quickly sold out, it was tough to argue with our deal. Don got the ticket sales, we got the exposure, and I got to emcee every major Boston Garden concert. All of it enhanced the "cool" image of John H. Garabedian and especially that of WMEX.

At the Boston Garden the night of the sold-out Ten Years After show, Don, who'd warned me that Lee made a sarcastic comment about my edit of the song, introduced me with some trepidation. Lee, a slender, good-looking English guy with blond hair that fell to his shoulders, didn't hide his annoyance. "So you're the guy who cut my guitar solo," he said, sticking out his hand.

I could understand how he felt but I didn't back down. "You're an incredible guitar player," I told him. "But we're trying to reach a wide audience, and hard-edged guitar solos turn some females off." He may not have liked my reasoning, but he didn't argue with it or the results. That single launched the band into stardom and helped make Lee a rich man.

Like Paul Ahern and the executives at Atlantic, Don Law had faith in my ear. A few months after the Ten Years After show, he popped by the station and handed me a five-inch reel of tape.

"I just got this from my friend Peter Rudge in the UK," he said sliding the tape over to me. "He manages The Who. They haven't had a hit in years, but he's hoping this might be something that could get radio airplay. It isn't even on a record yet. Would you mind listening to it?"

I took the tape, which had only one song on it, and the next day gave it a listen. I was a bit doubtful; it had been years since The Who had done anything. But when the speakers blared the first notes of "Won't Get Fooled Again," I knew the group was back. I called Don up immediately. "This is a smash," I said. "Can I play it?" Out on the WMEX airwaves it went, the first station in the world to play what would become an iconic rock song. Three weeks later it was number one on the WMEX request lines, and then Don brought me the

The legendary Don Law. Wonderful dry wit. Manager of the Boston Tea Party while a student at BU, he built the Xfinity Center amphitheater in Mansfield, and ended up Chairman of Live Nation, America's dominant concert promotion company.

band's about-to-be-released album *Who's Next*. I picked out "Baba O'Riley," which leapfrogged its predecessor to claim number one status.

Of all the hits we broke open at WMEX, though, the biggest ended up becoming the biggest hit of the year, reaching *Billboard's* number one song of 1971. Rod Stewart had been the lead singer of British groups The Jeff Beck Group and The Faces. After those groups broke up, he released a solo album, *The Rod Stewart Album*, which bombed, and then in 1971, nervously released a second, *Every Picture Tells a Story*. His label, Mercury Records, released two singles from the album to Top 40 radio but found little success at getting airplay. Failing to get traction, Mercury had stopped promoting Stewart or the record and his career seemed set to fade into oblivion.

My tiny four-room house in East Natick was often an informal musical laboratory. I played new music for close friends because I trusted their responses. Their reactions were often reliable indicators of whether songs had the potential to be a hit or not. That's what made me think that despite it being nearly five minutes long, Stewart's "Maggie May" might blow up. The fact that Mercury Records had issued it as the B-side to the single "Reason to Believe" was ironclad proof that record executives aren't always the best judges of either mass taste or advocates for their artists.

From the moment "Maggie May" hit the WMEX airwaves during that summer of '71, the request lines lit up. Within a day it became the most requested song on the station. Mercury, however, thought it was a fluke and tried to convince me that the real Stewart single I should be pushing was "(I Know) I'm Losing You." The vice president of promotion for Mercury Records actually flew to Boston to try to convince me to play it.

I was incredulous and began screaming and waving my hands. "No! No! Are you crazy?" I insisted. "'Maggie May' has been our number-one request for almost a month!" While watching the requests for the song pour into our request lines, he finally saw the light. He flew back to Chicago and put the full force of the label behind it. Over the next month it topped the charts and propelled *Every Picture Tells a Story* to become *Billboard's* number two-ranked album for the year. Meanwhile, while we blasted out "Maggie May" every ninety minutes as our number-one request, WRKO in its infinite wisdom decided to ignore us and not play it.

For me, "Maggie May" wasn't just a single we discovered, it was the first real proof that WMEX had turned things around. When Rod Stewart rolled into Boston to perform at a "Concerts on the Common" outdoor show later that summer, I was hired to emcee it. Stewart went through a round of old Faces and Jeff Beck songs, and then let the crowd get quiet. Then the familiar mandolin intro to "Maggie May" fired up. I was standing on the side of the stage when it happened. As he broke into "Wake up Maggie, I think I've got something to say to you," the crowd of ten thousand people immediately rose to their feet and started singing along with Stewart. I looked out with complete disbelief and a rush of joy went through me. They were singing along! All those people *knew the words*. I started tearing up. I was in awe.

"This is us," I yelled, turning to my friend Billy Stooke. "Nobody else in Boston is playing this song. This is all from airplay on WMEX!"

"You seen the ratings?"

Ed Hines, a VP at Columbia Records was on the line. It was late September and I was in the middle of my show. "The book just came out and you guys are number one."

"What the hell are you talking about?" I said, my heart starting to pound. "Which demo?"

"Every demo! You won in total audience," he answered. "It's unbelievable. You guys beat WRKO."

A chill went through me. I fell back into my seat. It had been ninety days since I was made program director and everything we'd done had taken WMEX, this washed-up, beaten-up,

In my programming office at WMEX in 1971 as we took the station from number fifteen to number one in Arbitron ratings in Boston in ninety days.

dead old Top 40 station that was ranked fifteenth in the spring ratings book, to number one. We'd done the impossible and blown past every other station in Boston, including the Bill Drake-programmed WRKO. As soon as I could, I put on a long song and rushed up the stairs into Mac's office and broke the news.

"No shit!" he said with a smile. "Let me make a phone call to get the details."

For the next few days, I was high as a kite. I mean, I sensed we were doing well, but didn't have any hard evidence to prove it. Now I did. Of course, 'RKO was at the ready to dilute the impact. A few months later, in an article in the *Rolling Stone* about the WMEX-WRKO battle, the station's general manager, Perry Ury, crapped all over our success. "John is a great radio man but don't get talked into thinking he's a white knight," he told the magazine.

It's funny, though, because within days of that summer book appearing, 'RKO suddenly started playing the unique WMEX album-cut hits we'd been pushing out, and Ury made sure the WRKO request lines, which had been taken out, were reinstalled.

For the next two months things hummed right along at our station and the spirit was wonderful. We continued to pump out great music, and there was this overall sense that we were knocking around 'RKO and the Drake formula every second we were on the air. It felt so triumphant. For me. For my staff. And especially for Mac. The universe had been restored. His station was number one again. "Good job," he kept saying to me. "We're back on top. That's how it should be."

Too bad it couldn't last.

On a cool mid-November evening I wrapped up my show and headed out the door. I had plans that night to have dinner with Don Law and my girlfriend, Neila Smith, a tall, beautiful red-headed media student at Boston University whom I'd met a few years before while she was president of the New England Beatles fan club. Somehow Neila and I had convinced Don to abandon his aristocratic tastes for just one night and instead of going to the French café on trendy Newbury Street, we dragged him to dinner at the Hilltop Steakhouse in Saugus, at that time the largest restaurant in America. Afterward, we drove back to the station so Don could pick up his VW microbus.

After saying goodnight to Don, I turned to Neila. "Do you mind if we just pop back inside," I said. "I need to write a memo for a new promotion which everyone needs to have in the morning."

I had just about finished writing it out when the blue station hotline lit up. When nobody answered, I finally picked up the call. On the other end was someone from Boston City Hospital who said she was calling on behalf of Mac's girlfriend, Ginger Green. "Mrs. Green came in with Mr. Richmond and she needs a ride home," the caller said.

I hung up quickly and grabbed my coat. "That's weird," I said. "I don't know what's going on but Ginger needs a ride home from the hospital and Mac doesn't. Something's wrong."

It was a quick ten-minute ride and pushing just past 11 when we arrived at the ER. We followed a couple of long hallways until we went through a set of double doors. Ginger spotted us and ran toward me, throwing her arms around me.

"Mac's dead!" she wailed.

A shock flashed through me. I stepped back from Ginger and held her by her shoulders, peering down at her red, tear-soaked face. I couldn't believe it. "What are you talking about?" I said. "What happened?"

In all the years I'd known Mac, he never looked really healthy. He had a ruddy face lined by stress and a bowling ball of a belly. The last few years of WMEX's troubles, especially, had taken their toll. Too much of a toll. Not even the run of recent success had been able to ease what he'd been through. After leaving the station that night he and Ginger went to dinner with a broker to discuss buying KQV,

On the way to a record company event sporting the then-trendy "hippie look" around 1971 with former girlfriend Neila Smith. Neila graduated from Boston University that year and went on to become a successful TV news anchor in Portland, Maine.

a Pittsburgh radio station. He then returned home to his Back Bay condo where he had a massive heart attack. It had all happened in the previous two hours.

His death changed everything for me. A few nights later I went on the air for the Sunday evening show and was barely able to get through it. My eyes watered up every time I had to say something into the mike and tears streamed down my face as listeners called up to express their condolences. Part of the emotion was selfish. I had poured everything I had into rebuilding this magnificent radio station. I'd made it my life. It felt like a gift to work there and for Mac, who had never questioned my approach or techniques, and supported all my decisions. Now, suddenly, he was gone, and everything felt uncertain and tenuous. What was going to happen to the station? What would become of all this great momentum we'd built up?

The answers came fairly quickly. With Mac gone, his surviving older brother, Richard Richmond, took over. To help him manage things, Richard

John Garabedian

In Woods Hole with my buddies headed for a weekend away in Martha's Vineyard. (Left to right) David Blease, Billy and Jimmy Harrison, Gary Blease.

brought in the general manager of one of Mac's other stations, WPGC in Washington, D.C. What a disaster that turned into for me, and for the station. Bob Howard brought an immediate sea change to WMEX. He looked like Captain Bligh, and like the captain of the *Bounty*, he had a management style that was built around his own personal paranoia. To try and offset his nervous personality he spoke in a hushed, even tone. He wanted everything that came out of his mouth to sound "important."

From the day he started, he began issuing orders. One of the first was the prohibition of all food and drink in the studio. Not even coffee, the lifeblood of every deejay, was allowed. He even went so far as to threaten to fire Ron Robin after he dared to eat a cookie while on the air. Then he turned to the programming. He turned on the newsmen and told them to make the news more exciting. "If it bleeds, it leads," he'd say, and actually told the news team to use more dramatic terms, such as substituting "commie reds" for "communists." Then, he called me into his office and told me to eliminate all the request lines. "We don't use them in Washington," he said, matter of factly. "Why do we need them here?" Finally, he instructed me to tell all the DJs to say "number one" every time they said the call letters.

I protested. "That's horrible, Bob," I told him. "We've spent the last year trying to get away from the fake, cheesy crap that killed the station before. Now you want us to return to it?" He didn't care and he had no understanding or appreciation for what we had accomplished. When I tried to gently remind him that he was meddling with what had turned the station from nothing into number one in the market, he just raised his hand.

"Frankly, I don't believe in ratings," he said.

The writing was on the wall. With Mac no longer running the ship, and Howard's irrational behavior in control, the future became black. At 7 a.m. one December morning I was awakened with a phone call at my house in East Natick. Neila was asleep next to me in my water bed.

"Hello?" I said, in a groggy tone.

"Hello, John," the whispering, urgent voice on the other line replied. "This is Bob Howard."

I sat up. I could have hung up right there. I knew exactly why he was calling. I took in a deep breath. "Yes, Bob, how can I help you?"

"Well," he said in that soft, condescending voice of his. "We won't be needing your services anymore. Thank you for everything you've done."

I took another deep breath. "Okay," I said, nonchalantly. "Thanks, Bob." I hung up the phone and rolled over to Neila.

"Who was that?" she asked, rubbing her eyes awake.

"That was Bob," I said. "I've just been fired."

I shut my eyes and went back to sleep. The rest of the day could wait.

16. Welcome to the Jungle

Guns 'n Roses, 1987

The Honorable James M. Langan was instrumental in helping me win the FCC license for WGTR. Under a former provision of Massachusetts law, he was allowed to serve simultaneously both as a judge and a lawyer in private practice.

I don't want to downplay what it was like to get canned. It sucked. Everything I had worked for and built up, all the sweat and hours I had poured into that station, had been obliterated by one ignorant asshole. But the ending was clear to me the moment Bob Howard had walked into the station and we had our first meeting. Still I could at least take solace in the fact that the more he changed things, the worse the station sounded. The ratings immediately plummeted into the abyss, and WMEX never again was a major station in Boston.

Which only helped me. I was a martyr. *Rolling Stone* published a feature article called "*Boston Tests New Music & Flunks Out,*" about my winning the battle with WRKO, and my ultimate firing. It was a huge lift. It was a hell of a lot better than any resume I could pull together. Bob Howard had fired me, but I had won. Job offers poured in. Stations in New York City, Chicago, and Detroit all wanted to hire me as their program director. But I didn't want to go anywhere. I was a Boston boy, loved my house in East Natick, my friends, and being close to the trees and woods of Vermont. The thought of being in New York City made me cringe. To me, living in New York City was like being in a prison with nothing but a bag of dirt, stress, and aggravation.

Besides, my push to get the WGTR license had continued forward. Even while I had been working to turn things around at WMEX, the battle with Natick Broadcast Associates raged on. In fact, it had become a full-fledged war. Back then, the FCC considered several specific factors when awarding a new station license among competing applicants. Was the ownership group local? How integrated was ownership in the actual management of the station? And what kind of community service did it provide? It also examined the background of the prospective owners. Did they have the character qualifications to be a licensee of the airwaves of the United States of America?

John Garabedian

Despite all the warnings from Judge Langan, I never imagined in my wildest dreams it would get personally ugly. But then I didn't know anything about Natick's lawyer and principal, Leon Fox, or as I soon began calling him, "Leon Pox." He knew what would get the FCC's attention and started digging. Eventually, he found the old search warrant that the Massachusetts State Police had executed at my East Natick house a few years before.

The fact that the police marked the search warrant with "nothing found" didn't stop Leon. He kept on digging and tracked down Jesse and Jamie, the two boys whose 3 a.m. questioning led to the police invading my home. Leon Fox met with them in person and got affidavits from them sworn under oath that stated that I'd been running around the room, drunk, rubbing their legs, and trying to entice them into the bedroom. I absolutely couldn't believe it when I read the documents.

"That's complete bullshit," I told Langan. "That absolutely never happened. It's completely made up."

Langan didn't doubt me. Besides, that wasn't my style. I didn't have to beg people to come to bed with me. But more than that, I was not public about my sexuality and certainly wouldn't have dared to be so reckless with my personal life that I'd jeopardize my radio career.

Langan went into damage control and hired a private detective to track down Jesse and Jamie. It took only a few days to find the boys, both of whom had become U.S. Marines. The detective located them at the Marine base at Parris Island, South Carolina. Then, Langan made his next move. "We're going to go see them," he said. "We'll get our own affidavits."

On the day before New Year's Eve of 1971, I flew down with attorney Pat Murphy, one of Langan's associates, and detective John Willis, a cigar-chomping old school type whom the judge turned to when he needed to find something out. He was like his fixer. Quiet but a real bulldog.

I was a bit apprehensive about seeing my two old "friends" in person. Frankly, I wasn't sure how they'd react to me and wasn't clear how mad I might be. Langan insisted that I be there because, as he said, "they'll have a hard time fabricating anything if you are in front of them." But he also pushed me to stay calm, no matter how things played out. He must have counseled Murphy on this because for most of the flight Murphy went over how the session should go. "Let me do the talking," he said. "I'm there to ask the questions. If I need you to chime in, I'll ask you. If I need something cleared up, I'll consult you. Otherwise, just keep quiet and be friendly. Keep your cool."

Willis had arranged the meeting and on a raw Tuesday afternoon, we trudged around the huge Parris Island Marine base and into an empty cafeteria, where Jesse and Jamie both sat. I barely recognized them. They were both in Marine uniforms, looking taller and fitter. Their lean teenage faces had given way to stronger, more chiseled looks. As the three of us walked across the room, the two men shot up from their seats. I was half expecting them to salute us. Both smiled when they saw me and at that moment any anger I might have had for them dissipated.

Murphy stuck out a hand when he got to the table, then threw down his briefcase in front of the boys and opened it up. "Thank you for making time for us," he said, pulling out the original affidavit to make clear there wasn't going to be any small talk or catching up. "Let's get started, shall we?" Willis grabbed a seat next to the lawyer and took out an unlit cigar and jammed it into his mouth.

Over the next hour Murphy pressed the two boys on what had happened at my place. About Joel's unexpected visit and the movie he showed. As they pored over the details of that evening, I caught occasional glimpses of Willis who seemed to chomp his cigar a little more furiously as Murphy delved deeper into the account. But from the moment Jesse and Jamie started talking about that night, relief came over me. Everything I remembered about what had happened matched exactly with what they recalled. Finally, against the wishes of Murphy, I spoke up.

"I'm glad you're saying all this now, but I don't get why you told the other lawyer something completely different," I said.

Both of the boys shook their heads. "We tried to tell him what happened, but he kept butting in," said Jesse. "Kept interpreting what we said, and then asking us different questions, like 'didn't this happen' and 'didn't he do something like this?'"

My father, 1971, in a Washington, D.C., hotel room during the FCC hearings while we were fighting for the 1060 frequency. Though he grew up in a different era and my lifestyle was foreign to him, he always gave me his full love and support through those stormy days.

Then Jamie interrupted his friend. "He also promised us that the least we'd get out of it was an all-expense paid trip to D.C. if we agreed to sign the affidavit."

It was all we needed to hear and we located a North Carolina notary public in Jacksonville to certify the new statements Murphy had written up, including the damaging affirmation that Leon Pox had fabricated and twisted the truth.

But the story was far from over. If I thought the government paperwork was endless, the hearings were mind-numbingly long. What had begun with me filing the original application in September, 1964, had brought us to late '69, consumed all of '70 and '71, and then moved into '72. Oral arguments before the FCC spanned a period of nearly three months. Then there were the pleadings and the exceptions to the pleadings. We were constantly flying back and forth between Boston and D.C.

Finally, in early '72, just a few months after I was fired at WMEX, Jesse and Jamie were subpoenaed. Leon Pox didn't look happy as the two young Marines strode into the examiner's room to testify. As soon as they opened their mouths, he knew he was in trouble. He started to squirm in his chair and you could see beads of sweat pouring down his face as they explained how they'd been coerced into making false statements. They still got their free trip to D.C., but Leon Pox's unethical craftiness came back to bite Natick Broadcast Associates where it hurt.

Those false affidavits essentially disqualified the group to be licensees of the Federal Communications Commission and paved the way for us to be awarded the license. In April of 1972, the FCC granted us the construction permit for WGTR. In trying to disgrace me, Natick's lawyer had made them ineligible. There was some noise about an appeal but, following Langan's advice, we offered to cover some of their legal fees if Natick's owners dropped the case. They did.

◀

During the summer of '72, as we geared up for the launch of WGTR, my little house in East Natick became central command. All day long, people I'd hired or consulted with streamed in and out of the home. Rooms became work-spaces. Counters and tables were turned into desks. The driveway was always packed with cars. It was not a sustainable situation.

With the help of my brother-in-law, Jack Carlson, we secured a $50,000 line of credit from Harvard Trust Company and then set out to find a permanent home for WGTR's offices and studios. I knew what I wanted—something which looked like a successful enterprise; roomy, classy, and in a high-visibility location in the community. It couldn't be in an industrial park, cold and soulless. No, it needed to be a place where if the advertisers, selectmen, the police chief, or the head of the gardening club came to do an interview, they would feel comfortable and be impressed.

I found the perfect spot in Natick Center one Sunday afternoon while driving down Route 135. It was a beautiful, century-old captain's mansion that had recently been listed for sale. Featuring three finished stories, all of the home's late nineteenth-century ornate details were still intact. My heart raced as soon as I took my first tour of the place and saw the magnificent interior entry. It was spacious and welcoming with extensive detailed wood paneling, arches, a huge stone fireplace in the grand entry, and a big sliding door that opened to a turret room.

As I poked through the building, I had the entire station visualized and laid out. First floor side rooms could become the sales and business offices while the four second floor bedrooms could be transformed into three studios and a newsroom. The third floor was completely finished and ready to be used as a separate living space. If I sold my little East Natick house to get the down payment and then temporarily moved into the third floor, I reasoned, I could make the deal work. Within a week I signed papers to buy the mansion for $45,000. A month later I had my East Natick house under agreement for $23,000, double what I'd paid for it five years before.

My first WGTR hire was Bob Lund, someone I'd known since my days as operations manager at WORC. Even though he was only twenty, Bob was a brilliant young broadcast engineer who was thirteen when I first met him, hanging out at the WORC transmitter in Auburn helping the chief engineer doing engineering maintenance. By the age of fifteen he had passed the complex eight-hour FCC exams and acquired his first-class commercial FCC license, something most people don't earn until they're out of college and in their twenties.

When Bob wasn't hanging out at 'ORC, he was hanging around with two friends, Jimmy Jenkins, and Mark Parenteau. The three of them built a small (and illegal) pirate radio station on the south side of Worcester. Bob eventually became one of my best friends and was one of the smartest people I've ever met. Nothing fazed him. Not even the workloads I sometimes had to throw at him. He took everything in stride and did it all superbly. Tragically, his life was cut short at the age of forty-three when he suddenly dropped dead of a heart attack, leaving behind his beautiful wife, Jill, and two young children, Andy, eight, and Stephanie, six.

Bob's first job at WGTR was to wire the whole building, three studios, a working newsroom, and the transmitter plant on Speen Street at the chicken farm. For most of that summer and fall he worked twelve-to-fifteen-hour days, snaking miles of wire through the plaster lath walls. It was the kind of detailed project Bob loved, and he was still going at it even as we debuted on air on November 12, 1972.

Bob wasn't the only great hire. From my old WMEX days I hired Wendy Furiga as music and traffic director and planted her in the front lobby. She was a bit abrasive and very sarcastic. I was constantly coaching her on how to improve her demeanor. *Instead of answering the phone saying "Whaddya want?" Try to say something like, "Hi, may I help you?"* She sort of got it, but Wendy naturally projected an air of confrontation and I took some joy in riling her up. Sometimes I'd drift through the lobby singing the Beach Boys song "Wendy." *Wendy, Wendy what went wrong?* "Cut that shit out!" she always screamed. "I hate that song!"

WGTR headquarters was in a 100-year-old captain's mansion on Route 135 in downtown Natick. The sketch was done by my talented sister, Jacqueline. Initially, I lived on the third floor.

Prior to launching WGTR, I'd been working as a programming consultant to the Knight Quality Station Group, which owned several stations throughout New England. At its Portsmouth, New Hampshire, station a young program director named Don Kelley was doing an outstanding job and really "got" what great radio was and should feel and sound like. WHEB had great ratings and sounded wonderful. Even better, he had grown up in Wellesley right next to Natick and knew the local area. Although I knew Norman Knight, the company president, would not be happy, I hired Don as WGTR program director and on-air talent.

Great local news coverage was a critical programming element we had to offer to bring value to a local listener in the MetroWest community. To build loyal listenership we had to be relevant and an indispensable part of our listeners' lives. That meant finding the right news director. Through either luck or accident I stumbled across that talent one hot July day in my car while listening to WCAP in Lowell, Massachusetts. When the station flipped to the news, I first thought they'd piped in a national network newscast. The newsman had this

John Garabedian

crisp, authoritative sound, polished and smooth. It immediately reminded me of Edward R. Murrow. "We've got to have that guy," I said to myself.

Jim McAllister was his name and after a couple of meetings, expensive dinners, and lots of beer, he agreed to become the WGTR news director. He was twenty-nine and an absolute news junkie. It consumed his life. During our initial interview he told me that his idea of a great newsman was someone who keeps the police scanner on even while he's having sex, and if he hears something important happening, jumps out of bed and goes to get the story. When Jim walked through the door for his first day of work, I smilingly handed him two scanners, one for the newsroom and one for his bedroom.

It turned out that Jim was even more committed to his work than he advertised. Because his apartment lease had a few months left on it, he lived in Nashua, New Hampshire, an hour away from Natick. But on Monday nights he slept on a foldout cot in the station kitchen so he could go to the weekly Natick and Framingham selectmen's meetings, which usually lasted until midnight. He was determined to have his fresh stories for the Tuesday morning newscasts. I'd come down at 7:30 a.m. from my third floor apartment, ready to start the day, and Jim would already be well into his work. The fact that initially we didn't have a budget to hire an afternoon newsperson didn't faze him. "I'll just stay here until we sign off," he said. No one had more commitment and dedication to excellence than Jim McAllister, although the rest of our staff was really not much different.

There were some familiar faces at the station, too. In an unexpected way the station also brought me closer to my family. Since I was eight years old, when my sister Doris was dating him, my brother-in-law, Jack Carlson, had been a mentor to me. While we chased the license and then built WGTR, he took me under his wing. Jack's family embodied the American dream—his father was a Swedish immigrant who'd come to America at age fourteen with just $50 in his pocket and built New England Erecting Company, a successful steel erection company. But Jack was determined not to just soak up his father's fortune. After he earned his degree from Harvard, instead of joining his father's company, Jack went out on his own and worked for another firm. When he eventually did join the family business, he staked out his own territory, launching Carlson Corporation, a

Christmas at the Carlsons with my big sister Doris and the incredible Jack Carlson.

new general construction firm that could feed steel jobs to his father's original company. Under Jack's leadership it eventually became the largest design-build construction firm in the world, with sales of over a half billion dollars annually.

As a manager and as a person, Jack was fair, kind, and always gracious to everyone. Jack's example made me realize those are the greatest qualities someone can have. I've always tried to be better at it, since I'm impatient and goal focused. It's fueled my success but it hasn't always made life easier for people who work for me. As a business partner, Jack helped me mellow my approach to management. Rather than micro-manage, I learned to let people make mistakes so they could have the freedom to grow and take ownership of their jobs. I learned all of that from Jack.

The Garabedian presence at WGTR also included my oldest sister Doris, Jack's wife, as public service director. However, the best family hire may have been my father. His first job was a temporary position. Prior to commencing regular broadcasting, the FCC construction permit required us to perform signal conductivity measurements of the new antenna system along radials twenty miles out. During these test transmissions the rules required us to announce the

John Garabedian

call letters and city of license every thirty minutes. Where could I find someone to sit in a transmitter shack in the middle of a chicken farm ten hours a day? As quickly as I could, I hustled my recently retired father into the FCC office in Boston one summer afternoon to take the test for his third-class operator's license. It didn't require engineering knowledge, just familiarity with general FCC rules. For two weeks that autumn we had him parked at the chicken farm. He'd sit there whistling, read the paper, look out the window. It was hilarious to be driving around town and hear his gravelly, untrained voice say, "WGT-ahhh, Natick." To keep him company my mother brought him lunch every day and would sit with him for an hour or so.

Once we were up and running, I actually ended up hiring my father full-time. I hadn't planned on bringing him aboard, but not long after his retirement, the furniture store chain he'd poured most of his working life into went bankrupt and he lost his pension. With weekly payroll, billing, invoicing, and accounting to do, I needed a business manager and I knew my retired father could more than handle the work. So I put him on the payroll. I arranged a barter advertising deal with Avis Rent-a-Car to provide him a free station car, gave him an office, a nice paycheck, and away he went. He worked for me until the age of eighty-five. Aside from Wendy, he was one of the first people you'd see when you walked into the station. And that was by design. I liked the idea that a stranger's first impression of the station was this distinguished-looking older man, and not some crew of crazy pot-smoking kids.

My father was an important asset to the station, but being there every day, working with me, and seeing how I worked, is the best thing that ever happened to our relationship. Until he came to WGTR we were never particularly close. I don't think my father ever really understood me. But seeing how much of myself I put into creating the station, how long my days were, the critical decisions I had to make under pressure, and ultimately the success I created, gave him an inspired view of who I really was. He would never say it, of course, but I know it made him proud. For the first time in my life we actually got along.

The other family member I hired was Kris Carlson, Jack and Doris's oldest son. Because just ten years separated us, Kris was less like a nephew to me and more like a friend. By his late teens, the two of us were regularly hanging out. He became part of the Vermont crew, getting high, engaging in deep philosophical discussions, and witnessing those gorgeous night skies. He looked up to me and because of my career became interested in radio. He had dropped out of Cornell University at the age of nineteen, and was now caught up in the launch of WGTR.

In early 1972, the major disasters that came with Kris Carlson were still a few years away. The more I talked about WGTR with him, the more he got excited about becoming a part of it. Kris was a born salesman and in high school had earned $50,000 one summer with his buddies in Weston running a lawn service. In order to prepare for doing ad sales at WGTR, Kris took an ad sales job at a small radio station in Beverly, Massachusetts. He was enthusiastic, bright, and very persuasive; the same qualities, I would later discover, that also make for great con men. By the fall of '72, Kris had hit the ground running, talking up the station with local businesses and signing advertising commitments.

◀

From the moment I conceived of WGTR, I knew it had to be a Top 40 station. As we got things started some of the obvious obstacles—the fact that we were only a thousand watts, or that we had to sign off at sunset—didn't bother me. After all, the rich MetroWest area of suburban Boston was where our revenue would be coming from. The biggest issue for us was that in addition to fending off a local competitor in Framingham's WKOX, we were also fighting for listeners going up against all the major Boston stations, like WRKO, WVBF, WHDH, WJIB, WROR, and WBZ with their long heritage, and high-priced air talent. But I've never been afraid to aim high and I had full faith we could dominate the local region.

Unfortunately our programming budget was a fraction of that of the Boston monsters. To compete, to sound big, to sound better, to attract the largest local audience we needed a different approach. At the time, programming automation was still new and primitive. Everything in radio programming was being done just as it had since the 1930s, with a live announcer sitting at a control board playing records. The earliest adopters of program automation had been "beautiful music" FM stations, where mechanical switch-controlled sequencers switched music tapes. Announcers could record their stop-down breaks between the pre-programmed music sweeps and commercials. But in 1972 equipment was quite primitive, with nothing more than a bunch of mechanical switches to determine the pattern in which the reel-to-reel tape machines were sequenced.

Still, the opportunities presented by the new technology stimulated me. Thinking about it, I realized that in a typical hour of Top 40 radio, commercials consume about ten minutes of air-time, and music another forty-eight. The rest of the hour is DJ talk. Yet for a four-hour radio show the DJ had to sit there for four hours just so they could talk for what amounted to eight minutes. It made me wonder why we needed to have live deejays actually sit at a control board for an entire show. Until that time, the only reason was to run the equipment; cuing up records, playing taped commercials, and pushing buttons. If that same deejay could sit down and just do the talk parts of each hour and let a machine do everything else, he or she could record an entire four-hour show in just ten or fifteen minutes.

It's what led me to invent the concept of "voice tracking." It was an untried idea but the upside, if it worked, was significant. Not only could I, as a well-known Boston DJ, be able to be on the air every day doing a four-hour show, but instead of hiring cheap, inexperienced, low-priced air talent, we could afford the best DJs to sound as good as or even better than the Boston stations. It enabled us to sound big, without a big budget. For a gear geek and business owner on a budget, it was the best of both worlds.

In April, 1972, Bob Lund and I headed down to New Orleans for the annual National Association of Broadcasters convention. There, in the massive exhibit hall, we scoured the room evaluating the latest automation systems, and we eventually came across a brand new product being introduced at the show by Shafer Electronics. It was called "System 903." It represented a significant breakthrough. Instead of using mechanical switches to sequence the tape equipment, it had a real computer. By today's standards it was teeny and limited, with just a 2,048-event memory. It had been designed specifically to replace the mechanical switch systems used by those early FM beautiful music stations. Executing that format was easy. The tape with the announcer would switch on after, for instance, three songs and say, "You're listening to such-and-such station." Then a few commercials, then back to three more songs. There was no "show biz" production, talkups over music, or dynamic personality. What got played in Omaha, Nebraska, was the exact same sterile thing that was played in Bangor, Maine.

What we needed, what we were pushing for, was a digital controller that allowed us to do real complex production with our voice-tracking concept, where the announcer came in over the song and actually introduced it so that it sounded live. After Bob and I spent considerable time discussing our flow designs with the Shafer engineer at the convention, he told us that with some rewiring of the memory board he could make the "903" do what we needed it to do, even though it would work totally backward from the way it had been designed.

The other issue was that in order to go that route we also needed expensive tape equipment to play those tunes, commercials, and voice tracks. We were still living in an analog world. Getting music to play from computers was still twenty years away.

By chance I saw an ad in *Broadcast* magazine in which ABC Radio was selling its old automation system for WABC-FM, "Love-FM," in New York City. The equipment list included three Ampex model 440 record-playbacks and seven Ampex 445 playback-only machines that used professional grade ten-and-a-half-inch reels of tape. The price was only ten grand. Each machine was worth more than $3,000 alone. The price even included the seven-foot tall racks that held them.

On a late summer day, I rented a U-Haul truck and hired Kris Carlson to come along to drive to New York City early the next morning to pick up the machines. After sorting out the paperwork at ABC headquarters in Midtown Manhattan with Sidney Small, the ABC business manager, we headed to the WABC transmitter plant in Lodi, New Jersey, to get the equipment. For a radio guy like me, it was like going to Oz. Inside the big building was WABC's massive 50,000-watt GE transmitter which covered the entire nation on their clear-channel 770 frequency. They also showed us the legendary EMT 140 plate reverb unit, a ten-foot long device that gave the station its dynamic concert-hall sound. After all those years of listening to it from Boston, North Carolina, and Miami and marveling at the big WABC sound, it was such a trip to be looking at the machinery that created much of the soundtrack to inspire my evolving radio career.

🔊

"OK, everybody, get ready," I shouted. It was just pushing noon and every member of the WGTR staff was upstairs, crowded in Studio "B," waiting for the big event. It was November 12, 1972, and we were minutes from going on-air for the first time. This was like the opening of a Broadway show, and the excitement was palpable. Even my heart was racing as I stared at the clock and nervously played with the volume sliders on the big control board in front of me. I sat in the middle of a big horseshoe-shaped table, with a turntable on either side of me. Right in front was a big clock counting down the seconds. The whole

Studio "C" at WGTR recording tracks for my show. "Voice-tracking" is universally used in radio today, but we actually invented the concept and designed the equipment to run it in 1972. Programmers from all over the country flew in to see how it was done; they didn't believe it was possible.

thing felt like a dream. And yet it felt natural, too. Everything in my life had pointed to this event. All the learning, all the frustrations and disappointments, triumphs and successes.

For a moment I allowed myself to soak in the present. Worrying about whether the station would succeed and whether we'd lose money—all of that was in the back of my brain. It could resurface later. For now, I was just gearing up to launch my own radio station and fulfill a goal I'd had since I was a kid.

I looked around the room. My mother and both my sisters were there. Even my father had a little smile on his face. It hadn't just been a long eight years; it had been a wild few months. It seemed like I'd only gotten a few hours of sleep over the last several days as we endured a ragged, frenetic pace to the finish line. There had been the issue with the program lines from the transmitter to the studio, which had unexpectedly gone dead a few days before, as well as glitches with getting the new, custom-wired computer automation system operational that forced us to debut with completely live talent during the station's first few days.

Still we were ready. I glanced over at Bob Lund, who managed to take a break from his continuing wiring marathon to enjoy WGTR's birth. He looked more exhausted than I felt. "You think anyone is going to be listening?" he asked.

Bob shrugged his shoulders. Not even sheer exhaustion could sap him of his cool, dry demeanor. "We'll find out," he said.

With that, I signaled for everyone else to quiet down, flipped on my mike, and had everyone in the room shout out a giant "Hellloooo" over the intro bed of "My Sweet Lord" by George Harrison, the number one song in the country at the time. WGTR was officially launched, and I finally had the freedom to do exactly what I wanted on radio.

Even with uncertainty that hung in the air, there was a confident sense that the days of glory were coming on strong. 🔇

17. Sunshine on My Shoulder

John Denver, 1974

This looks posed because I'm all dressed up, but it was following a meeting at the bank and actually the first time we fired up the WGTR transmitter (a Gates/Harris BC-1H). Engineer Bob Lund had brought a camera to record the moment.

Out of the gate, WGTR was a winner. Kris Carlson did a superb job building excitement and signing new advertisers for the station, and we soon added a second sales rep, Craig Howard, who had just returned from Vietnam serving as a Green Beret medic. Kris and Craig were both outstanding achievers during those early days. From the moment we started, the two pounded the pavement hard, putting the station on the radar of every business in town. By January of '73, less than three months after we first went on the air, we were in the black. The excitement that had infused the station in the run-up to its launch grew in our MetroWest area of Boston as we found our footing and started making real money. The station was double-digit profitable starting in our third month.

Everything I'd learned about radio from Bob Bryar and Mac Richmond, both what *to* do and what *not* to do, as well as the stuff I'd gleaned from the more challenging experiences I'd had at places like 'PTR and other stations, drove what we did at WGTR. It was alive, with energy and color. We weren't held back by convention. If someone had a good idea, we ran with it. And if it didn't work out, we went in a different direction. We were nimble, unafraid to make mistakes or be daring.

And we did a decent job of doing both. As it had at WORC, audience participation and interactivity drove what we did. One major programming feature we developed was something we called the "*On* Li*ne*," an hourly feature which gave listeners a dedicated phone number they could call and record a short message, comment, or spout off about anything on their mind. Each hour we'd play one of those short comments. It was like a big community message board, with people griping about news events, celebrities, local issues, or the TV shows they hated. *I hate it when these idiots who don't know how to drive in the snow get out on the road and make it hell for the rest of us.* Those kinds of things. We also

John Garabedian

Sales manager Kris Carlson in a publicity shot outside the WGTR newsroom in 1973. He fell in love with one of our salesmen, Tina Becker, a stunning twenty-three-year-old woman who worked under him. They quit and moved to La Jolla, California, to start a new life. When his new business failed and their relationship ended they returned East.

debuted the Friday nude beach report in the summer, a lost dog update feature, and, of course, the listener request lines.

In spring of 1973, we did the first-ever live radio broadcast of the Boston Marathon, although it kind of fell in our lap. Since the Marathon route ran right in front of the station, it was easy to just lean out the open studio window with a microphone and yell down to news director Jim McAllister, who was on the sidewalk doing live interviews. That year there were only eight hundred runners. It was just prior to the explosion of the sport of running. Compare that to recent Boston Marathons, with nearly forty thousand runners.

Within two years, as the running boom exploded, we attacked the race from the ground and the sky. WGTR staff was staked out every five miles. Mobile phones hadn't been invented yet, so news director Jim McAllister, wearing a headset microphone, was put on a bike equipped with a remote transmitter. His assignment was to follow the pace car. Jim had assured us he'd trained for the thing, but every time we cut over to him it sounded like he was on his last breath, huffing and panting as though he was more worn out than the runners.

Up above, Rick O'Kane, a young commercial pilot we'd hired to do traffic reports, was following the lead runners in the station airplane. Often times, though, he couldn't see a thing. He'd try and fudge it a little, say something about where the pack was, but deciphering any real detail among the thousands gathered along the route was almost impossible. Even the reporters at the selected stakeout points had trouble seeing anything through the throngs of well-wishers.

It was all made more comical by the fact that unless you had a friend running, no one really knew the actual names of the runners. It was like a *Saturday Night Live* skit.

In our second year of broadcasting we created a huge contest promotion called the "Record-Breaking Fun Summer of '74." For a whole week we broadcast live from Natick Mall, inviting people to come down to try and break a Guinness World Record to get in its record book. Lis-

That's me leaning out of the studio window broadcasting the 1973 Boston Marathon as runners ran down Route 135 in Natick in front of WGTR. That year there were only 1,573 runners, compared with over 30,000 in 2015.

teners entered and tried to set the mark for the stupidest things. Throwing a street sign. A forty-yard dash with a baby stroller. A cantaloupe hurl. Sitting on a football. Longest Frisbee throw. One woman we came to call Sue the Washboard Lady unsuccessfully tried to set the record for the longest time playing the washboard. It was dumb but entertaining, and the crowds were there every day.

Perhaps our silliest contest came in 1975, right before Thanksgiving, when we did a big turkey giveaway. We partnered with Owens Poultry Farm in Needham and invited listeners to call up and record their best turkey call. We recorded them for a week, and then sent Don Kelley out to the turkey farm with a tape recorder to play back the human gobbles. In one hand he held the player, in his other another tape machine to record the reaction of the birds. Whoever did the impression that elicited the best response won a free turkey. It seemed like a brilliant idea but on the afternoon Don arrived at the farm it immediately began to pour. Don stuck it out there for a good hour, trying to get just one turkey to offer up a response, but the turkeys wanted nothing to do with him. The only thing Don managed to get was a cold.

Like it had been at WORC, sometimes the most entertaining people associated with our station were our listeners. During those first few years we were on the air, we developed a dedicated following who made WGTR a part of their

John Garabedian

Finding jewels that will excite listeners from among the hundreds of songs released each month is a thrill. "You Light Up My Life" by Debbie Boone (shown) was number one for a record-setting ten weeks, directly resulting from WGTR airplay. Its popularity spread to Boston stations and then nationally.

daily lives. One of the most amusing was a crazy woman we nicknamed the Goulash Lady. She was a short, chubby, middle-aged lady who always dressed in black. She appeared without fail whenever we did a remote broadcast. She didn't interact with us; she just stood there and stared, arms crossed, like she was getting ready to make a hit on someone. She was also fond of our "*On Line*" feature. She'd call up and in her thick Hungarian accent she'd go to town, angrily complaining about something. Nobody could ever understand a word of what she was saying, but it sounded funny as hell. Don Kelley would then edit it down to something short that made no sense and we'd put it on the air. People thought it was a character we played and didn't believe us when we insisted she was a real person.

Adding to the station's atmosphere was the music. The hit songs from that period were great. The same interactive research principles I'd learned at WORC and brought to WMEX, I hammered home at WGTR. Requests, not record sales or national charts, drove what we played. Even so, new music wasn't something we shied away from. In 1974, we broke the disco single, "Rock the Boat" by the Hues Corporation. Half our listeners had never even heard of disco at that point, but they loved the song and it eventually became the number one song in the country. There were other national hits, too, including "Dance With Me" by Orleans, and the disco crossover, "Love to Love You Baby" by Donna Summer.

Don Kelley, WGTR program director, went on to greatness, later inventing the "Mix" format while at WYYY in Baltimore, then took Greater Media's "Magic 106.7" from the bottom to the top of the Boston ratings and kept it there for twenty years.

When we could get them, we had celebrities and recording artists come into the studio to plug their record or a show. In 1975, Frankie Valli stopped in at the studios for an afternoon interview to promote a Four Seasons concert at a nightclub in Framingham. Valli and the group were on the comeback trail. Their new single, "Who Loves You," had become the band's first hit in five years. Don Kelley did the interview and after a little back-and-forth opened up the phone lines. "The next ten people who can get through at 655-1060 win tickets to the show and dinner," Kelley said.

For the next ten minutes the phones lines remained lit. Then, without warning, everything went dead. Not a single call. Valli played it cool, but you could tell Don was getting uncomfortable. He strung together some questions, played more songs, and managed to get through the thing unscathed. It was only later we found out that we had received so many calls that we had blown out the entire phone exchange. The incident even made it onto the front page of the *Middlesex News* the next day. Every number in the area had gone dead because an army of listeners had been trying to call.

Even with ad sales we tried to break convention. For decades, the sixty-second commercial was the gold standard. If the client ever asked about buying a thirty-second spot, stations typically charged them eighty percent of the minute rate, even if it was only half the air time. It just didn't make any sense to

"Leo", the amazing WGTR automation system, with newswoman Roseanne Pawelic. The round Sono-Mag "Carousels" held commercials and current hits and were digitally addressable from the Shafer 903, a major breakthrough. Audio and transmitter controls are shown in the right rack.

me. My concern was minimizing the reasons people would tune out our station, and by running thirty-second commercials we could slash the length of ad breaks. Usually listeners only paid attention for the first thirty seconds of a minute spot anyway. Television used mostly thirty-second ads, I thought, why couldn't radio? So I knocked the discount to sixty percent of the full minute price, then I told our sales team to push thirty-second spots and explain to the advertiser that for a given budget they would get nearly double the exposure and impressions for the same money. It was a win-win. Local businesses could reach more people more times for the same money, and we could reduce the duration of commercial breaks while actually earning twenty percent more per commercial minute. Less commercial time meant less tuning out, longer time-spent-listening, and bigger audiences.

All of this—the entertaining contests, the music, the top-shelf personalities, slick on-air production, the way the station sounded and felt—made WGTR an immediate success. By year four, we had become the most listened to radio station in the MetroWest region across all demographics, beating all of the Boston stations and local competitors WKOX and WVBF-FM in Framingham. It felt great. All the struggling and hard work had paid off.

And I was getting bored.

My passion, vocation and avocation, is creating new projects and building things. The whole process is exhilarating. I loved those early, lean, uncertain years when we were just getting WGTR off the ground. Back then, every day it seemed, we were adding something new, doing something different. It's like building a house. There's the planning, design, and then the construction. You move in and it's done. Maybe you hang up a few paintings and decorate the place, but the heavy lifting, the really exciting work, is over. Now you just have a house. What fun is that?

I was getting anxious and looking to build something again. What that meant and where it would lead, I had no idea. 🔇

18. Seasons in the Sun

Terry Jacks, 1974

Tommy Nicoletti.

My friend Doug Sears needed a favor. Doug was a Harvard Divinity School student who had become part of my circle in the early seventies. He was intelligent, good looking, and adventurous with a heart of gold, always looking for ways to help people. He'd volunteer at homeless shelters, counsel abused kids, and lent a hand to people with drug issues. Doug had a genuine commitment to being able to make the world a better place.

It was an early September afternoon in '74 when he reached me at the station. "John, I need your help on something," he said, after a few pleasantries. "There's a kid here in Cambridge who's been kicked out of his home and needs a place to stay. Nice kid. Fourteen. But his home life in the housing projects has come undone and he has nowhere to go. If he stays in Cambridge, he's bound to get in with the wrong crowd."

I let out a laugh. "And so you thought the Hotel Garabedian might have a vacancy?" I said.

"He just needs a stable place to call home for a while," Doug said. "He's a hard worker and I know he'd be happy to help you out around the house."

I did have the room. After a year of living in the station attic, I'd started house-hunting and eventually ended up with a beautiful four-bedroom contemporary with a private beach on Lake Fort Meadow in Marlborough. Doug had been there several times. He knew I had the space. And he knew me, too. He knew I wouldn't immediately say no.

"I'm not sure, Doug," I said. "I'd really want to meet him first. Then I'll think about it. Okay?"

"Great!" he said. "I'll be there in a half-hour." Then he hung up. I was stunned.

Doug meant what he said. About a half hour later Doug strode through the WGTR doors with a tall, blond-haired, blue-eyed kid, dressed in jeans, a white-T,

A Vermont weekend in my half-built cabin with the lovely plywood walls. Jim McAllister (front), his future wife Kay, and my foster son Jimmy Townsend (back). Jimmy called two years ago to announce that his oldest daughter had a baby "…and John, you know what that makes you?"

and a big smile. "John," Doug said stepping aside, a little, "I'd like you to meet Jimmy."

Jimmy stuck out his right hand. "Nice to meet you," he said.

Over the next twenty minutes Jimmy told me a little about his life. He hadn't been dealt an easy hand. His father had left the family when he was young, leaving Jimmy's mother to raise six kids in a housing project in East Cambridge. She eventually found a new man for her life, but that only made her grow distant from her kids and soon Jimmy and his siblings were forced to fend for themselves. Jimmy and his new step-father didn't get along and eventually he was thrown out on the streets of Cambridge. It killed me to think that a nice kid like him had already been through so much. Doug could see how I felt and when Jimmy left to go the bathroom, he ramped up his lobbying.

"He's got every reason to have a chip on his shoulder, John," he said. "Life hasn't given Jimmy any breaks. But you won't find a nicer kid. He just needs a place to live that isn't crazy, a home that isn't in turmoil. You won't regret it. Honestly, try it for a week."

Doug had me and he knew it. When Jimmy returned, I leaned back in my chair and shot the kid a smile. "What do you think about living in Marlborough?" I asked him.

Jimmy ended up being an anomaly in my life. After watching my two older sisters bring up six kids, I never felt the pang to have children or a family. In fact, I never really enjoyed being with kids. They are like annoying little wild animals and I lack the patience to be around them.

With Jimmy, though, I didn't have to play the role of the strict dad, and maybe because he'd been through so much in his short life, he didn't create difficulties, or overstep boundaries. I gave him a bedroom, made sure he got to school, that there was food in the house, and that he had a little pocket money. He was amazing, completely self-reliant, outspoken yet courteous, polite, warm, and appreciative. He mowed the lawn when I asked him, kept things clean, went to school every day, and rolled with whatever social scene might develop at the house. It really helped that Jimmy's older brother Chucky was gay, so I didn't

My foster son Jimmy Townsend with his first-born daughter. That little girl is now married and a mother, making Jimmy a grandfather.

have to explain my lifestyle to him. He just didn't care. After coming under so much fire from living in the housing projects in Cambridge, he was street-smart and had learned to be accepting, of allowing people into his life who weren't like him. And yet he could handle any kind of personality and was no pushover. We soon grew close and eventually the Commonwealth of Massachusetts named me his foster father.

Jimmy ended up living with me for over two years. But at the age of seventeen, he wanted to reconnect with his biological father, who had moved to Iowa when Jimmy was a young child. During one summer vacation, Jimmy went to visit him on his farm. They hit it off and Jimmy decided he wanted to be closer to his dad and moved in with him. But not before meeting Tammy, a really sweet girl from Cambridge whom he ended up marrying. He's still there, they're still happily married, and we continue to stay in touch. Last August Jimmy called to tell me his oldest daughter just had a baby. "That makes me a grandfather," he beamed. Then he paused and let out a laugh. "And you know what that makes you, John?"

"Don't say it," I said, returning his laugh.

Over the years, Jimmy has told me numerous times how much he appreciates what he learned from me and the impact I had on him in becoming the person he is. It is a wonderful reward for sharing two years of my life and giving him the peace, security, and stability he needed.

🔊

Preston Claridge was the headmaster at Fessenden Academy, an exclusive all-male private school in suburban Boston. One July afternoon, Preston called me up and in his elegant Harvard accent asked what my plans were for the weekend. "I've got a trip planned to Provincetown this weekend," he said. "My friend Stan Sorrentino owns the Crown and Anchor Hotel and is looking for advice on some real estate. He's always a lot of fun. Would you like to join me?"

That Saturday morning I headed to Natick with Jimmy to meet Preston at the WGTR studios. As Preston's green Chevy Nova came down West Central Street and pulled up in front of the WGTR building, I noticed Preston wasn't driving—instead I saw this gorgeous kid, I thought probably nineteen or twenty, in the driver's seat. He clutched the wheel with his right hand, letting his arm hang down the outside of the door.

They pulled into the driveway, and when the kid driving stepped out of the car I gulped. He was over six feet tall, with wide shoulders, narrow hips, blond hair, big lips and a muscular frame. "John, say hello to Tommy Nicoletti," Preston said as we stood next to the car. This kid was simply too good-looking. I didn't know if he was straight or gay, but I figured he was probably used to people gawking at him and empowered by it, so I decided if I wanted to attract him to me I'd play it cool and completely ignore him. "How ya doin'," I said, trying to sound indifferent to his presence. Then I pointed to my van parked in the driveway. "Let's hit the road."

The 135-mile drive out to Provincetown at the tip of Cape Cod was over three hours. A spring heat wave had hit New England, and everyone with wheels seemed to be making a break for the Cape. Approaching the Sagamore Bridge, Route 3 turned into a parking lot. The drive also felt a bit tense because even though I was dying to get to know Tommy, I was doing my best to ignore him. Except for occasional glances, I didn't even so much as look his way. If he asked me a question, I gave a one-word answer or just let Preston handle the talking.

For a hot young stud who was used to being the center of attention, I could see it drove him crazy. My technique was working.

Tommy had a cool edge to him that reflected his upbringing. Adopted as an infant, he'd grown up on the south coast of Massachusetts in Somerset. His stepfather was principal of Durfee High School in Fall River, the largest high school in Massachusetts. The old man was strict and didn't

Provincetown, Massachusetts.

give any allowances for deviating from his rules, which were many. Tommy, though, had a severe distaste for authority that came matched with a somewhat violent streak. After a series of school fights and run-ins at home with his father, his parents gave up on him and booted him from the house when he was fourteen. He then landed at a Massachusetts Department of Youth Services reform school on Georges Island in Boston Harbor, a place for delinquent youth. It wasn't long, though, before Tommy took to the streets, hustling his way through Boston for survival, which is how he met Preston.

Tommy had never been to Provincetown, but old Preston certainly had. It was one of his favorite spots. By the mid twentieth century, P-Town had already undergone its transformation from a quaint art colony and quiet fishing village to an outrageous and popular gay and lesbian summer destination.

It could be a crazy place and was on its way to getting even crazier. In 1977, town selectman Paul Christo was arrested and charged with committing an "unnatural sex act" at the Atlantic House bar. Christo's crime was using a belt to beat a man tied head-and-foot while another guy gave him a blowjob on top of a pool table. All of this happened front-and-center to a crowd of cheering, drunken onlookers. Christo's little foray made front-page news, but it was no big deal to local voters. Not long after, he was re-elected to a second term as chair of both the board of selectmen and the finance committee.

John Garabedian

The A-House wasn't the only club where you could find a "guys-gone-wild" scene. A few doors down, the much larger Crown & Anchor Hotel had developed its own wild reputation. The elegant hotel complex was owned by Preston's buddy, Staniford Sorrentino, a larger-than-life character who had a rotund frame and packed a love of food that was only matched by his love for the drag queen scene. All kinds of them paraded into Sorrentino's nightclub—a Kentucky horse breeder, a Rhode Island sheriff, a seventy-something cross-dresser who had an impressive collection of high heels.

Once a year, Sorrentino brought the whole drag queen scene to a head with his annual drag contest. From all over the country, contestants flew in to try and capture that little crown. But once the winner was announced, the prancing, drunk bitches turned into real brutes and sometimes began fist-fighting over the results. Fists, wigs, and dresses occasionally flew around the club and into the parking lot. Overlooking it all would be Sorrentino, laughing out loud and shouting out, "Oh, this is too much!" He loved every second of it.

Notorious Boston crime boss Whitey Bulger was allegedly a friend of Sorrentino and liked to frequent the Crown. That shocked nobody because Sorrentino didn't exactly lead the straight-laced life himself. Eventually, he was arrested and convicted by the IRS on tax evasion charges of skimming big money from the business and not declaring the income.

Yet Sorrentino, a former opera singer, was intelligent and gracious and knew how to play the role of a great host. He took us to dinner and invited us to come back later to his big "Paramount" nightclub on the beach for rounds of free drinks.

At the club I hung with Preston, Jimmy, and Stan, all the while I kept ignoring Tommy as I nursed my rum and Coke. Tommy sucked down several gin and tonics and constantly had a Marlboro cigarette lit as he wandered around the club and the pool. As it was getting late, suddenly, without warning, he came over to me wearing a big sombrero he'd found somewhere. He put it on my head and said "Come on," grabbing my right arm. "Let's dance."

"I don't dance," I said, turning to him directly for the first time all day.

"So," he said. "You can't start now?" He grabbed my hand and pulled me reluctantly out on the floor.

Tommy was completely masculine; a guy's guy who packed a tough, rugged appearance that gave way to a warm, charming side if he liked you. It was a side that began to reveal itself slowly on the dance floor. The rest of the night, Tommy stuck by my side. In-between sips of his drink he asked me questions about music and radio, trying his best to get some small talk going. I had softened, too, and I began to actually engage him in conversation. At midnight, after the bars had closed, one of Sorrentino's friends, a guy named Peter Ryder, who owned the famed Boatslip Beach Club farther down Commercial Street, invited us to go back to his place for drinks. I think he would have been happy if only Tommy had accepted the invitation. As soon as Peter joined us I could clearly see he liked Tommy. His eyes grew wide as soon as he saw him, and every time he said something Peter directed his gaze at him. But Tommy wanted nothing to do with Peter or seeing his apartment. "Just some tired old queen," he muttered to me. As Peter led us through his place, Tommy "accidentally" kicked over a filled trash basket, looked at me, and smiled. I really loved his independent attitude.

The next afternoon our groggy crew piled into my van for the long drive back to Natick. About halfway through, Tommy, who'd been asleep in the rear, woke up and moved up to sit on the floor next to me, between the two front seats of the van. We talked non-stop the rest of the way. It felt so easy and natural, as though we were two old friends. He peppered me with questions about the radio, my life, the music I liked, and the musicians I'd met. If we could have kept driving and talking for the next two days, I would have. I wanted his number but was too uptight to ask for it and unsure how to play it with Preston. Were they together or did he just hire him for the night? And yet I felt something electric with Tommy that I hadn't had with anyone since those early days with Joe. I could have been misreading it, but he really seemed to be attracted to me, too.

I was still thinking about him the next night when I came home from work. No one was home and I was tired from work. I made a Black Russian and took a seat at the kitchen counter when then phone rang. It was Doug Sears.

"John, I have some terrible news," he said. "Remember that boy who was with Preston when you went to Provincetown?"

"Yeah," I said, "Tommy," feeling suddenly alarmed.

"He was involved in a terrible car crash this morning in Provincetown," Doug said. "He was with his fifteen-year-old boyfriend Michael Flanagan, and one of them was killed, the other critically injured. I'm not sure which."

My heart sank. "Oh, Jesus," I said. "What happened? What the hell were they doing in Provincetown? We just came back from there yesterday."

Doug was short on the details. "Apparently Stan Sorrentino flew them down from Boston last night," he said. "I don't know much else about it," he said. "The police haven't released any names, so we're not even sure which of the boys is dead."

I thanked Doug and hung up. I sat there in silence for several long minutes before reaching for the phone again. I needed to call Cape Cod Hospital and find out if Tommy was the one who lived...

"I'm calling to find out the condition of Thomas Nicoletti," I asked.

"Who's this calling," they responded.

"Er, I'm his uncle," I said.

"Hold on," the voice on the other line said. For what felt like an eternity I waited for the woman on the other line. Come on, I kept muttering, just get me a damn answer. Finally she picked up the line. "His condition has just been lowered from critical to serious," she said, "but he will require specialized surgery and is being moved to St. Luke's Hospital in New Bedford."

A few days later the full details began to emerge, and to no one's great surprise, Sorrentino was at the center of it. It turned out that Tommy had left quite an impression on him, too. The day we returned to Natick, Stan had contacted Tommy through Preston and hired him to come back for a paid "visit." He flew both Tommy and Michael to Provincetown from Boston, under fake names, and then had them out all night, feeding them drinks. After, they all went back to his house for what Stan really wanted them for. Up all night with no sleep and fucked up on pills and alcohol, Tommy ran out of cigarettes.

While Stan headed out early to do some business, nicotine-starved, determined Tommy, who only had his learner's permit, found the keys to Stan's big new Mercedes 450. He and Michael hopped in and took off in search of some Marlboros. With true Tommy determination, he sped down 6A, hitting what the police estimate was ninety miles per hour before coming up on a sharp curve and wrapping the Benz around a utility pole. The accident killed Michael instantly and knocked power out to P-town for the next several hours.

The following Sunday, I headed down to St. Luke's Hospital in New Bedford to visit him. He didn't look nearly as bad as I feared. Although he'd lost some weight, the scars were minimal. The biggest issue he faced was the loss of movement in his lower right leg.

Tommy eventually was able to walk, but due to irreversible nerve damage, he always had a slight limp. Six weeks later, when Tommy was finally released, his parents still wanted nothing to do with him. So Preston arranged to rent him a room at Doug Sears' apartment in Cambridge. Tommy hated it there. According to Tommy, Preston was lurking around the apartment nightly looking for favors. After a few days of that, Tommy called me up.

"When are you going to come over and take me out for a ride?" he said.

It had been a few weeks since I'd last seen him and while it was great to see Tommy move around, he was a shell of his original self. He was down a good thirty pounds and just had a lost look on his face, like he was still trying to make sense of what had happened. Over dinner, Tommy's tough guy demeanor melted and he completely opened up. He told me about the struggles he had with his family and with school; how those he was close to had always disappointed him. As he talked, I saw a lot of myself in him. The frustrations Tommy had in finding the real value in life were the same for me. Authenticity was important to both of us. He was an old soul. But it was only at the end of the night he told me his age. "I'm sixteen," he said with a grin. I was shocked!

As I started to drive Tommy back to Cambridge he shook his head. "I can't go back there," he said. "Preston is there all the time and while he's harmless, he's a pain in the ass. I don't want anything to do with him." He then looked over at me, "Can I stay with you?"

I swallowed hard, torn between really wanting to be close to him but afraid of what I might be getting myself into.

◀

John Garabedian

Tommy Nicoletti at eighteen. After a crippling car crash, he died following a stroke at age fifty-three.

Our relationship became everything I could have hoped for, and Tommy and I were together for two years. We just clicked. He was smart and always fun. We both were sarcastic and didn't accept the bullshit that people and life dished out. Tommy liked to question everything and could quickly do an accurate read on anyone he met. We went to Vermont on the weekends, and when I closed on purchasing the land from Angus in 1976, he was right there by my side, swinging an axe or a hammer to help me. To help him feel like he had a future and to put some money in his pocket, I gave him a job at WGTR as the station's music director.

He had an obvious ear for a hit, but the station was also due for a change in that position. After years of putting up with Wendy Furiga's growing bitchiness, I'd had enough. She'd gotten arrogant to everyone and kept forgetting I was the boss. After I let her go, she went on to become music director of WBZ and eventually WHDH in Boston, but lost both jobs due to her continued arrogance and negative attitude.

I realized what it looked like. Could my sixteen-year-old boyfriend do the job or fit in? But people really liked Tommy. He was self-confident, a straight-shooter, loved the radio station, had a cutting sense of humor, and didn't waste time with any kind of office politics. And he respected the fact that when we were at the station, he worked under Don Kelley, the program director, to avoid a "boss-worker" relationship between us.

But in bringing our worlds so closely together, we ran into problems. By the time he turned eighteen, Tommy began to resent what he perceived as his dependency on me. He lived in my house. He needed me to taxi him around. I did my best at work to not come across as an authority figure, or the older guy who knew it all, but I later imagined that must have been how he started to see me, feel a loss of control, and fear the loss of his independence. For exercise and to get around, he bought a really nice mountain bike. Sometimes after work we would get home and he'd grab his bike and go out for a ride. Tommy needed the space and those rides became the only way he found it.

And then I screwed up.

One hot August night Tommy decided to take a spin around town. My friend Matt Marsello and I hadn't seen each other for a while and had made plans to go out for dinner. When we came back, Tommy still hadn't returned. Matt and I smoked a bowl or two and then the next thing you know we got intimate. There was nothing I wanted less than for Tommy to come home and see me with somebody else.

He didn't. Or at least I don't think he did. When I woke up the next morning, Tommy wasn't there. Not the next day, either. Or even the next week. He never stepped foot in the house again. It was weeks before I managed to find him. He'd moved in with a buddy in Boston, and when I did finally catch up to him there was a chill in the conversation and our talk just remained on the surface. *How are things? What are you up to?* To this day, I don't know if he walked in on Matt and me or he just decided he needed to start the next chapter in his life.

Whatever his reasons, Tommy's sudden departure from my life left me hurting like hell. The change had been instant. Tommy was there 24/7 and then he

John Garabedian

wasn't. It felt strange. Like the ground underneath me had shifted and I needed to adjust to the new footing.

Going to work didn't help, either. The station only reminded me that he was out of my life. I tried my best to hide the hurt I was going through, but anyone who paid even a little bit of attention could see I wasn't myself. Even my father. About a week after Tommy had left, he and I were in his office going over some

Dinner in Boston in the mid-seventies. Clockwise, Max-anne Sartori, Billy Squier (before he was famous), Mark Parenteau, myself, and Tommy Nicoletti.

bills. He looked up and in a kind voice said, "You look kind of down. Is it because you lost your friend?"

I paused for a second, and then back at him. "Yeah," I said sadly.

My father wasn't a dummy. Although we had never gone near the subject, he knew what was going on. He took a deep breath. "Well," he said. "If you want some advice from me, next time, find someone without any *problems*."

With that, he returned to the business of looking at the papers in front of him. I never forgot that advice. It became a prerequisite for any business or personal relationship in my life. I hate drama; I hate problems, and since then I avoid or distance myself from people who bring either into my life. 🔇

19. Take It to the Limit

Eagles, 1976

My father at his desk in the rotunda at WGTR. Behind him, the paneled lobby and Wendy Furiga's desk.

I've always lived with a certain built-in urgency to not sit still. I'm not happy unless I'm moving or building something. "Johnny and his projects," my mother used to say when I was a kid. Contentment is a tricky thing. There's a peace that can be found in it, a living-in-the-now aspect that can bring about a level of happiness. But it can also dull the senses and forge a forgetfulness of what it feels like to push forward to create things, to find new goals and go after them. I had seen how my father's aversion to risk had withered his ambitions and faded whatever dreams he may have had as a kid. Perhaps he inherited his Scottish mother's stoic personality. But he pushed on in a job he never loved, living through the Great Depression in a life that at times may have not felt like his own. Like many people, he spent his life in a job that only earned him a paycheck and not the fulfillment of a dream. He worked for people he found incompetent and unappreciative. Although he was a well-respected and successful executive in the home furnishings industry, financial security was the thing that drove him, providing for his family. Maybe my mother saw that, too. Perhaps that's why she pushed her children to go after what they wanted.

He was a good guy, but I didn't want to be like him. When I was young and thought about where I wanted to take my life, I never dreamed of doing just one thing, making it a success, and then riding it out until I was ready for retirement. I saw a buffet of interests which fascinated me, multiple mountains to scale.

That's one of the reasons why, as WGTR's success continued, I began to think about what was next, for the station and for me. I had grown up with Boston radio. Stations like the old WMEX, WHDH, and WBZ had been my first introduction to the medium's power. Millions of people listened to those stations and were entertained and influenced by them. As a kid I'd dream about working at one of them.

The Massachusetts Broadcasters Association made annual lobbying trips to D.C. to visit with our congressional delegation. As a director, I was part of our delegation. Senator Ted Kennedy (shown) was one of the most charming people I have ever met.

By 1976, WGTR had delivered everything I had hoped for. We were making money and the business was worth a couple of million dollars and employing a full-time staff of fourteen people. We had paid off our loans. I was able to draw a decent salary and pay my dad even more. The station sounded excellent and we dominated radio listening in our local market. But we were limited by our thousand-watt, daytime-only coverage that relegated our signal only to Boston's western suburbs, and we had to go off the air at sunset. I wanted to do more and widen its signal to make it a major Boston station.

It wasn't a small idea, and absolutely no one thought it could be done. It would require major engineering tricks to be able to demonstrate to the FCC that we wouldn't cause prohibited interference to any existing stations. To find out if we could, we contacted one and then a second leading broadcast engineering firm in Washington, D.C., who specialized in FCC work. One told us we would never get approved for nighttime operation, and the other said we might get 250 watts at night; but that during the day we'd be limited to 5,000 watts. That wasn't going to be enough to completely cover the Boston market.

In 1976, The National Association of Broadcasters announced it would be sponsoring a three-day directional engineering seminar in Cleveland, under the direction of Carl E. Smith. Carl Smith was a legendary broadcast engineer who had invented the directional antenna back in the 1930s, and his formulas were actually adopted into the FCC rules, specifying how directional antennas must be designed. I immediately sent Bob Lund to the seminar. He was a brilliant engineer, and I was figuring he might find a possible solution for boosting WGTR's power.

After returning, Bob did some calculations and discovered a hidden feature in the FCC antenna formulas that the two engineering firms had overlooked: If the height of an AM tower exceeds 180 degrees, a zero null is produced, which can be controlled by adjusting the height to protect a co-channel station. Using a computer program, Bob wrote on our now-primitive DEC VT78 (with 16k of memory, and 8k reserved for the operating system), the two of us taking turns working day and night running antenna pattern designs. Each pattern run took more than a half hour to calculate and print. We eventually concluded that if we used five 540-foot towers 250 feet apart, in a straight line, we could indeed get a nighttime power of 5,000 watts and a daytime power of 50,000 watts.

Knowing this, however, and pulling it off were two very different things. Getting that power increase meant buying a huge amount of land, clearing and stumping it, building five massive towers and a building, and buying a 50,000-watt transmitter and associated tuning and phasing equipment. It meant more proceedings before the FCC, and getting local zoning approval. Altogether, the changes would cost close to a million dollars. But with the instant success of WGTR and our continuing prosperity, everyone was on board. Jack Carlson, Judge Langan, my father—they trusted my judgment and saw the huge returns and increased station valuation a major Boston signal could bring.

Building out the transmission facilities was just one part of it. Programming was the other. I would have loved to continue as a Top 40 station, but all over America, AM radio in the mid 1970s was undergoing a sea change as music formats began a migration to the FM dial. In Boston, WVBF-FM adopted a Top 40 format and had even started achieving the kind of ratings shares WRKO regularly pulled in. WJIB-FM was getting big ratings with soft music, and WBCN-FM had switched from classical to album rock. In a 1972 interview with *Rolling Stone*, I had stated that AM radio would be stripped of music stations within a decade, and now in 1976 my prediction was coming true.

It would have seemed unfathomable just a few years before. Since its birth in the 1930s by inventor Edwin Armstrong, FM had suffered more disappointments than successes. Even with a series of FCC regulations to try and prop it up, FM failed to gain traction with station owners and consumers. Even in 1965,

News director Jim McAllister with the big red WGTR news-mobile. It was a former Avis Rent-A-Car shuttle bus at Logan Airport, but we turned it into a big, rolling billboard from which we could do live broadcasts.

ninety-eight percent of radio listeners tuned in to AM stations. AM was what everyone listened to. FM was just background noise.

Then Tom Donahue appeared on the scene. In the annals of radio history, Donahue was a visionary who saw just how under-played album rock music was on radio. This was despite the fact that more people had begun buying albums instead of 45 rpm records. In 1967, Donahue took a dumpy little San Francisco foreign language station, KMPX-FM, and turned it into the country's first album rock station. With rock moving into a more evolutionary era, bands like the Doors, the Yardbirds, and Procol Harum had a home for tunes that weren't simply two-minute singles. Suddenly, listeners had a choice between The Archies and Led Zeppelin.

Other KMPX clones, with their free-form playlists and political commentary, soon sprouted up around the country. In Boston, WBCN came on the air in mid-1968. Others followed, setting the stage for AM's ultimate demise as a home for music. The revolution was underway.

As someone who'd grown up with Top 40 radio, I still completely believed in the format. But the writing was on the wall for WGTR. If we went into the Boston market with 50,000 watts and Top 40 on the AM dial, there was a good chance we'd fail. All that hard work, all the value we'd created over the years, would evaporate.

As I evaluated which programming format would succeed in our newly expanded market, what stuck out was that every other U.S. top ten market had two successful all-news stations. Boston only had one. It was WEEI 590, which broadcast with a meager 5,000-watt signal from Medford, which was barely listenable in the western half of the Boston market. We were staring at an obvious opportunity. Lots of news aficionados lived right in the western suburbs where

WEEI was unlistenable: Waltham, Newton, Natick, Framingham, Weston, Burlington, Bedford, Lexington, Needham, Norwood, Dedham, and Wellesley.

The decision to go all-news was exciting but sad at the same time. There was the thrill that came with building a whole new format but also the quiet resignation over what we were leaving behind. Gone were the music, contests, and antics; all the fun and frenzy that comes with a great Top 40 station. While responsibility for the final decision was mine and I saw no practical alternative, some weren't ecstatic about the change. Don Kelley, Bob Lund, even Jim McAllister, the news junkie, felt like we were attending a wake on that last day in 1980 WGTR played music. Like we were saying goodbye to an old friend. That whole afternoon we only played "Bye, Bye, Miss American Pie" by Don McLean. It had been suggested by someone as a joke, but then we ran with it. For us, anyway, it really was the day the music died.

Did it fail? Well, that's a whole other story. And it gets quite personal.

In the middle of 1976, before the serious work of making WGTR a 50,000-watt station began to take shape, I was once again scouring through the FCC's table of allocations one evening when I noticed an open TV channel assigned to Worcester. From those early days of watching Milton Berle, I'd never quite shaken the television bug.

Worcester, though, wasn't prime TV country. Because the city is surrounded by seven hills, it sits in a bowl. The FCC rules required that a television station must provide a clear line-of-sight signal over the entire city of license. That meant any station licensed to Worcester had to place its antenna tower near Worcester. Those hills wouldn't allow the signal to reach Boston adequately. Marginal coverage meant poor ratings, which meant that making money was difficult with a Worcester signal. It's why the only commercial TV channel licensed to Worcester was owned by the Catholic Church, which used it to air its Sunday mass and other religious programming.

Being the nerd I was and digging deep into the FCC rules, I found an obscure provision that allowed an applicant to apply for a license in any community with-

John Garabedian

in fifteen miles of the city of allocation reference point, usually the main U.S. post office. One night, sitting at my kitchen table in Southborough, I got out a map and drew a fifteen-mile circle around Worcester. The City of Marlborough fell within that radius. Because Marlborough was in Middlesex County, it made it a "home station" to the Boston market, and the antenna could provide complete Boston coverage. That vacant TV channel suddenly looked incredibly valuable.

In 1978, we filed an application with the FCC for channel 66. I really had no idea what we'd do with the license. That decision could be made later. Opportunity doesn't wait. Unlike my conservative father, I always operated with a belief that if you wait for all the answers to emerge before you act, you'll miss out; that some of the best opportunities in life can't be planned in exacting detail. To find out where you're going, sometimes you just need to head out in a general direction to find a path. That's how I approached the TV project.

But now with the TV application filed at the FCC, other ideas popped up too. While taking flying lessons, I was required to complete a three-leg solo cross-country trip of more than a hundred miles per leg. On a beautiful spring afternoon, one leg took me to Nantucket Island, thirty miles south of Cape Cod. I'd never visited the place before but liked it immediately. There was a charm and beauty I loved discovering even from the air as I flew over its wide, sandy beaches, open land, historic colonial architecture, and cobblestone downtown streets. Upon returning to my office that day I whipped out my worn copy of the FCC rules and discovered an FM allocation on Nantucket for 93.5 MHz that no one had ever applied for. Bob Lund and I moved immediately to apply for it.

By the end of 1977, we had three applications filed with the FCC—one for the WGTR power increase to 50,000 watts, another for the channel 66 TV license, and the third for what would become my second radio station, WGTF, 93.5 FM.

Each of those projects would come to represent something different for me. With the WGTR power increase, there was the opportunity to become a major player in the Boston market. The TV license offered the chance to navigate a totally exciting new media territory. The Nantucket FM station was a fun little project that would cost very little, could eventually become something of value, and give me the opportunity to build something easy from scratch again.

Planning the Nantucket build was fun. Jim McAllister's landlord introduced me to Nantucket Airport manager Kenny Holdgate, who was beginning construction of a new airport operations building. He offered to rent his old offices: two small rooms in the FAA tower building that would headquarter the station, and at no extra charge, permitted us to put a forty-foot mast on an unused forty-foot-tall radar platform to mount WGTF's antenna. The $135 monthly rent even included free electricity, and with our 3,000-watt transmitter running twenty-four hours a day, we later figured out the electric bill would have been $300, double what we were paying for rent.

The biggest challenge was programming. Nantucket had a year-round population of five thousand residents. Finding an experienced air staff on the island was out of the question. Since WGTR would have a full news staff, I figured that we could format the new station as all-news fed from our WGTR news staff back in Natick, hire some local person to do a local news segment, and use automation to run it. A repeating thirty-minute "edition," with a morning, midday, and evening version could repeat in each time period, giving everyone a chance to listen at the time of their convenience.

The local news segment, Nantucket weather, marine forecast, and the national stories—they filled out the bulk of a thirty-minute package. It was all delivered on a three-carousel device that held seventy-two tape cartridges. To change the tape cartridges and update the segments, I hired Bill Reis, the jovial airport janitor, and his teenage sons, Joey and Andy, to change the tapes three times a day.

In finding a local news person to give WGTF a local flavor, we lucked out. Someone recommended a retired woman named Martha Walters, who had worked as women's programming director decades before at WNAC radio in Boston. She was absolutely perfect! A complete social butterfly, Martha went to all the right parties and social affairs and could report in detail on every one. Martha was a virtual clone of Lovey Howell from Gilligan's Island. She packed an aristocratic Nantucket air that was both real and ridiculous. But she was great at her job. If there was a dinner party, a car crash, or a garden club function, she knew about it. Every afternoon at three, she drove out to the airport with her little English Terrier and recorded three five-minute local news segments for the evening, morning, and midday editions that were part news, part social gossip.

But all of that was to come. In early 1979, within a two-month period, the FCC granted all three approvals, the power increase to 50,000 watts for WGTR, the construction permit for channel 66, and the license to build the Nantucket FM station.

My father, the stoic business manager, said "That's great, but who's going to pay for all this?" he liked to ask, repeating the same question he'd asked my mother all during my childhood.

I shrugged my shoulders. "I'm working on it; don't worry," I told him. "There's a way. There's always a way."

I had every reason to feel confident. Business was strong, and the license grants had suddenly increased the market value of the company by millions of dollars.

Life is funny. One moment you're muddling through the boring details of daily life. The next moment, something unexpected changes up your life.

In early August, 1976, I walked into Roche Brothers supermarket in West Natick. It was pushing five on a Friday afternoon and I was in a hurry to get going for the trip to Vermont to work on the cabin. My little Mazda B2000 pickup was loaded with tools and in the passenger seat was my friend Billy Harrison, who'd joined me for another trip to Vermont to help pound nails for a couple of days. But first I needed to cash my paycheck at the supermarket.

"Give me a minute," I said to Billy, hopping out of the truck.

When I walked into the store, I happened to glance to the pay phone and saw this guy, maybe nineteen or twenty years old, dressed in a jean jacket, with long, dark hair and movie star good looks. Whoa, I thought, who is this? He saw me and flashed a big smile. I smiled back, then nervously turned away and made my way to the line at the service counter. Should I look back? I thought. As I stood in line, I turned around, just to get a look at him again, and like before, he caught me looking over and smiled again. I could feel the back of my neck getting hot. Having already embarrassed myself a little I decided to have some fun. As I walked to the door I self-consciously smiled at him, then I jumped and clicked my heels, like I was doing a dance. He laughed, and then kept his eyes on me as I made my way out the door to the parking lot.

When I got back to the truck, I let out a big sigh.

"What's the matter?" Billy asked, arching his eyebrows.

"Oh, nothing," I said sort of kiddingly. "I think I just fell in love."

Billy groaned. "You weren't even gone five minutes," he said. "What are you talking about?"

"Oh, nothing," I said. I didn't even try to explain it. How could I? It did sound ridiculous. Who falls in love while waiting in line at a supermarket service desk? But that whole weekend it was all I could do not to think about this kid and how stupid I was to be so uptight and not introduce myself. I made my mind up that the next time I saw someone who interested me I wouldn't be so shy.

On a Wednesday night in late October, I was planning for another weekend in Vermont, where an early bout of snow had hit before I got a chance to close in my cabin. It had been a frantic week and I was running behind schedule, which was made worse by my last minute realization that I needed to swing by the Natick Sears and grab a circular metal saw blade and new set of wrenches. I bought my stuff and was heading through the men's department toward the parking lot when two young guys came down the aisle from the other direction. As we passed each other, I glanced left in their direction. One of them, who was really good-looking, locked eyes with me and grinned a big smile.

I thought for a second and remembered my resolution not to be afraid to start a conversation. Do something, John, I muttered to myself. Get his attention. As I turned around to look, I saw they had passed into the tool department and were about to turn down another aisle. But the kid I'd noticed had turned around and was still looking at me. So I threw my arm in the air and beckoned for him to come back. Surprisingly, he spun around and jogged toward me. I suddenly had no idea what I was going to say. Then, when he got close I trotted the old line, "Where do I know you from?"

He smiled gently. "Roche Brothers," he said.

I couldn't believe it! It was him. The same kid!

John Garabedian

A momentary silence fell between us before I found my voice again.

"What's your name?" I asked.

"David," he said, sticking out his hand. "David O'Leary."

I shook hands with him and introduced myself. "You live around here?" I asked.

"Yeah," David said. "Right over on Speen Street." By now, the kid he was with, his older brother, Billy, had caught up to us. After David introduced us, I explained to David that I was building a cabin on a mountain in Northern Vermont. "Can you operate a hammer?"

"Sure!" he said.

Not wanting to be too forward, I said, "Well, if you'd like to come up some weekend, I could use a hand."

"Okay!" he said enthusiastically, "I'd love to."

"Hold on," I said, fumbling through my wallet for a business card. "Call me if you want to go some time."

David looked at the card. "You work at WGTR, huh?" he said. "Cool station. I listen to it all the time."

For the next month, I really hoped he'd call. Every morning on the way to work as I drove down Speen Street, I'd think about him and wonder which house was his.

Around Thanksgiving of that year, the work on my Vermont place continued. The days were getting cold and I had bought a big cast-iron Franklin fireplace to heat the place. But it was a heavy thing I couldn't possibly lift alone. I tried to enlist some help from my friends, but everyone had plans. Hmmm, I thought. Maybe that kid David can help me. I looked in the phone book and found an O'Leary on Speen Street in the phone book and called.

"You remember me?" I asked when I reached him on the phone.

"Yeah, of course," he said.

"Well, I know this sounds crazy and it's last minute but I'm headed up to Vermont and wondered if you wanted to go," I said. "I've got this big stove that needs moving and I can't do it alone. You interested?"

"I'd love to," he said.

"What about your parents?" I asked. "Do you need to ask them?"

"Oh...yeah," he sighed.

David got the okay to go and later that evening I picked him up at his house. It was the quickest drive to Vermont I'd ever made. We talked the entire time. He told me about his family, school, and the music he liked and then recounted a tour he'd taken of WGTR a few years before when he was in junior high school. That night, it was well past 1 a.m. when we got to Cabot and stepped inside my frigid cabin. He loved the place, didn't mind the cold, and didn't complain the next morning when we hauled that four-hundred-pound cast-iron stove into the house. It was his first trip to Vermont, but I could tell he liked it. That Sunday afternoon as we were packing up my truck, he looked out at the woods.

"Do you think it would be okay if I cut down a Christmas tree to bring back to my house?" he asked.

"Sure," I said,

We didn't see each other much the next few months. He had an after-school job, as well as a girlfriend, and was caught up with high school life. But in May, around the time he turned sixteen, he called me up to say hi and eventually we began hanging out a lot. He came over to the station, we went out to eat, the movies, visited friends, and made more trips to Vermont. We weren't romantic or anything like that. We were just two guys who got along and who enjoyed and were drawn to each other. We connected because we shared similar views about people and life.

David told me he thought most kids his age were idiots and that he struggled to connect with them, a feeling I understood because it was my story also when I was a teenager. In a way, we found refuge together from life's insanity with the respect we had for each other's highest principles and of figuring out life's real rules. I know what it probably looked like, some thirty-five-year-old guy hanging out with a teenager. We talked about that and neither of us gave a shit about what others thought of our relationship. He was an exceptionally amazing person. We enjoyed each other's friendship and intellect and that's really all that mattered.

It went back to what my mother always taught me as I was growing up, "If you believe something is right, it's right. Don't let anyone talk you out of it." I had become confident enough that I didn't care what someone might think of me or my friendship with David. I had left behind letting other people set the limits for what

John Garabedian

I could do. And oddly enough, David felt the same way. I was astonished at the strength of his character and intelligence, as well as his confidence in who he was.

Looking back on it now, I think we both saw ourselves as refugees from a crazy society. Neither of us could identify with the way most people lived, thought, and acted. He didn't respect kids his own age and saw through their immaturity. He was an old soul that way. Bright and philosophical, he wanted to be around someone who was the same way. In David, I saw somebody I completely admired and respected, somebody with many exceptional qualities I wish I had. And I think he felt that way about me, too.

As the months rolled on, we connected more and more. At one point, when he was still sixteen, David asked if he could move in with me. Part of me wanted to say yes, but I knew it could be a disaster. "You've got to do all the regular high school things and go through those experiences, or else you'll hate me by the time you're eighteen," I told him.

David was the fifth of nine kids, four older brothers and four younger sisters, and life at his house could get crazy. His father was tough, sometimes too tough. On a Sunday night in early October of 1978, my then girlfriend, Linda Hart, and I arrived back at my house after an afternoon hanging out in Boston. We were sitting at my kitchen table talking, when the phone rang. It was David, and he was in tears.

"What's the matter?" I said.

"It's my dad," he answered. "He just beat the shit out of me." He paused and then asked, "Can I come stay with you?"

I froze. I didn't know what the hell to say. He was still only seventeen, but we had become very close. I loved having him around me and I couldn't allow him to be subjected to physical abuse. How could I turn him away?

"Sure," I said warmly, trying to play it cool around Linda. "Come on over. But park down the street on that dirt road right after my property. That way, if the cops come looking for you they won't see your car."

When I hung up the phone, Linda, who was leaning against the counter with her arms folded, looked at me with a curious smile. "Who was that?" she asked.

"Oh," I said, "It was David. He's having some family problems and I told him he could stay here."

In 1978, Atlantic Records invited the Boston radio community on an open bar boat trip around Boston Harbor to debut the new J. Geils Band album. (Left to right) Former WAAF PD Lee Arnold, my former girlfriend, the lovely Linda Hart, myself, J. Geils, and WBCN's Charlie Kendall. ©*Ron Pownall/RockRollPhoto.com*

"Oh, that's a shame," she said. Then Linda looked at her watch. "Well, I should probably get going."

I walked her to the front door and gave her a kiss. She started to leave but then turned back around, looked at me, and stated fearfully, "I'm never going to see you again."

It was such a weird statement. I mean, she knew I was bi and knew David and I were close, but I didn't understand where she was coming from. "What are you talking about?" I asked. "Of course we're going to see each other again. That's ridiculous."

She shook her head. "Goodnight," she said sweetly, and then walked to her car.

I stood in the doorway for a minute, unsure of what the hell had just happened. I watched Linda drive out of the driveway and then closed the door and sat down to wait for David.

Damn if Linda wasn't right. She knew before I did that things with her were over and that a whole new life for me was about to begin with David. Women are

John Garabedian

David O'Leary shortly after moving in with me.

amazing like that. They really have a sixth sense. Unlike most men, most women notice subtle details, pick up on things, notice the stuff men just completely overlook. I'd never tried to hide the fact that I also liked guys. But with David she sensed that something much bigger was at play. David wasn't just coming over to escape his dad or maybe move in for a little bit. He was coming to my home in Southborough to be with me. It's thirty-eight years since that night, and I haven't seen Linda since.

David and I were together for over ten years. In my entire life I've never met anyone who is a finer, more perfect human being. He has an amazing combination of intelligence, street-smarts, kindness, warmth, sincerity, generosity, talent, charm, moral strength, and honesty. When I was inducted into the Massachusetts Broadcaster's Hall of Fame in September of 2014, I was honored that it was David who introduced me.

Since that chance meeting in Roche Brothers all those years ago, David and I have remained best friends. No matter what kind of success or hardship I've faced, David has always been like a rock, giving me perspective and setting an exceptional example for how to live life.

◀

One of the things Jack Carlson always hammered home to me was that thousands of businesses start and soon fail. They look good on paper, they can even become profitable and be doing great volume, but they run out of cash. And if they grow too quickly and the increased expenses aren't met by a parallel increase in sales and collections, they go under, quickly. Cash flow and capital reserves, he often said, make all the difference.

My friend Kenny O'Keefe, managing partner and COO of Vestar Capital, once said, "You know, John, no matter how well you plan and how much padding you put in your budget, everything always takes longer and costs more." Building the new 50,000-watt transmitter facility was a major undertaking, and it used up a lot more of our cash reserves than we had budgeted. We bought forty acres of land along Route 126 in Ashland, had it clear-cut, stumped and graded, plowed in twenty-five

Building WGTR's 50,000-watt transmitter plant required hauling giant reels of cable and other equipment to the forty-acre Ashland site. The WGTR newsmobile became a heavy equipment hauler, although we had to fight with news director Jim McAllister to get it away from him.

miles of number ten copper wire for a ground system, and erected a building and five 540-foot towers.

At our increased power and running the all-news format at WGTR, we also dramatically ramped up the cost of doing business. There were the lease costs for the towers and transmission equipment, the huge electric bill, and a substantially larger staff. We bumped up our sales team from five to a dozen people, and added a small army of on-air talent and news writers. Plus, we needed to make a splash with advertising to let Metro Boston know we were a brand-new choice for all-news, which further exploded costs.

At the time, the radio industry had recently abandoned call letters for more common words, the kind of stuff that's everywhere these days. Mix 104, Kiss 108, Magic 106—catchy brand names that made it easier for listeners to remember the stations and identify their content.

With the new identity, we didn't want to be left behind. So I came up with the brilliant idea of calling it "G-1060." We invested in expensive ads in the *Boston Globe* and bought big billboards on major highways around the city to get the name out: Boston's new all-news station. It turned out, though, our smart name wasn't all that ingenious. The art work for the billboards didn't read "G-1060,"

John Garabedian

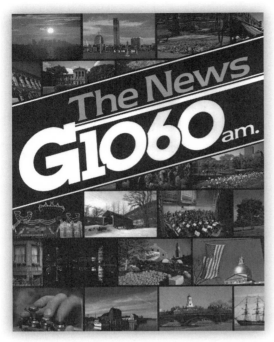

The trouble with the all-news WGTR logo began from the start. Instead of the design reading as "The News, G-1060," people read the logo as saying "The News, Globo," and thought it was some ad for the *Boston Globe* newspaper. It was a complete waste of money.

because the artist deleted the hyphen and designed the logo as "G1060," making the "1" look like an "L." Unfortunately, people glancing at it had no idea it was a new radio station and read it as "Globo," thinking we were somehow connected to the *Boston Globe* newspaper. Sales candidates would come in and the first question they'd ask was, When did the Globe get into the radio business? We couldn't figure it out until Don Kelley took a look at our billboards. We scrambled and changed it to "All News Radio, WGTR," but it was too late. The moment had passed and the budget was too drained to run a new campaign. In a sign of things to come, the budget was getting tight and I was getting nervous.

As we were about to launch the new all-news format, news director Jim McAllister resigned. His fear was that with the new responsibilities he would be over his head and didn't want to fail. It was a terrible thing to happen, since Jim was a great newsman, but no matter what I said, I couldn't convince him he would do great.

Once the format launched, our all-news on-air product we delivered was excellent. Rick Simonson, Malcolm Alter, Janice Glynn, Ron Bradbury, Roseanne Pawelic, and Harlan Levy sounded fantastic and were consistently on top of the biggest local and national stories. Audience response was solid and building.

Unfortunately, we'd been overly optimistic with our sales and cash flow projections. We had hired a highly experienced Boston sales manager named John Pappas to run the sales department, but we failed to recognize the long ramp-up time a new sales team would need—especially with a new, unproven product.

Successful radio ad salespeople make a lot of money and once they become established at a particular station it is nearly impossible to pry them away. So we had to hire newbies, most with no radio sales experience. It involved extensively training them and then giving them the time to build their client relationships and either become successful or wash out. As the weeks went by, more cash was going out than coming in.

We were also getting kicked around in another way. Ever since we filed with the FCC for approval to increase power, Westinghouse Broadcasting, the oldest broadcasting company in America and owners of WBZ in Boston and KYW in Philadelphia, had challenged our signal, saying it would cause nighttime interference with the Philly signal in New York. The evidence was questionable, but they were determined to hurt us to protect WBZ and they had the money, lawyers, and engineers to fight.

To advocate their cause, they brought in a consulting engineer named Jack Moffett. Moffett began demanding we take "cross-radial" measurements, which are not required or even defined by the FCC rules but provide a microscopic data analysis that can show microscopic blemishes in almost any station's signal pattern. It was a ridiculous request, and Carl Smith, our engineering consultant, warned me that we were in for a real disaster if we agreed to it. They could show interference in places where there really wasn't any, he told me.

As WGTR kept burning through cash, a character from the past suddenly showed up. My nephew, Kris Carlson, who'd done a fantastic job as sales manager when we launched the station in 1972 had left in 1974 to move to La Jolla, California, with one of our key salespeople, Tina Becker, who had become his girlfriend. He then started a health food restaurant. The enterprise was funded by his father, Jack Carlson, but eventually flopped, along with his relationship with Tina, and when he moved back east, we had a conversation about him rejoining WGTR as sales manager.

We needed to do something. To make payroll, we now had to borrow money from Carlson Corporation, Jack's company. The whole thing stressed the hell out of me. I was putting on weight, not sleeping, feeling depressed. No matter how hard I worked, no matter how much time I put into the station, righting the ship

John Garabedian

was going slowly. But sales were definitely increasing, and by November of 1980, we were within $5,000 of breaking even. Even so, I'd frequently wake up at two in the morning and stare up at the ceiling and wonder if there was something I'd overlooked. Had we made a mistake by going all news? Would we run out of cash? For the first time in a long time, I felt stuck, even a little unsure of myself.

And then things got complicated.

Needing a job, I figured Kris would return from his failed business and be delighted at the opportunity to make some real money and step in once again at something he had previously succeeded at as sales manager. Kris, however, had other ideas. While he was talking to me about the job and the sales issues, he was also talking to his dad, telling him that he should be the one running WGTR. I had failed, he argued, and if things were really going to turn around, a major shakeup was needed. Even though we were inching closer to becoming profitable, and even though Kris had never run a successful business in his life, he portrayed me as "a great programmer but not a good businessman." Then, on a Wednesday afternoon in September of 1980, Jack called me.

"I want to meet with you and Kris and go over things," he said. "Thought we could meet at my office in Wayland."

I didn't have a choice. I was at Jack's mercy. He had stepped up for me, even though his own business had taken a beating in the recession. The next afternoon, I found myself sitting around a big table with Jack, Kris, and Jack's in-house lawyer, Alan Lamport. From the moment I entered the room, I felt a strange vibe. It got stranger as we moved through the session.

Over the next several minutes, Jack, in his usual gentle, calm demeanor, began talking about solving the cash flow issues and changing up management. Maybe the company would be better, he said, if I stuck to my strengths in programming and allowed someone with a fresh viewpoint to run the day-to-day operations. I looked around the room with a puzzled expression.

"Who are you thinking?" I asked.

Jack looked over at Kris, who smiled. "We think maybe it's time to give Kris a shot at it," he said. "He's got a good head on his shoulders. Knows the station, knows the business."

After being deposed at WGTR, I was moved into this third floor attic office.

I was devastated. Without any kind of warning, they were taking WGTR away from me, relegating me to some secondary position in which I'd have to answer to Kris. I didn't even know what to say, or how to push back. The majority voting interest I'd been assured of getting when we had formed the company had never been passed on to me. Now, it was being used to take the station out of my hands.

"Guys, we're almost there," I stammered. I looked at Jack. "You've seen the numbers. Expenses are $90,000 a month and this month we'll bill $85,000. We're not that far from breaking even."

Jack wasn't having any of it. He leaned forward in his chair. "John, you've had a year to turn things around and it's not working," he said. "We need to try something else."

Within a week Kris had moved into my office at WGTR. I was bumped to the third floor like some crazy person. Every day I'd come to work and every day I walked past my old office and wonder what the heck I was going to do. I was a captain without a ship.

Kris had no magic tricks up his sleeve. In fact, he had no clue what to do. From the moment he took over, WGTR floundered far worse than it had before. Sales quickly plummeted to $25,000 a month, then to $15,000. Maybe if Kris

John Garabedian

Assembly of the WGTF satellite dish at Nantucket airport. While pulling cables, a cabbie helped David O'Leary replace a 300-pound manhole cover and accidentally dropped it, crushing David's big toe. (Left to right) David O'Leary, Jill Lund, and Bob Lund.

was the hungry twenty-something he'd been when he had first started with me eight years before, the situation would have been different. But he wasn't. Instead, he'd become this smug, entitled thirty-year-old who was confident he could coast along on his charm and "brilliance." In late and out early, that was his workday. It was unbelievable watching him fail. All the while he assured his father things were going to improve. He just needed a little more time to "clean up all the mess John had created." I went from being frustrated that I couldn't turn things around quickly to being depressed that I'd been deposed, pushed out of the project I'd spent my entire adult life building and running. And now an inch from the finish line, my legs were broken.

The future looked bleak. I had absolutely no confidence Kris could succeed and knew I needed to figure out the rest of my life and career—who I was and where I needed to head.

I finally went to Jack and told him I wanted out of the corporation. My feelings about how things had transpired at WGTR had cooled and now I just wanted to strike out on my own. An appraisal of the station by Blackburn & Company showed it to be worth $2 million. Although I didn't have voting control, I still owned fifty-seven percent of the stock and we had little debt. I thought I could convince him to sell WGTR, but Jack didn't want to consider taking his son's new project away. Instead, he wanted to go the opposite direction and dump more money into the operation. To do that, however, he pushed to dilute my shares. I wasn't even angry. I just wanted out.

I eventually proposed a deal: I'd give up all but ten percent ownership of WGTR in exchange for complete ownership of both the Nantucket station and the TV license. Within a month we signed papers on it.

Finally out on my own, I made the Nantucket FM station my focus. I performed an engineering study, went through FCC rulemaking proceedings, and succeeded in bumping its power to 50,000 watts to get the signal to Cape Cod. Because of the power increase we had to move to a new frequency, 96.3, and we built a new transmitter facility on an FAA beacon tower in Madaket at the west end of the island. We then petitioned the FCC to reallocate the old 93.5 frequency to Harwich Port on Cape Cod. But life is funny. For no reason except coincidence, today I own the 93.5 frequency once again as WFRQ, "Frank-FM."

While I worked developing the Nantucket station, I watched as Kris continued to fail to turn WGTR around. Eventually, in desperation, they fired the whole news staff and turned programming over to a satellite streaming service called "Stardust" that specialized in oldies music. It wasn't an original idea. I'd done the same thing with the Nantucket station. Then, to give the operation a fresh image, Kris changed the call letters of the station to reflect the new Stardust format. The station's new name became "WSTD." I howled with laughter when I heard that.

"Oh, my God!" I told friends. "They might as well call it 'syphilis radio.'"

In the end, the station I'd spent so many years building was sold in 1982 to a group from Texas who just wanted its physical assets; the real estate, the station equipment, and the towers, which they turned around and sold for a profit. It was a sad end, but a fitting finality to something I was just happy to finally have behind me. ◀×

20. Learning to Fly

Tom Petty, 1991

1948 Piper Vagabond I bought as a wreck for $10,000, then spent $95,000 restoring it to museum-quality condition. It has no electrical system, but cruises at 95–100 mph with a little Continental 65 horsepower engine.

By the late seventies, the near-weekly four-and-a-half-hour drives to Vermont were becoming weary. I still loved being up there away from everything, but the travel was a pain. Because interstate I-93 was only partially finished, the journey north became this mix of highway-and-backroads travel. In the summer I had to fight through swarms of people headed to New Hampshire's Lake Winnipesaukee. In winter it was hordes of skiers, and in autumn it was leaf-peepers making their way through New Hampshire's Franconia Notch. Stretches of the road became a virtual parking lot. Then as I'd looked up at the sky, I'd see all that space. Up there, there was no lineup of Winnebagos to slow me down. "What I need is a freakin' plane," I exclaimed during one particular grueling stretch. Everyone got a good laugh about it, but it was hard to completely abandon that thought and soon it stopped being a joke.

Then I happened to bump into Diane Foxwell.

For years she'd been the executive secretary to Norman Knight, president of Knight Quality Group, the small New England radio conglomerate for which I'd done consulting work in the early '70s. One Saturday in early August of '77, Mark Parenteau was doing a WGTR live broadcast from an indoor bazaar in Framingham. I had stopped by to check out the event and was wandering around when I heard my name called out.

"John!" shouted out a familiar voice. I looked over and there was Diane, waving excitedly at me.

"What are you doing now?" she asked when I came up to her.

"Well, I own this radio station in Natick and we're doing a live broadcast," I answered. I looked over the table she was standing behind, which had a scattering of flyers and pamphlets with planes on them. "What are *you* doing now?"

"I married this great guy, and we're running the flight school at Hopedale Airport," she said. Diane then pushed a pamphlet toward me. "You ought to come down and learn how to fly."

I looked up. "And you ought to run ads on my radio station," I answered. "Let's do a trade!"

That's how it all started for me. A simple swap. A year after I ran into Diane, I was a licensed pilot and my Vermont commute was reduced to an hour.

Practicality had driven me to the sky, but the beauty and serenity I've found in the sky is what's made flying a passion of mine over the last forty years. Up above the clouds, above the mayhem of life and chaos, I discovered a peacefulness that's tough to replicate on the ground. When you're flying you're forced to be right there, focused on the present, doing one particular thing. I imagine it's like doing yoga (something I've never done). There's a focus required to pilot an aircraft which you can't deviate from. Whatever personal issues or nagging business problems might dog you, you push to the side because the plane requires your total attention. I love that.

As I got deeper into aviation, I developed a love for classic and antique planes from the forties, fifties, and sixties. But since your very life depends on these aircraft being in good shape, I decided the ideal thing to do would be to buy run-down airplanes cheaply and then completely rebuild them to better-than-new, museum quality. At one point, I owned twenty-two planes. My homes in Boston, Vermont, and Cape Cod each now have private runways. I know it sounds ridiculous, but each of my planes is like an old friend. They all have personalities and serve different purposes. The little single engines like the '41 Piper Cub, '47 Vagabond, or '39 Aeronca Chief are great for a sunset flight along the Cape shores and beaches. The bigger ones, like my Maule, Piper Super Cub, Stinson Voyager, or the Piper Pacer, are more roomy and comfortable. For a longer journey that requires speed or instrument flying, I hop in the Navion Rangemaster or the twin-engine Piper Geronimo. In their own unique way, they're easy to get attached to.

That goes for the first plane I ever bought. In late January of '79, after several months of renting, I found a three-year-old, low-time Taylorcraft that a

Taking off from my Vermont airstrip in my 1946 Taylorcraft.

stonemason outside of Detroit had put up for sale. It was a beauty, in Daytona White with Madrid Red striping and N-numbers. Unlike every airplane I had flown before, this one was a taildragger, with a tailwheel in the rear instead of a nosewheel in the front. Taildraggers can be tricky to land because the center of gravity is behind the pilot, not in front of him. I'd never flown one before and wasn't interested in trying to make that inaugural flight coming home from Michigan on my own. I started asking around for an experienced co-pilot.

A buddy of mine eventually pointed me to a young guy from Wayland, Jimmy McKenzie, who worked for a banner tow company in Lawrence, Massachusetts. He was just twenty-three years old but had been flying since he turned seventeen and my friend assured me he could land a taildragger with his eyes closed. I offered to pay his travel to Detroit plus $200 if he'd help me fly my new plane home.

I had the plan in place and had bought two one-way airline tickets, but two days before we were scheduled to fly out I received a call from an apologetic Jimmy.

"I know it's last minute but I can't go," he said. "There's an election in New Hampshire on Tuesday and we were hired to fly banner tow all day on Monday for big money for one of the candidates."

John Garabedian

Classics: my 1941 Piper Cub J-3L and 7AC "Champ" on the grass, mountaintop runway in Vermont.

I was stunned. "What am I going to do?" I asked.

Jimmy had a plan. "My boss said if you can make it to Lawrence Airport tomorrow, he can teach you how to fly a taildragger," he said.

I didn't have a choice. Sunday morning I trekked up to Lawrence to meet the legendary Wayne Mansfield. Flying was a part of Wayne's DNA and his family involvement in it went back two generations, to the early years of aviation. His grandfather had been a barnstormer in the 1920s, his father had started the banner tow company, and Wayne had carried on the tradition. He was in his late thirties and carried himself in this free, nonchalant way, like he had nothing to prove.

It was a chilly February afternoon at the airport when I arrived where a white and blue Taylorcraft F-19 just like the one I was going to buy sat waiting for me. Our takeoff proved smooth. "That was nice," he said. Then Wayne turned toward me. "Hey, wanna try a loop?"

I shot a look at him with eyes as big as grapefruits. "That's okay, Wayne," I said. "I'm not really into acrobatics." I wasn't concerned about my stomach; I was really worried about my life. The Taylorcraft we were in was based on a design from the 1930s. With its wooden wings, it wasn't made for stunts. But that didn't stop Wayne, who took over the controls. "It's not a big deal at all, John," he said with all the confidence in the world. "Watch this." And with that he put the plane into an accelerating descent to pick up speed, then pointed the plane up, shooting it toward the sky, then over the top, before circling it back down. I thought I was going to lose my breakfast.

Wayne let out a good laugh. "That worked out okay, now didn't it?" he said.

I nodded. "Yeah," I said with uncertainty.

"Great," Wayne said. "How about we try a barrel roll?"

I knew Wayne wasn't really asking and just closed my eyes as he gave us a spin, turning the plane over one complete time. When we were right side up again, I turned to my co-pilot. "Jesus, Wayne," I cried out. "If this is the warm-up, I'm scared as hell about what the lesson is going to look like."

Wayne laughed hard once again. "Just breaking you in a little," he said. "Now let's learn how to fly this thing."

Two hours and nearly a dozen takeoffs and landings later I was just barely comfortable enough to think I could fly my new plane home from Michigan. It took another year and a hundred hours of flying time before landing a taildragger didn't terrify me. Today, though, they're my favorite type of airplane to fly. They're sporty, but more important, they're made to land on rough terrain, like my grass Vermont landing strip.

Pilot error is the leading cause of aviation accidents and over-confidence drives many pilots to fly into conditions beyond their capability. It was only a few months after my lesson with Wayne Mansfield that, on a flight from northern Vermont, I had another stomach-churning flight of my own. In early 1979, I needed a new sales manager for WGTR. One of the better candidates to come up on my radar screen was a guy named Dennis Jackson who was working at WJOY, a radio station in Burlington, Vermont. I agreed to fly up there to meet him on a Wednesday in mid-January for an interview. The flight was impossible to complete in visual conditions, with snow in the forecast and Vermont's Green Mountains obscured in the clouds.

At the time, I was taking lessons from my friend Jim Stickney to get my instrument rating. I still needed a few more hours of actual instrument flight time to prepare for my FAA flight test, and I asked Jim to come along so I could get in some instruction time. The flight north was easy, and after the interview, Jim and I grabbed dinner in the city before heading home. It was pushing seven in the evening and a cold drizzle had started to fall as we arrived back at Burlington International Airport and climbed into my Cessna Skyhawk.

The conditions had seemed manageable at takeoff, but as we began climbing into the clouds the plane's indicated airspeed started dropping. "Shit," I said to Jim. "I forgot to turn on the pitot heat." He smiled as I flipped on the switch and watched as the airspeed indicator increased. For a few minutes, anyway.

At about three thousand feet, we were rocked by a loud bang. Then another. Jim looked out.

"Ice on the propeller," he said. "It's sheering off and hitting the wing."

As we continued to climb, the icing only intensified. We shined a flashlight onto the wing struts, and, sure enough, about a half inch of ice had accumulated. Airframe icing kills people two ways: one is the extra weight it adds to the airplane, but the worst effect is that it changes the shape of the wings so they are no longer their original shape and can't hold the aircraft up. The plane then can suddenly tumble and go into an unrecoverable spin. That's what we were facing; at night, in the clouds, in freezing rain, over the Green Mountains.

The forecast had called for the tops of the clouds to be at four thousand feet. But now we were still in the clouds at 4,700 feet, our air speed had dropped to sixty knots, and we were barely gaining altitude. The plane's exterior was also coated. The wings, propeller, most of the fuselage, were all iced up. "Better tell Burlington Approach what's happening and that we want to return to the airport," Jim said calmly.

I got on the radio and the controller on the other end turned us around. "I'll put you over the highway," he said "In case you need to land."

We picked up airspeed to prevent a stall but were descending through the clouds for what seemed like days before we finally broke out and were vectored direct to Burlington International. It was a beautiful sight to see the lights of the city, the airport beacon, and the sparkling airport runway lights. We blasted onto final approach, touching the Cessna Skyhawk down at a blazing 120 mph to prevent the wings from stalling due to the heavy ice, which would have resulted in a fatal out-of-control crash.

As a pilot there's simply no time to panic when you're in the middle of a thorny situation. Your mind blocks out the stress, you focus, and go into survival mode. But once you're on the ground and in the comfort of the pilot lounge, that's a different story. What might have happened starts running through your mind. As the Skyhawk's wheels touched down on the runway, my shoulders dropped and my whole body loosened. I hadn't realized it,

This little single engine 1976 Taylorcraft F-19 was instrument-equipped and carried us back and forth day and night over thirty miles of open ocean to Nantucket in both good weather and bad.

but I'd been as tight as a clenched fist for a good five minutes. I looked over at Jim, who looked just completely relaxed.

"I never doubted you," he said turning toward with me a modest grin. "That was a great lesson on what can happen in icing conditions."

In those early flying years, I was certainly more adventurous and less cautious than I am now. If something went wrong with the radio station, I didn't think anything about flying to Nantucket in some pretty marginal weather. If the station's transmitter went down, there wasn't a tech crew I could call to get it back up online. I was it. Either I fixed the thing or the station remained off air. It was that simple. I shudder to think of all those winter nights or foggy evenings I navigated my little single-engine Taylorcraft more than thirty miles of open ocean over the frigid waters of Nantucket Sound with one little hundred-horsepower Continental O-200 engine pulling me along. It makes me wince to think what would have happened if the engine quit. Today, I wouldn't fly at night or in low instrument conditions in anything but a multi-engine plane.

◀

Beginning in our early years, David always flew with me. I guess it's no surprise that he eventually caught the flying bug as well. He wanted to take lessons, but I didn't want to be the one who taught him. I wasn't a licensed flight instructor, but even if I had been, it could have put a severe strain on our relationship. Like I was the dad teaching his son how to drive. Bad idea. Neither one of us wanted that.

I did, however, suggest that rather than renting a plane for his lessons, he should just go out and buy one. The cost would pretty much be the same, but at the end of it, he'd own his own aircraft. David loved the idea and for several weeks in early 1979, he combed through *Trade-A-Plane*, a trade publication filled with ads and classifieds for airplanes and airplane parts. Then, one morning in early April, David burst into my office.

"I think I found my plane," he exclaimed, showing me an ad in a dog-eared copy of the most recent issue of *Trade-A-Plane*. On the page, he'd circled a listing for a 1946 Taylorcraft BC-12D. "It's in Michigan. Only fifteen hours on it since a total rebuild five years ago."

A week later, David and I boarded a flight at Logan Airport in Boston and flew to Detroit, where we rented a car for the three-hour drive north to Lake Isabella. The owner of the plane, a middle-aged petroleum engineer, worked for Gulf Oil. He'd overseen its rebuild, but because his work kept him on the Gulf of Mexico, he'd barely flown it. Outside of a few Sunday trips, the plane had sat in his hanger since it was restored.

It was really beautiful, with a stunning dark green finish that looked like it had just been done. David and the guy took it for a test flight and returned excited as ever. "It's nicer than I hoped for," he told me.

That afternoon, David and I climbed into the plane for the trip back home. The fuel gauge on a 1946 Taylorcraft is a rigid wire attached to a floating cork sticking out of the fuel cap on the nose. About two hours into the journey, we saw that the fuel level had dropped considerably.

"We can't have used that much," David said, peering at the gas gauge. "Right?"

We didn't want to take any chances. We didn't know a thing about possible issues with the plane. Maybe there was a leak. Maybe the gauge was off. It didn't matter. We had planned to go straight to Buffalo for the night but that now seemed impossible. I whipped out the Sectional aeronautical chart to see where we could

David O'Leary at Marlborough Airport after buying his first airplane (parked next to mine). The propeller had been sent out for inspection.

land and fill up. "Looks like we're going to have to make a stop in London, Ontario," I said.

We just made it. The fuel indicator had inched uncomfortably close to the bottom as we hit the runway. There was another problem. I had to *really* urinate. As we came to a stop, I opened the door to jump out so I could take a piss when a customs agent shot out of his office. "Get back in the plane!" he barked.

After the official looked over our identification, I was finally allowed to hit the bathroom and David was permitted to fuel up. We bolted for Buffalo, where we spent the night, before taking off early for home and arriving at the airport in Marlborough right after lunchtime.

John Garabedian

David's new plane was due for its annual FAA inspection in another week and he arranged to have it done at Marlborough airport. With the excellent condition it appeared to be in, it seemed like it would be an informality. A week later, David received a call.

"The wooden propeller is not airworthy," the mechanic said. "There is some wood rot. You're going to need a new one." David sighed and signed off on purchasing a new one.

A week later, another call came in. "Better come over," David was told. "We need to show you something. There's a big problem."

The situation wasn't overstated. The plane had passed inspection but when Jeff, the line boy, went to wash it, his fingers went right through the fabric covering the fuselage. A test of the cotton fabric showed that the entire covering including the wings was trash. Apparently the moisture from the dirt floor inside the metal hanger in Michigan had compromised it, causing it to rot. And we had just flown eight hundred miles in an airplane with rotten fabric!

David was devastated. He'd spent $5,500 on the plane and now was looking at another few thousand to fix it. "What do I do?" he asked me as we stood looking at the damage.

"Why don't *we* do it?" I suggested. "It can't be that difficult."

David smiled kind of curiously. "You mean, the two of us?" he said.

"Sure," I said. "How hard can it be?"

That next day we loaded up the WGTR newsmobile, the huge retired Avis shuttle bus we'd picked up, cleaned up, and had painted a bright red with the letters "WGTR NEWS" all over it. With tools, rope, and bungee cords, the two of us headed to Marlborough Airport and spent the day taking apart the plane. Off came the wings, then the tail feathers, which we slid into the back of the bus. Then we towed the fuselage on its wheels back to our garage in Southborough.

I wanted to help David save every penny I could, so in an effort to cut his costs on the fabric, I got on the phone and worked out a deal with a company called Superflite in Chicago. We received the recovering materials, and in return they received a free Caribbean cruise with Carnival Cruise Lines, whom we had trade credit with through WGTR.

Over the next six months, David and I worked away at covering the plane. My garage became a sort of second home for us. Weekends and weeknights—whenever we had a spare hour—we were out there getting it covered. When we finished, the plane looked unbelievably beautiful. Like it had just been marched out of a showroom.

David ended up keeping the plane for about two years. Since it had no electrical system, the engine was started by hand-propping its propeller, which got old, quickly. It was also a taildragger and David wasn't a fan of landing it. He sold it in '81 for a profit and moved up to his next plane. 🔇✕

21. Dirty Water

Standells, 1966

The spacious-but-dimly-lit WBCN control room. The ambiance here was spiritual, enhanced by the station's great cultural heritage. Some ambitious engineer installed this thirty-six channel mixing console, yet we only used seven channels and no one knew what the rest of the knobs did.

By 1982, the migration of music radio from the AM dial to the FM airwaves I'd predicted in the 1971 *Rolling Stone* article was nearly complete. In music-loving Boston that was especially so, where WBCN had helped pioneer radio's free-form album rock concept. It had launched in 1968, just prior to the Woodstock era, and then powered through the decade that followed with trippy music and spaced-out, street-sounding deejays stumbling over one another.

There was no debating WBCN's cool reputation. Since its start, the station's sound embodied Boston's alternative culture. It was daring, a little ragged, even out of control at times. That was true of its headquarters at 1265 Boylston Street, located in the shadow of Fenway Park, on the first base side. The former home to a car dealership, the WBCN studios sprawled out across a single floor where a long hallway marked by posters and gold records wrapped around a large central studio. That big room, with its couches and chairs, art work and incense burners, was essentially a hippie den where people hung out or passed out from exhaustion or other things.

Just off the rear of the main studio was the station's prized jewel—its record collection. It was a mammoth run of floor-to-ceiling shelves stuffed with vinyl. Little Richard, Aerosmith, Long John Baldry, Muddy Waters, Pink Floyd—every rock and blues record you could imagine had a home there. But it was the one that didn't get played that got the most use. In the back of the library, in an isolated shelf space, was a framed Jefferson Starship gold record that was used exclusively for cutting lines of coke. The thing had been ravaged so badly by razors you could hardly see through the glass. It was the stuff of legend at the station and deejays, musicians, and whoever else wanted to get high used it. All the biggest musicians and local talent knew about the Starship record.

After his sold-out Boston Garden show, we ended up in Bob Seger's suite at the Cambridge Hyatt. Bob loved the J. Geils Band, so Mark called Peter Wolf and he came over in a cab. "My nephews in Detroit aren't going to believe I met you," Seger told Wolf. (Left to right) Mark Parenteau, Seger, Wendy Furiga, and myself.

WBCN's appreciation for new music made it a haven for up-and-coming bands, who forged a tight relationship with the jocks before they hit it big. Those friendships endured even after those groups began selling out arenas. The Police, Led Zeppelin, and U2 owed their early American following to the attention WBCN gave their first records, and none of the bands forgot it.

In September of 1979, the Clash came into the studio after a big show at the Orpheum. Toward the end of the interview, members of the world's coolest, most famous punk band were singing at the top of their lungs a version of the Village People's "YMCA" live on the air. For local groups like the Cars, Aerosmith, the J. Geils Band, WBCN became a second home. You'd pop into the station kitchen and there would be Steven Tyler grabbing a coffee. Like he was some kind of regular, which he was.

The talent extended to the jocks. J. Geils Band front man, Peter Wolf, got his start at the station as an on-air talent, and by the late 1970s, WBCN had a lineup of deejays who had become local stars in their own right. Charles Laquidara and his "Big Mattress" show in the morning, Ken Shelton on middays, and Mark Parenteau in the afternoon. Mark started at WORC with aspirations to become a famous Top 40 deejay, but he eventually forged his own path on FM radio, fusing together comedy and music into his program. The biggest name comics and rock stars were always visiting his show. Some were prearranged visits. Others were not.

Around 1980, John Belushi stopped by unannounced. He was in Boston, running around with some of the same coke dealers Mark was friendly with, when he decided to visit. He knocked on the back door and when the newsman opened it up, Belushi and his posse plowed past him and stumbled into WBCN's main studio. "I've been listening to the station and wanted to talk to you,"

Belushi blurted out to Mark. For the next hour, it became frenetic radio. Host and guest babbled back and forth on air, then when Mark went to a song or commercial break, he and Belushi went to the back of the library to scratch up the Jefferson Starship record some more.

My own connection to WBCN stretched back to its beginning, when the station's founder, Ray Riepen, approached me in 1968 about becoming his first program director. Riepen was an unlikely counter-cultural hero. A Midwestern-er and a trained lawyer, he came to Boston in the early 1960s to get a master's degree at Harvard Law School but was soon lured to Boston's music scene. In 1966 he opened the Boston Tea Party, an underground rock club on Berkley Street that became the stage where many now-legendary English bands first played in front of American audiences.

As the rock scene evolved, Riepen saw the excitement that Tom Donahue had created with a cutting-edge album rock music format on FM stations in San Francisco and Los Angeles. Ray believed the same thing could be replicated in Boston. In late '67, he approached the owner of a struggling classical station, WBCN-FM ("Boston Concert Network"), and offered him money to let him take over the station with album rock programming at eight o'clock each night. On March 15, 1968, WBCN's new alternative nighttime programming went on the air when Joe Rogers (aka "Mississippi Harold Wilson") debuted with Frank Zappa and the Mothers of Invention's "Nasal Retentive Calliope Music." Boston radio was never the same after that.

Riepen was a media connoisseur. On a recommendation from an associate, he'd listened to WORC, knew my work, and called me up one day at the station to see if we could chat about his new venture. It was a cool October night in '67, when I parked on Boylston Street in Boston and met with Ray at a jazz club.

"People are buying albums these days," he argued. "Not singles. That's where music is headed. But the Top 40 stations like WRKO are only playing 45 rpm singles. If we play albums, we'll beat them."

It was hard for me to get excited about what Riepen was selling. Being a part of something brand new, moving back to Boston, working in FM—that was great. But I knew from the interactive request lines at WORC that people had favorite *songs*, not albums. And only a couple of songs on most albums were actually any good. The rest sucked. As I explained to Riepen, the audience will tell you what they like, and if you want a large audience you need to find out specifically what those songs are. It was clear he just didn't understand.

Still, I was interested in working for him, until he told me what he could pay.

"I can offer you six dollars an hour," he said.

I shook my head. "I can't do that, Ray," I said. "That's not enough. I'd be taking a big pay cut."

So instead of being a part of the WBCN revolution, I watched it from a safe distance. For a while, at least.

By the late seventies, WBCN had attracted a modest advertiser base of head shops, music retailers, waterbed stores and other "hippie" retailers, but hadn't achieved any kind of major ratings success. It was considered very cool, but it was really the most talked about station nobody listened to much. Everyone cool under thirty wanted to listen to it because it was so avant garde and tuned in socially, but they migrated back to Top 40 radio for the big hit songs. The long, opinionated, radical, political diatribes from the deejays, the station's left-wing news reporting and frequent really weird music selections meant it consistently struggled to ever grab more than two percent of the Boston radio audience. By comparison the highest ratings among listeners under thirty was to Top 40 WRKO with a twenty share. Clearly, people under thirty *said* they listened to WBCN, but they *actually* spent most of their time listening to WRKO.

Then WCOZ blasted on to the scene and upended everything with a format built around less talk, familiar, hit rock music, and a catchy slogan "Kick-Ass Rock 'n' Roll...and No Disco."

By 1979, WCOZ had undermined WBCN's rock format monopoly and eaten into its meager ratings as well as its profits by presenting a tight format of the biggest rock hits. The fact that WBCN was struggling was of no great surprise to me. Whenever I listened to the station, I just wanted to yell. The deejays lacked any previous radio success or discipline, nor did they have the understanding of how to entertain and hold an audience. They'd go on these mind-numbing personal rants. Or there were these idealistic programs that made no sense. Saturday night at eight, for example, there was "Letters From People In Jail," which featured the tedious reading of endless letters from criminals.

The music programming was even more of a train wreck. If you liked the song by the Fugs that just played, then you certainly *wouldn't* like the Judy Collins song that came on after it or "Songs from Humpback Whales," which interweaved actual whale recordings into something that resembled music. In between, the deejays droned on about politics and Vietnam or babbled their opinions about some other humanitarian crisis, which most of them had absolutely no expertise to be talking about. It was brutal.

The 'COZ team stuck to the big rock hits by Led Zeppelin, The Who, Rush, and Stones: popular songs that large audiences wanted to hear. The results were impossible to refute. In the summer of '81, WCOZ pulled in a 11.1 share, while WBCN eked out a miserable 2.1.

Mark Parenteau knew how I felt. Sometimes we'd get together after his shift to grab a bite and inevitably talk turned to radio and the station. Mark gave me room to get on my soapbox and deliver my diatribe about how the station's vibe was great, but the music and the gabby DJs were too sloppy and loose. "Don't you want to work for the number one, most-listened to station in Boston?" I'd ask him. "Until those things are addressed, WBCN's ratings won't improve."

Mark didn't disagree and without me knowing it had been lobbying WBCN's new general manager, Tony Berardini, to sit down with me to discuss how I thought the station could significantly improve. Tony had arrived in Boston after managing bands in the Bay area, including a stint as road manager of Jefferson Starship. After his arrival, he and Mark had become fast friends, and while he had a keen understanding of the eccentricities of the WBCN staff and he knew the station's strong local image was an asset, he was unsure how to empower his crew to begin making significant advances in the ratings.

My Top 40 background may have made Tony wince, but Mark is nothing if not persistent, and finally Tony surrendered and agreed to a get-together. In April of 1982, the three of us met at Sol Azteca, an outstanding Mexican restaurant on Beacon Street in Boston. Between bites of carne asada, I launched into what was right and what was wrong with WBCN.

"Everyone *wants* to listen to WBCN because it's cool, but the music sucks," I told him. "Ninety-five percent of the music is obscure and unfamiliar. Those unfamiliar album cuts may be the deejays' favorites, but it's pure crap to most of the listeners. You've got to play the familiar hits, the songs your target audience loves." Tony listened intently, sipping sangria while I got more amped up and waved my arms all over the place. "And the deejays talk way too much, and usually about nothing the average listener gives a shit about," I continued. "Every time they talk for more than thirty or forty seconds in a break, you lose half the audience. It's like the inmates are running the asylum. They may be very nice people, but they know absolutely nothing about how to grab and hold an audience."

Berardini didn't get defensive, but as someone who'd originally come to WBCN as a deejay, he had to walk a careful line. He'd worked side-by-side with the people he now managed and knew that to get anywhere with his team, he couldn't just come down like Hitler and order change.

What Tony knew well, and what I respected and reminded him, was that WBCN had something massive to build from. "People in Boston love the station and *want* to listen to it," I told him. "The station image is great. But between the crappy music and gabby, hyper-political deejays, you're constantly giving them reasons to tune out.

As we talked, Tony asked questions looking for ways to implement a structure for music presentation. Mark knew it wouldn't be easy. The WBCN crew was made up of strong personalities and of opinionated people who were used to complete autonomy on the air. It would take someone with masterful management abilities to pull it off. In Tony, though, along with his program director, Oedipus, who both knew all sides of the operation, the station had the perfect team to make the changes at WBCN.

Slowly, Berardini, Oedipus, and Parenteau began skillfully convincing the key players to incorporate the suggestions and implement a flexible structure that allowed the deejays considerable freedom in programming their shows, while still maintaining a structured musical flow that could attract and hold a quickly growing audience. Without losing the station's cultural essence, the deejays talked less. The music library was tightened and streamlined, and actual research was put into finding out which artists and titles the listeners really wanted to hear. By that fall, the station sounded significantly better.

From that initial dinner conversation, Berardini and I stayed in touch and became friends over the next several months. Then, when a couple of weekend slots opened up, he and Oedipus asked me if I'd like to "have some fun" and go on the air. The entertainer in me needed an outlet. It had been a good three years since I'd worked as a deejay. I was busy, entrenched in running and expanding the Nantucket station, but I couldn't say no to the offer.

It was awesome and an honor to be a part of the WBCN exploding scene. The nearly three years I spent on the air there were absolutely some of the most rewarding and exciting times I spent in radio. I felt that old rush again at being a part of a station that was cutting edge, one that was completely tied into the culture of Boston, with an intelligent, tight format that gave the on-air talent latitude to entertain and be creative. All I had to do was deejay—there were no management responsibilities to load me down.

I wasn't the only one who relished the WBCN environment. The creative atmosphere there was loaded with exceptional talent and helped launch many high-profile careers. Two members of Charles Laquidara's "Big Mattress" morning show crew, Billy West and Eddie Gorodetsky, went on to Hollywood fame and success. West became the voice of Ren and Stimpy, Bugs Bunny, Elmer Fudd, as well as a number of the characters on *Futurama*. He was also a cast member on *The Howard Stern Show*. Gorodetsky's career as a producer and writer has been just as impressive. He's worked as a writer and producer on TV hits like *Big Bang Theory*, *The Fresh Prince of Bel Air*, and *Saturday Night Live*, as well as executive producer on *Two and a Half Men*. He's been nominated for six Emmy Awards and won one. It is possible they never would have developed their talents without working years in the WBCN creative culture alongside the brilliant morning host, Charles Laquidara.

When I started working at WBCN, one of the things that began to bother me was that it had an unfocused public image and no clear statement that said exactly what it did or what it stood for. Its slogan at the time was "360 Degrees of Rock and Roll." To me that said "we play anything," which is the same as having no position at all. What the station needed was something that reflected its great rock heritage and its mainline connection to Boston's music, culture, and vibe.

"I don't know what the hell that means," I kept telling Oedipus. "Does it mean you'll play anything? That's the old image we're trying to get away from. We need something simpler and more direct, a slogan that connects the station to the city and says what it stands for." This thought challenged me and for weeks kept rolling around in my head.

Then it came to me, a double entendre: "WBCN, The Rock of Boston."

"It says exactly what the station is all about," I said. "You hear it and you know what it means. We're the cool, respected rock 'n' roll establishment in Boston radio and we have an important, legendary past." Berardini and Oedipus loved it and started using it almost immediately. It remained the station's tagline for twenty-five years, until WBCN signed off for good in August of 2009.

A few weeks later I realized I had given WBCN and Infinity Broadcasting, its corporate owners, something of great value and I hadn't been compensated for it. So I sent Oedipus an invoice for $10,000 for "creative services related to creation of 'The Rock of Boston.'" Nothing was said for a week. Then coming home one night, I found a large UPS box sitting on my front doorstep. It was from 'BCN. I took it inside and opened it up. Inside was $10,000 of Monopoly money and my invoice marked "PAID."

Part of WBCN's strength, what made it such an institution in Boston, was its commitment to being local. You didn't hear it and think, yeah, this is the same thing they get in Chicago. It oozed Boston. It promoted and sponsored local concerts and put its muscle behind Boston bands it believed in. The "Rock 'n' Roll Rumble" and "River Rave" became popular annual events. On Sunday mornings, newsman Matt Schafer produced and hosted a fantastic program called "The Boston Sunday Review," which went in-depth on a range of different topics, from the AIDS crisis to how to make wine at home and how coffee worked in your blood stream. The show was designed to satisfy the public affairs responsibility of the FCC license, but Schafer did a brilliant job of making it a program people actually wanted to listen to. "Boston Sunday Review" enjoyed top ratings every Sunday morning.

With all this happening, the ratings started to skyrocket. In the fall of '82, the Arbitron radio ratings revealed what many of us already suspected—WBCN had pulled ahead of 'COZ. From there, the station never looked back. Within two years, 'COZ changed its call letters to WZOU and switched its format to Top 40. Then in 1984, Boston's legendary rock station beat everyone! It was finally and for the first time number one, Boston's most listened to radio station, with a 9.3 share of total audience. WBCN had finally realized the hopes that its founder Ray Riepen had dreamed of, doing it in the manner I first expressed to him in 1968, and I felt extremely gratified to have been an important part of that success.

◀

That new success only ramped up the WBCN scene. With morale up, there was even more of an excuse to party. During one legendary incident, Mark Parenteau traded lines of coke with Tom Petty. The story has become urban legend with many versions told, but Mark Parenteau detailed exactly what really happened. It came at a time when radio stations had turntables with four speeds. You could go from 78 to 45 to 33 to 16 RPM, the latter of which was used for playing transcriptions. During Petty's visit, Mark had a dealer string out a long line of coke on the platter, in a circle like a barber pole, then fired up the turntable at 16 RPM. The game was to snort as much coke as you could before you couldn't stand it. Whoever did the most was declared the winner. Tom thought that was the most hilarious thing he had ever seen. Later that year, he wrote Mark a Christmas card telling him he tried to do it again but couldn't find a turntable which had a 16 RPM setting.

As evident by that well-used Starship record, coke was always around. At WBCN we even had our own official dealer, a slender thirty-something friend of Mark's who looked vaguely like an undernourished, bearded John Lennon and went by the name of "Thumper." Mark liked to refer to him as his "high priest and spiritual advisor." He worked as a waiter at Paul's Mall jazz club and rented a room from two young Wiccan women in a creaky old mansion in Brighton off Commonwealth Avenue behind the Massachusetts State Police headquarters. Every week or so, a few of us would head over to his place to get buzzed and hang out.

In the press booth at Gillette Stadium watching an Aerosmith concert. (Left to right) David O'Leary, Nick Lehage, his partner, Aerosmith manager Tim Collins, my pals Joel Sampson and Mark Parenteau.

Thumper was a pack rat. He was very intelligent and studied everything, so every square inch of his room, including the floor, was piled high with magazines, newspapers, electronic toys, and computer parts. It always became an adventure to walk through, let alone find a place to sit where you wouldn't stick to something. In one corner sat this crappy old tube TV that only worked in blue and orange. Thumper always had it on and if I was high I had to check myself to make sure I wasn't losing my mind.

During one memorable visit, Mark, David, and I rolled into Thumper's after a concert and stayed until five in the morning, snorting lines. Our relationship with him was simple: He gave us free coke and we gave him inside access to the famous people who rolled through WBCN. As the night wore on, Thumper got slower and slower with his generosity. Every time he made a move that we thought was to lay out more lines of coke, he wheeled back around to go into some dissertation on one of his pet theories, like how frosted light bulbs are good for you, or his vegetarian prejudice against eating "dead animals." (Mark once remarked, "Why not? They'd eat you.") It was getting late, and I glared at Mark, who rolled his eyes as he sat on the floor, with his knees pulled to his chest. At one point Thumper, started looking around, as if he was going to grab his Deering grinder with the coke in it. A rush ran though us in anticipation. But no, Thumper simply reached down on the floor to pick up the pizza box where he had some pot, to separate the seeds. Mark jumped to his feet angrily. "Come on, Thumper!" he yelled. "Put out some more lines. After all, I got you the 'BCN account!" I fell over laughing. Only Mark. But hell, it worked. We were back in business a minute later.

I knew, though, that kind of thing couldn't continue. If I wanted to achieve anything, or at least stay sane, coke could not continue to be a part of my life.

Food, drugs, booze—it's not hard to develop cravings and become dependent on them. Before he quit, my old friend Tim Collins, who managed and successfully recycled Aerosmith, once told me that he didn't think he was addicted to coke because he didn't shoot up with a needle. But of course he was only fooling himself. Once he found himself doing an eight-ball a day he knew he had a problem. He eventually quit and then got all the Aerosmith guys into rehab. He ended up saving their lives and reviving their careers.

In 1985, I quit cold turkey. They say that to quit doing drugs you have to get away from the people, places, and things that remind you of them. But temptation is everywhere. Just a few months after I quit, I was hanging out at my house when I received an unexpected visit from a friend of mine, a Massachusetts judge, and a young Harvard student he knew named Daniel. They had been at an event at Harvard University drinking lots of wine, were half "in the bag," and wanted to go flying. Out of the blue we decided to fly to my house on Nantucket for the night. It was pushing nine when we piled into my twin-engine Piper Geronimo. Flying under starlight, we made the forty-five-minute flight to the island for a late-night dinner in the bar at the Jared Coffin House. After we arrived and settled down at my waterfront house, the judge asked Daniel to show me a small foil packet from his pocket.

"Look what I have," he said, revealing two large pink rocks of coke.

The judge didn't hide his excitement. "Oh, yes," he said, looking at us both with a big smile. "Let the night begin."

I stared at the packet with a blank expression. Here is my test, I thought. I knew that if I did even a taste of the stuff that night, I'd be back in. "You guys enjoy yourselves," I said. "I'm having a nice Scotch!"

"More for us," said the judge, still smiling.

By 2 a.m., the two of them were babbling like baboons. I had to call it quits and went to bed. The next morning, I got up around eight and they hadn't moved an inch. Daniel and the judge were both still sitting there looking like crap, quacking away like a couple of insane people. I was so happy I'd made the decision to quit and had the strength to stay clean. 🔇

John Garabedian

22. Begin Again
Knife Party, 2015

The WGTF transmitter room was the airport manager's former office in the Nantucket Airport Tower Building. The adjoining room was the studio where Martha Walters recorded her daily local news segments.

After walking away from WGTR in 1981, I wasn't sure how life was going to unfold. It was a total gamble. I'd given up ownership of something that still had significant value for the ownership of a little, unprofitable FM station on Nantucket Island, and a construction permit from the FCC that permitted me to build a new Boston TV station. It was thrilling and terrifying. The stakes couldn't have been any more real. If these two ventures didn't launch, if I couldn't make them successful, I ran the risk of losing everything I had—my home in Southborough, which was collateral for the loan to take the Nantucket FM to 50,000 watts, my airplanes, my place in Vermont. I'd put everything on the line.

I was almost forty years old and rebooting my life. My dad, who'd spent almost his entire career with the same company, just shook his head. "You really sure you know what you're doing?" he kept asking me. I wasn't. I just knew I couldn't continue with the way things were.

But more than running away from something, this was really about what I was running toward. One of the exciting parts about building WGTR had been assembling the station's team; putting together a roster of talent and playing coach—making assignments, developing strategy. I loved being able to lead like that, developing results, and enjoying the reward of seeing how it all came together.

With Nantucket, though, there was only David and me. I relished that challenge. I didn't have to worry about investors or a lot of overhead. If we wanted to take it to a country format, we could. If we wanted to make it a 50,000-watt monster to blast all of Cape Cod, I just had to make sure the numbers worked and execute well. I was back to building something, not simply managing it as a caretaker.

Our home in Southborough became station headquarters. Everything was run out of there. On an early DEC Robin computer I pounded out spreadsheets

John Garabedian

Nantucket Memorial Airport. We mounted the WGTF antenna on an abandoned radar platform and located the studios in a two room office in the FAA tower. The rent was $135, which included the transmitter electricity, which we figured cost the town of Nantucket over $300 a month.

and sales projections, and David handled the program logs, commercial production, payables, payroll, and billing. If the transmitter went down or I needed to be on the island for a sales meeting, I hopped into my little Taylorcraft F-19 and flew from Marlborough Airport to Nantucket. I was working harder than I had in years, but I felt lighter, happier. We'd often work 'til midnight and then collapse in bed, exhausted and bleary-eyed, then wake up at seven or eight the next morning, ready to jump right back into things.

David didn't begin working with me on the Nantucket station right away. After I left WGTR, he stayed with Kris for another few months, and if I had any reason to doubt my reasons for bolting the station, I only had to observe his demeanor every time he headed off to work. At WGTR, we had initially hired David as a commercial producer and after I left, Kris promoted him to program director. David is usually always positive and upbeat, but in his own polite way he frequently let on that working for Kris was a living hell.

"I just don't understand what Kris is doing," he often said. "Without you there, the place just seems rudderless. There's no direction. Morale is tanking."

Then, early one Saturday afternoon, David came into my office. His face looked puzzled, like he'd spent the entire morning thinking about something. "I need to talk to you," he said, taking a seat.

I pushed the papers on my desk to the side and gave him my full attention. "Sure," I said, a little nervously. "What's up?"

David took in a long breath. "I can't work for Kris anymore. It's not the same place without you there." David isn't a quitter and I could tell by his slumping demeanor he'd beat himself up pretty good for not being able to make the situation work.

"What do you think you want to do?" I asked.

In the driveway in Southborough. David O'Leary and his '68 Chevrolet convertible with the radiator leak. Rushing off at 5:15 AM to his first radio job signing on WJMQ (AM) in Norfolk, the radiator ran dry and the engine seized. He hitchhiked the last mile to the station and still got on the air on time.

David looked me in the eye. It was obvious he'd already thought about that as well. "I want to work for you," he said. "I see what you're doing with the Nantucket station and I want to be a part of it."

I smiled. David always had impeccable timing. The truth is I had already thought about bringing him aboard. But I didn't want to put us in a "boss-worker" relationship for fear it could upset our incredibly perfect personal relationship. But as things with the station had progressed, I was feeling stretched for time. I needed someone to manage the day-to-day operations so I could concentrate on bigger picture things like implementing the power increase, getting more involved with our sales operation, and developing the TV license. David was only twenty-two years old, but I trusted him completely, had total confidence in his judgment, intelligence, and work ethic. I knew he would be great at running the day-to-day operations of the station.

John Garabedian

David entering music data into the DEC VT-78 mini-computer. It enabled us to totally automate WGTR, including traffic and billing. That little 1978 computer only had 16k of memory, with 8k reserved for the operating system. Data was stored on four very noisy 8" floppy drives.

"I have actually been thinking I need help," I said. David's eyes brightened. "But I can't pay you what Kris does. What I can do is give you a piece of the station. If things work out, you'll come out way ahead. But there's no guarantee."

David wasn't bothered by it at all. "That's fine with me," he said, with a laugh. "I could care less about the money."

Over the next several years, David and I worked as closely as any couple could. We added a second desk to the home office in Southborough, bought another computer, and every morning, after coffee, we walked down the hall from the kitchen and got to work. It was honestly one of the most delightful stretches of my life. There was none of the drama or high stakes emotions that had accompanied my earlier relationships with Joe or Tommy. Life with David was easy, warm. We understood each other so well. He could stand up to me if he disagreed with something, and backed off when he knew I needed space. He was responsible, open and honest, and had street-smarts and ethics.

There was something else that brightened up my life, too. Nantucket restored my confidence. I'd been rattled by how things had ended in Natick. I couldn't figure out where the blame lay. Was it all my fault? Was Kris right? That I really was incompetent to run WGTR? With the Nantucket station I saw a business opportunity, but it was also a personal test. I needed to make this work, to know that I could again build something that was successful and fun.

Nantucket proved redemptive. Each month brought a little more success. Sales climbed and the eventual power increase to 50,000 watts enabled us to blanket Cape Cod, which had thirty times the population of Nantucket. David and I were more than behind-the-scenes forces. We did many live broadcasts of major Nantucket social events, which made us visible and helped build sales by showing we were a part of the Nantucket community. One of the most fun events was the Nantucket Christmas Stroll, a holiday weekend that the local stores had launched to lure summer people and visitors back to the island after the summer season. We'd fly down Friday, then early on Saturday broadcast live from the heart of downtown. Between songs we'd interview shoppers, put store owners on the air, and stick a microphone in Santa's face soon after he arrived by Coast Guard boat to a throng of little kids.

David O'Leary giving a tour of WGTF and the transmitter room of our tiny two-room headquarters in the FAA Tower Building at Nantucket Memorial Airport.

One year, a Nor'easter slammed Nantucket, bringing it to a total standstill. There was no leaving the island and even more alarming, there were no available hotel rooms. That night David and I ended up sleeping on a foldout couch in the little WGTF transmitter shack by the FAA tower in Madaket. We lay there listening to the wind howling as it blew against the 350-foot tower. It was a really magical experience.

Nantucket high school football games were another big thing. To cover them, we hired a former coach, a square-jawed guy named Vito who had never used a microphone in his life. No matter how many times you went over how the equipment worked, he never got it. Without fail, Vito would call up nearly every Saturday morning in the fall to go on about how the "machine seems broken." That meant that David or I would have to immediately make the 120-mile trip just to turn on some switch. This is how you do it, Vito. Flip this right here. He'd nod confidently, but a week later he'd call us up again.

It was easy stuff to grumble about in the moment, but dealing with an absent-minded ex-football coach or navigating a mass of holiday shoppers was all

John Garabedian

so much more preferable to staring down shrinking cash or dealing with anxious business partners.

As the calendar turned to 1984, my attention began to focus on doing something with the TV license, which stood to expire in a year if nothing were done with it. Thus it was time to cash out and sell the Nantucket station. The deal had come together quickly. I put the station on the market in March, and four months later, on a Friday afternoon, David and I were in a twentieth floor Bank of Boston conference room on Federal Street in downtown Boston signing WGTF-FM over to a group of Cape Cod businessman for over a million dollars.

After the closing we walked out of the office building with a huge cashier's check in hand and stepped into the late afternoon sun that splashed down on the Boston sidewalks. I felt so light and free. "Not a bad way to end the week, huh?" I said to David, putting my arm around him.

Other feelings rose to the surface, too. As David and I walked back to the car, thoughts of my mother came to mind. Her faith in me had never wavered. Even during the darkest periods of the whole WGTR experience, she did what any great mother does, and saw me as a success. "My Johnny." That little phrase, still bursting with pride, continued to fall out of her mouth. I didn't confide in her a lot, but she could tell when I was struggling and her unconditional love always made me feel there were plenty of great possibilities ahead. She didn't always understand why I did things, but she could appreciate my restlessness, my need to always keep moving, my urges to try something new. She was the same way. At the age of seventy she enrolled at the Museum School at the Boston Museum of Fine Arts for sculpture and earned her Bachelor of Arts degree.

I know she would have been proud of how things had developed with the Nantucket station. She would have loved hearing what I built and would have beamed when I told her about our big payday. But she never lived to see us sell it.

One morning in September, 1981, at 7 a.m. I woke to the phone ringing. It was my sister Doris.

"Hello, dear," she said, somberly. "We just had to take mother by ambulance to the hospital and it doesn't look good."

I sat up straight. "Doesn't look good?" I said, "What does that mean?"

The day before, she had complained of a pain on her left side, near her stomach. "Probably just a muscle strain," she kept saying and with her usual determination pushed forward and cleaned the house. The next morning she woke up coughing, asked my dad to get her a Tylenol, and then passed out. My father called the ambulance and a while later she was pronounced dead at Woburn Hospital at the age of seventy-nine.

It was such a strange time for our family, for me especially. She'd been a singular energetic force of love, hope, optimism, and confidence for our entire family. I'd never imagined life without her, and then, suddenly, she was gone.

My mother had always said that she didn't want an open casket funeral. "I don't want people gawking at me," she said. "I don't want them looking at me lying there with all that cheap make-up plastered on."

We honored that wish. But two days before the funeral, Doris and Jackie arranged a final private viewing for the family at the Bedrosian Funeral Home in Watertown. David, whom she called "my second son," asked to go, and on the evening of the viewing we made our way to the funeral home to say our goodbyes. We were led into a large, empty, wide-open room normally used for wakes. It was cold and a bit clammy—and in the back was the open casket where my mother lay. I stopped in the doorway, unsure of what to expect, or how I'd feel.

David gently put his hand on my shoulder and together we slowly walked forward, my eyes fixed on the coffin as we crossed the long room. There was no denying her death any longer. When we finally reached the casket I peered at the face I knew so well. I looked at her and blinked away a few tears. David put his arm around me. I shook my head and took a deep breath. I turned to David. "She's not there," I said to him. "That's her body, but she's not in it." He nodded his head, understanding what I meant.

It wasn't easy to articulate. What I saw was my mother's body, but not her. The spirit and aura, the person, was completely gone and we were looking at this empty vessel. The woman I'd known, my mother, with her radiant personality, was completely missing. I'd never encountered that before. I'm not sure what

John Garabedian

My mother was an unforgettable character and impossible not to love. Even in her late seventies, we never knew what her real hair color was because she always colored it. She used to say, "I'd die for my children," and we all knew she really meant it.

happens after death, but what I was looking at that evening was not my mother. It was only her body. She was gone. It was really strange.

My good friend Arnie Ginsburg described it perfectly when I first told him about my mother's death a few days later.

"The hardest part is that you want to call them up and tell them something, and you can't," he said.

My father died fourteen years later at age ninety-four. I didn't feel the same loss, and I think a lot of it was that my mother's death had prepared for me what it was like to lose a parent. And he had lived as long a life as anyone could wish for and in great health. But I was also closer to her. She had always believed in me and encouraged my full-throttle approach to life. Everything is possible. Do what you love and do it without fear, and always do the right thing—it was a message she delivered and ingrained in all three of her children. 🔇

John Garabedian

23. Road Runner

Modern Lovers, 1977

The first anniversary poster for V-66. There wasn't a second anniversary. *Photo by Leo Gozbekian.*

In 1983, in the midst of building up the Nantucket FM station and being John "Gara-BCN" on the radio in Boston, I started thinking more seriously about how to develop my television license. The clock was ticking. I needed to do something with it by 1985 or it would revert back to the FCC.

So the search began for programming, something that could grab an audience and make money in a top six television market like Boston. I talked to many people and attended NATPE, the National Association of Television Programming Executives annual TV programming convention, where I searched for content. It was bad news. Absolutely nothing was available in the Boston television market. Virtually every old rerun, movie package, and syndicated programming series was locked exclusively up by the other eight Boston television stations. And there were no networks available. Here I was with a license to build a 3.8 million-watt television station in the sixth-largest TV market in the country, but with no programming available it was worthless. It was a serious crisis.

I've never enjoyed gambling. It always seemed like a dumb and expensive waste of time. What was the point of spending hours casting your fate to chance with no control over the outcome, and with microscopic odds of winning? Programming radio or TV is a much greater challenge that takes skill. It is like a sport. You have to plan your approach, hone your skills, and use every ounce of experience to execute and achieve the winning goal. But like gambling, it often costs a lot of money, the outcomes are uncertain, and it involves making decisions based on the amount of risk one can stomach. That's what I was up against with my TV license. If there was no conventional programming to be bought, then the only solution was to create new programming.

For two years, the music industry had been abuzz by its newest broadcast jewel, MTV. With its twenty-four-hour music programming, the network had upended how music artists and record companies could reach consumers. It was powerful and smart.

And I wasn't a fan.

I thought MTV was a great idea with terrible execution. While watching your favorite hit songs in music videos was exciting, MTV came across like all the bad radio stations I'd worked at and listened to over the years. It was blatantly obvious it was not produced by experienced television people, but by unimaginative radio people with no talent for showmanship or visual entertainment. MTV was dumbed down, with no personality, no culture, no fun.

It wasn't live. You had no idea where it came from. There was no sense of place. Where was it shot? Was it New Jersey? Idaho? The moon? The VJs didn't help. They came on after a couple of songs, babbled something inane about the video that had just aired, then introduced the next one. This was the age of Michael Jackson's iconic "Thriller," so the videos were certainly cutting-edge, but there was nothing sticky MTV did that made the video environment come alive. MTV in its early years looked like it had a charisma bypass.

MTV was the creation of Time-Warner president Steve Ross, who not only ran Warner Brothers Records but also ran Warner Cable, a major cable television system. As an incentive to lure people to sign up for cable TV, Warner needed exclusive channels not offered by over-the-air TV stations. At the time the only cable channels were CNN, TBS, and HBO. To lure more cable subscribers, Ross launched MTV, then VH-1 and Nickelodeon.

I loved the music video concept. It was really a TV channel targeting the hard-to-reach under-thirty viewer. For years, bands as far back as the Beatles, Bob Dylan, and Elvis Presley had made short films to support their singles. But they never found a regular outlet to showcase these mini-films. The singular brilliance of MTV was that it finally gave a 24/7 home to this content. They didn't have to go out and commission these videos to be done. They didn't cost MTV any money. They were already made and the record companies were only too happy to hand them over to promote the sale of records. The bands got promoted, the single got a boost in exposure and sales, and MTV had all this free programming to air.

Cable, however, was still in its infancy. Even in cities like Boston, New York, or Chicago, cable penetration topped out at less than thirty percent. Viewers may have wanted their MTV, but less than a third of them were actually getting it. Meanwhile, over the air, channels were still king. The more I thought about it, and the more I realized we had a rich college and nightlife culture flourishing in the Boston market, the more I began to wonder if a local music television station might be our programming content solution.

Part of what intrigued me about creating a Boston music video station was the city's music scene itself. By the mid-1980s, Boston had come into its own as one of the best music scenes in the country. There was WBCN tying it together of course, but the club scene was also thriving while the airwaves were dominated by major groups with Boston roots like The Cars, Aerosmith, J. Geils, and Boston. These weren't one-hit wonders, they were groups who produced a steady stream of big national hits and gold records and had huge local fan bases.

My idea was to draw on all this incredible music and culture that was being generated in Boston, then package the content in a hot new television station that had an embedded local flavor. We'd have local VJs, local music, and events, and regularly broadcast from local Boston venues. There'd be viewer participation and a strong focus on locally made videos. Sure, we'd surround it with the big Michael Jackson productions, but mixed into the flow would be up-and-coming groups like Extreme or Modern Lovers. We'd bring the charisma of WBCN or even the early interactive excitement of WORC to the TV screen. And unlike MTV, which was limited by its meager thirty percent market penetration, we'd be doing it over the free, open air waves to anyone in Boston with a television set.

In late '83, I sat at my primitive DEC Robin computer in my home office in Southborough and buried myself in spreadsheets. I brought everything into focus—the transmitter, the antenna, building space, studio equipment, advertising, sales, promotion, and working capital. Then there were the major people costs to factor in—the producers, technicians, salespeople, office support crew, business and accounting people, VJs and engineers. When I was done crunching the numbers, I landed on a sobering figure: $10 million dollars of capital would be required. It felt like a hell of a mountain to try to scale.

How was I going to raise that kind of money? David and I were running a little FM station on Nantucket, an island of five thousand people. How could I get investors to gamble millions of dollars and bet on a guy who had never even worked at a TV station, let alone run one?

I needed a credible team. Actually, I realized I needed one unique person in particular: a guy who had the credibility, knowledge, and connections to help me put this whole deal together.

That night I picked up the phone and gave a call to Arnie Ginsburg.

"A television station, huh?" said Arnie, his voice raising a bit with excitement.

"Not just a television station," I told Arnie. "A music video station. Think MTV but better. One designed exclusively around Boston's pop culture market." Then after going through the hot points and answering some tough questions, I honestly laid it down. "Arnie, I can't really do this without you."

My offer was simple. Ten percent of the company with no investment. Arnie took a couple of days to think about the deal, but I suspected he'd come aboard. Although Arnie likes a new challenge and loves Boston, he's not a risk taker. Since that first encounter at the old 'BOS studios all those years ago, we had become friends and stayed in touch. I'd visit him many times at his Ogunquit, Maine, waterfront home, and pick his brain about the radio business and current trends. He was still known in Boston as "Woo Woo," but it had been years since the Night Train had dominated the airwaves. In fact, it had been some time since Arnie had been on the air.

After the debacle with Mac Richmond and his departure from WMEX in '68, Arnie had moved into station management. By the early 1970s, WBCN had named him general manager. Following that, he joined Richie Balsbaugh as a major investor in Pyramid Broadcasting Company to found Boston's now-heritage Top 40 station KISS 108. Arnie became senior vice president.

That whole Woo-Woo thing dogged Arnie a bit because it was *the* thing that people thought of when his name got mentioned. Like it was the only thing he'd done. People really loved him. But his talents went far beyond knowing how to play the kazoo. Arnie was extremely analytical and as smart a businessman as I've ever known. Arnie didn't just have on-air cred, his name carried weight with the money people, too.

One of the people Arnie thought we should meet with was Kenny O'Keefe, former head of the broadcast lending department of State Street Bank, who'd come over to Pyramid as its chief financial officer. Kenny had a friend in New York who'd just closed a private partnership investment of $8 million to build a brand new UHF TV station in New Orleans.

"They used Kidder-Peabody, a Wall Street investment bank to pull together the deal," Kenny said. "We should set up a meeting to see if they'd be interested in what you guys want to build."

Kenny lined up the meeting and on a cool spring morning in '84, the three of us hopped in my twin-engine Piper Geronimo—the one extravagant gift I'd allowed myself to buy after we sold the Nantucket station—and flew to New York City. Kenny had been dead-on with his timing. Wall Street was in love with MTV. It was hot, it was making money, and Kidder thought investors would find it a sexy investment. After months of due diligence and two dozen trips to the firm's Wall Street headquarters, Kidder-Peabody agreed to underwrite the deal for $10.5 million.

With the investment bank commitment behind us, Arnie and I took to the road. Traveling with David Hunter, Kidder's sales manager, and senior VP Mike Anderson, we flew all over the country to meet the brokers who would sell shares of the new Channel 66. Our pitch was straightforward—for seventy-five grand per unit, they could get 140 people in on the ground floor as limited partners in the next big thing in television. "Thirty years ago people were advised to invest in steel mills and railroads," David told them. "Today those things are all bankrupt. This," he'd add, tapping the table, "is the wave of the future." By the early fall of '84, we had the 140 units sold.

As Kidder lined up the investment capital, Arnie and I got to work on building the station we planned to call V66. There were dozens of large details, like construction of the 1,450-foot tower in Hudson that would transmit a 3.8-million watt signal, making us the most powerful TV station in Boston. In Framingham, we found a stunning, brand new office building next to the Massachusetts Turn-

Upstairs at the Metro nightclub (now House of Blues) for one of several V-66 launch parties. Here I am with Arnie Ginsburg, left, and KISS 108 CEO Richie Balsbaugh, center.

pike entrance designed by renowned architect Robert A.M. Stern. There we leased sixteen thousand square feet on the top floor for studios and offices, which we had to design and build before the end of the year. Then there were thousands of smaller decisions, like wall colors and carpet choices and furniture. I couldn't avoid having a hand in all of it.

Staffing was the most essential part of building a successful operation. There were many reasons for V66's rapid, early success, but the people we brought in for management and talent were absolutely critical to achieve it. Business affairs and budgets needed to be skillfully watched, the sales people had to develop the revenues, while the program and production crews had to give the station its vibe.

We really lucked out. The two most important hires were David Beadle, director of programming, and business manager Merril Buchhalter. Arnie found David through an ad we placed in *Broadcasting* magazine. David had a TV news background but had also created and produced a daily music video show in Atlanta. David admitted he wasn't the embodiment of cool—he looked more like a college professor than someone involved in music television—but he was intelligent and knew exactly how to manage program and production departments, find and hire great talent, and manage, develop, and direct them to do their best work.

Merril Buchhalter was someone to whom I'd known for over fifteen years. We'd first crossed paths in 1969 at WBCN when Ray Riepen moved her over from *The Phoenix* newspaper to take over and fix WBCN's dismal accounting department. It had been under the direction of an older hippie woman who reeked of pot and lived in a Winnebago parked outside the station on Stuart Street. Merrill got the books in order and became one of the steady behind-the-scenes faces at WBCN. By the early 1980s, the station's new owner,

Infinity Broadcasting Company, had named Merril business manager of the entire company and put her in charge of accounting for its national group of stations. But the grind of working for Infinity and its demanding boss, Mel Karmazin (Mark Parenteau nicknamed him "Meligula," after Caligula, the ruthless Roman emperor), eventually got to her and after three dinner meetings when I offered her the chance to join us at V66 as CFO and business manager, she leapt at it.

Chief Financial Officer Merril Leferman (nee Buchhalter) at the V-66 closing just after we sold the TV station to the Home Shopping Network. She's smiling because our investors ended up making a 155% return on their investment in under two years.

The position of music director was a critical hire. We needed someone with personal connections to all the top-level record label executives and artist managers. Those relationships were crucial when it came to acquiring the videos and booking appearances by major artists. We found our person in Roxy Myzal, a woman who had spent her entire career working closely with record labels and artist management. At the time we found her, she was the music director at WXLO, New York, at one point America's most listened-to radio station. Roxy programmed the V66 video rotations so that they featured a majority of big-name acts, but with a proper flavor of new, up-and-coming musicians, and outstanding local artists. She also ended up hosting two popular programs—a music news update we called *The Roxy Report* and our *New Music Show*.

Then we had to find the VJs, and that was hard. When I had first started thinking about who we'd bring aboard, I assumed we might grab some of Boston's most well-known radio personalities. They had name recognition, were experts at talking about music, and had knowledge of the local area. But most of them were simply awful in the auditions. The things that work in radio—an exaggerated, high-energy way of speaking and the over-emoting—all comes across as completely fake on TV. They were out of their comfort zone. Plus,

John Garabedian

most didn't have the looks for TV. Viewers prefer to look at attractive, stylish-looking people who represent the look of the times, not fat, fifty-year-olds with mullets.

After an extensive search and dozens of auditions, we went with a lineup of mainly young, unknown talent. Perry Stone came from WAPL in New York; Mary Jo Kurtz was a street reporter for a Harrisburg, Pennsylvania, television station; Bill Stephens was the former morning host at Magic 106.7 in Boston and TV weatherman on Cape Cod; and Ian O'Malley came to us from Anchorage, Alaska, where he was hosting a video music TV show.

Then there was David O'Leary. His hire caused some consternation. He was, after all, my boyfriend, and that seemed to threaten David Beadle. Even though Arnie and I were involved in approving the finalists, we'd left the selection of VJs to Beadle. It was his terrain—but when he started coming up with reasons for why he didn't think David O'Leary would work out, I challenged him.

"He's got more name recognition in Boston than anyone else we've hired," I told Beadle. "He's really good-looking, he's been on WAAF and WBCN for four years, and he's got the right personality for the station. He's funny and entertaining, doesn't take himself too seriously, knows music, and people warm up to him. And did I mention that he's really good-looking?"

Beadle tried to dig in his heels a bit more, but after David prepared a new audition tape on his own, which did impress him, Beadle eventually relented. Later, when we polled viewers for their favorite VJs, Mary Jo and David O'Leary consistently came out on top.

Finally, in early February of 1985, we were ready to go on air. Or, at least it looked that way. The transmitter was still being tweaked on the night of February 10, the day before our scheduled live debut. The night before Arnie, David Beadle, and I went out for a late dinner in Framingham. For a few guys gearing up to launch something big, we certainly didn't look like we had something to celebrate. I'd ordered chicken marsala, but hardly touched it. I was overtired and stressed.

"We're supposed to be on the air tomorrow," I said. "Tomorrow! Is that going to even be possible?"

The master control room at V-66 just prior to launch. (Left to right) Arnie Ginsburg, program director David Beadle, sales manager Bill Wayland, and myself.

Arnie shrugged his shoulders. "We don't have a choice," he said. "We've already got Channel 4 lined up to come out and do a live shot from the station. We have to be on the air by the afternoon."

In his jaunty manner, David Beadle looked up. "Well, if we have to be live by the afternoon, we might as well go on at six in the morning because we are going to need all the practice we can get."

I let out a big laugh. "OK!"

That next morning, at exactly six, Bill Stephens welcomed whatever sunrise viewers we had to the new station. "We're on *television*," he said, sounding almost surprised. "Good morning." Next he fired up V66's first video, the Steve Miller Band's "Abracadabra." I watched in awe as this new station that we had jammed together in under two short years officially took off. "Round and round and round it goes," Miller sang. "Where it stops nobody knows."

From the moment V66 hit the air, there was an immediate buzz about it. People knew MTV, but they'd never seen anything like V66. The VJs didn't

John Garabedian

just introduce songs, they ran the show. They sat behind a desk and ran all the controls, even switching on the videos. We didn't hide that. Viewers actually saw them doing this stuff. Part of it was economics—it cut down on operations cost—but the main reason was it also gave the station a personality; it showed that our VJs weren't just plastic talking heads like the MTV personalities.

For two radio guys like Arnie and me, designing a complex television studio operation was way beyond our experience or expertise. We had hardly spent any time in a TV station, let alone run one. Fortunately, we were lucky to have my friend Peter Fasciano and his company, Vizwiz, as our consultants. Pete was a real genius who would later go on to create the original design for the Avid video editing system, now used to produce nearly every major film and television show.

Technically, Pete helped us become possibly the most advanced TV production facility in America at that time. Everything was completely automated and executed using a "La-Kart" playback system and custom software on an early Apple II with two floppy disc drives. The automation software controlled the camera shots, switching, video playback machines, and special effects.

Still, the launch had a certain number of growing pains. At one point, I remember David O'Leary coming on without any sound. The camera faded and his mike became hot. He had no idea. He was gabbing about something to one of the production assistants while Van Halen's "Hot For Teacher" video went out over the air. It was just loud enough that he seemed to be doing a duet with David Lee Roth.

I got on the phone and called down to the studio. "David, you know your mike is on right now?" I said.

"Nooooo," he said, nervously. He said something else to the PA, then fell silent. It was followed by an apologetic, "Oh."

Another time, David was on-air and behind him was this large fake wall that had a collage of band posters on it. They were all stuck together in this giant mass. But somebody didn't use enough adhesive spray to stick them. Just as David started to introduce Duran Duran's "A View to a Kill" the thing started to peel off from the top and roll down on top of him like a giant blanket. It was hilarious. David tried to fend the thing off, but it was useless. The posters consumed him and he just started laughing, as did everyone else in the studio. This is the kind of thing that made V66 stand out. Years before Facebook and Twitter, we generated a major street buzz that quickly spread and built unimaginable appeal and mystique.

The fact that we didn't take ourselves too seriously, that we were able to laugh off those on-camera flubs, was in part because many of us had come from the kind of radio where loosey-goosey entertainment was encouraged. Arnie, David, Roxie, Perry, Bill, Ian, myself—we'd all spent our careers in the radio business. The VJs didn't rely on a teleprompter to march them from one intro to the next. It was live as live could be. They knew how to ad-lib and roll with whatever was presented to them to sound cool and bring excitement to the programming. What universally came across was an attitude of "fun."

Our radio backgrounds impacted the station in other ways, too. We took actual viewer requests and tabulated which ones were the most popular. In "Video Wars," a local band like Lizzie Borden and the Axes squared off with "Shout" by Tears for Fears. After the videos played, viewers were told to call in and vote. Many times the underdog beat out a big-name artist, which helped create a passion for the videos and the channel.

Not every important new video we *wanted* to play, however, could get aired on V66. MTV was now three years old and the idea of new local music video TV stations threatened them. They were afraid and they had the power to flex their national muscle and lock up exclusive rights to important releases. It became an ongoing battle and we had to develop creative ways to work around the MTV monopoly. When Prince, one of the hottest artists of the time, released "Raspberry Beret," we soon discovered that MTV had a ninety-day exclusive lock on it. Rather than wait three months to broadcast the video, I instructed our production director to produce a V66 version of the video in our studio. The result was outstanding. Then we did it with Starship's now-classic, "We Built This City," which we made around the concept of Boston's rock 'n' roll history. It became our most requested video.

In 1985, Dire Straits released the single "Money For Nothing" from its album, *Brothers in Arms*. The song became a monster hit, and the cool cutting-edge cartoon animation made it one of the era's landmark videos. Time-Warner owned MTV, and the song and video were released by its sister Warner Brothers record

Live on V-66 in the main studio with Kenny Loggins, right.

company. "Money for Nothing" quickly became our most popular request, but we couldn't play it. Frustrated, Roxy had enough and hit the phones, eventually making contact with the band's manager. He was pissed that his expensive video was being held back from getting full exposure and he told Roxy, "Screw the label. Tell them I told you to air it."

Within twenty-four hours of our first play of the video, Roxy received a call from a rep at Warner Brothers. MTV was irate. "I don't know what you did, but you just started World War III," he told Roxy. She didn't buckle. We just stripped out the video's MTV logo and continued to play it. When singer Mark Knopfler sang "I want my MTV," we substituted the singing with, "I watch it on the 'V.'"

We also discovered some great videos and songs that MTV stupidly rejected. In the spring of 1985, we received a new video for a song called "Take on Me" by an unknown Norwegian band called a-ha. It had yet to receive a minute of air time and radio had also passed on the song. Roxy called me into her office. "John, take a look at this," she said firing up the video. "It's really cute and the song has a great hook."

It was outstanding! As I watched, I fell in love with the characters, the production, and the tune. It combined live action with animation, and packed this endearing story line about a guy trying to win the heart of this girl. We'd never seen anything like it. We put it on the air that day. Immediately viewers reacted to it and it became our most requested video. Not long after, KISS 108 in Boston added it to its music rotation, with hundreds of radio stations across the nation quickly following. Weeks later, MTV woke up and started playing it. The final kicker came at the 1986 MTV Video Music Awards when "Take on Me" won six Moonmen.

V-66 billboards were everywhere around Greater Boston.

Probably our biggest coup for legitimacy as a station came in the summer of 1985, when we secured broadcast rights to air a continuous broadcast of Live Aid. Other local stations showed excerpts, but we aired every hour of the event live all weekend from both London and Philadelphia. We even ran a contest and sent viewers to the Philly performance to see the show and meet The Cars and other performers. It was one of our highest rated broadcasts.

Six months after V66 launched, we were reaching nearly two million homes, which was close to ninety percent of the Boston market. The station had a huge, enthusiastic following of fans. So did the VJs. David O'Leary and Mary Jo became superstars. They'd show up at an event and people would scream out their names.

At first the recognition was fun. But eventually it became annoying. When David O'Leary and I went out to dinner, strangers would inevitably walk up to our table to start a conversation. Unlike me, David was always completely gracious. He would ask them their name and where they were from. Then I would quickly say, "Thanks for coming over" to give them a clue to go away.

But the recognition was a mark of success, and the whole thing was magical. Arnie, David Beadle, and the whole staff were in awe of what the station had become, the excitement it had generated. Too bad that time was not on our side.

In the spring of '86, Roxy reported that someone had stolen money from her pocketbook. As she usually did, she left it on the floor in the music office

Radio programming guru Rick Sklar, taken in 1979, in the ABC Superadio studio in New York. When ABC management realized it would take five years to become profitable, the entire project was scuttled, costing millions to buy out the high-priced long-term talent contracts.

next to her desk and after stepping away for a minute, came back to find that somebody had gone through her wallet. Arnie, David Beadle, Roxy, and I had a meeting in Arnie's office to discuss it. We all suspected one of the interns, but without any clear evidence we couldn't point the finger. I was pissed, not just because somebody had stolen cash from sweet Roxy, but that we were even dealing with this kind of negativity in our organization. I hated this kind of stuff.

After Roxy and David left, I slumped further in my chair. "You know, Arnie, honest to God," I said. "We might as well be running a shoe factory. We don't get to do the fun things. All we do is manage budgets and problems."

Life at work had become administrative and repetitive. Day after day I was mostly dealing with budget pressures, looking at sales figures, and contending with personnel problems. With nearly one hundred employees, it was non-stop. It was all made worse by the fact that the sales numbers were not coming in where we had forecast them. Television revenues are dependent on ratings. A typical Boston UHF station pulled in a four or five viewer share, which generated millions in advertising sales. We were being viewed by a couple million people a week, yet our share of audience never rose above a three. We were stumped.

Rick Sklar, our media consultant, suggested we do perceptual market research to determine what people's attitudes and viewing habits were, and how they used V66. We hired one of the leading media researchers in the world, John Parikhal from Joint Communications in Toronto (plenty of jokes about *that* name). Night after night, we sat behind a double-blind mirror watching and listening as a moderator led groups of heavy television viewers in the twenty-to-thirty-year-old age group through questions about what they watched, how often they watched, and what they especially liked on TV. When it got to V66, the moderator probed deeply.

After listening to dozens of people, we discovered the root cause of our problem: It was the videos themselves. The problem lay with "time-

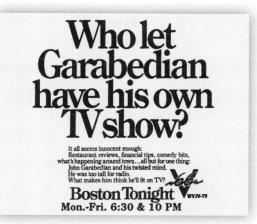

Typical print ad we ran for "Boston Tonight."

spent-viewing," that important metric that measures how long the average viewer watches something before changing the channel. Typical V66 viewers would watch a couple of videos, but when one came on they weren't interested in or had seen a few times, they'd grab the remote control and hunt for something else. If it was a Red Sox game, we would lose them for hours. Even if it was a comedy or *The People's Court*, they'd be committed to watching a program for a half hour or more. They simply weren't staying tuned to us for extended chunks because, like YouTube today, we didn't have programming with a beginning, middle, and end to hold them. Like YouTube, we were offering little four-minute elements. That killed our time-spent-viewing metric and the possibility of getting high time-spent-viewing, which meant low rating shares, which meant lower sales figures. That forced us to drastically re-think our station concept.

Since there was no commercial programming available to buy, the solution was to develop and roll out a lineup of original shows. We brought in Tank, the sports director at 'BCN, to host a nightly sports talk program with Bill Stephens, a sports fanatic. Mary Jo was the centerpiece of a program we called the *Superstar Show*, which focused nightly on a featured artist or band. She'd give a historical review of their careers, updates on what they were doing at the moment, show their videos or backstage clips of the group making the videos, and if we could, interview them live in the studio. Even I got in front of the camera and hosted *Boston Tonight*, a nightly, thirty-minute show with guests and rotating features that covered things happening around the city. We ran ads for all the shows in the local papers.

Ratings immediately began to pick up, but sales still lagged. Some advertisers wanted to see a longer stretch of good numbers. Others had committed their budgets. Meanwhile, as sales slowly increased, we continued to burn through cash. Those new programs had increased the ratings, but they'd also greatly ramped up program production costs. We were in a race against time. We all felt like we were hanging on for dear life. That's because we were.

◀

"Arnie, Merril's ready for us," I announced over the intercom to Arnie's office. I had asked Merril Buchhalter for a meeting to review our budgets.

We sat down and Merril went straight to it. "I've projected expenses and updated our sales forecast," she said. "We have enough cash to get through Thanksgiving, but not Christmas."

I gulped and Merril continued. "And even if we made the end of the year, you know what would happen next," she said. "We go into January and then be in first quarter when sales are especially weak. We'll never make it to April without a major influx of cash."

I looked over at Arnie, who had a pained expression on his face.

"We've got two choices," I said, leaning back in my chair. "We can go back to the investors and raise more money. That will be embarrassing, and a lot of work for an outcome that we can't guarantee. They'll really press us on why we couldn't deliver what we promised. Or, the second option is we can sell." Arnie's expression became even more pained.

The words fell out of my mouth like a lead weight. I hated that option. Hated disappointing our staff, knowing all the hard work everyone had pumped into the station. My favorite ending would have been, we built it, our ratings went through the roof, other stations like it came online, and the cash came pouring in. That was the dream ending I wanted. But looking at Merril's analysis, it was obvious that selling was the best option. We couldn't cut budgets or the ratings would disappear. Our sales team was improving, but the effort to raise funds from the investors to get to positive cash flow would have been a major headache and a bit of a gamble. Since our fiduciary responsibility to the investors was to minimize risk and give them a big return on their investment, the choice was clear.

The next morning we advised our investment bank, Kidder-Peabody, of our intent to sell the station. The next call I made was to a TV station broker in Florida, who by chance also represented the Home Shopping Network (HSN). Its owners were looking to acquire TV stations in the ten largest markets in the country. Frustrated at being at the mercy of cable providers to give them channel positions to reach larger audiences, HSN had started buying up TV stations that already had a channel position on cable. Fortunately, back when we first started, it was Arnie who had pushed our presence on New England cable systems. Arnie had been living with cable at his home in Ogunquit, Maine, for years and had told me, "Once you're on cable, if the station isn't in the cable package, it just doesn't exist." Arnie worked diligently to get us prime low channel number positions. It was easy for him. The local cable system managers, all of whom had grown up listening to "Woo Woo" on the radio, were happy to give him anything he wanted.

Those low channel numbers proved to be important assets to HSN and helped pave the way for us to negotiate a price of $20 million for V66.

Our investors loved the deal. In under two years, they received a 155 percent return on their money. For the rest of us, however, it was an emotional goodbye. In early August of '86, I called the staff of my *Boston Tonight* show together in a conference room and told them we were canceling the program and that their jobs were being terminated. The night before, I didn't sleep very well. Some twenty-five people, from photographers and writers, to producers and editors, had their lives turned upside down that day. There were many tears that morning. I cared about them and hated having to let them go.

I felt the same way about the station itself. For three intense years, V66 had consumed our lives and finally made the concept of music television come alive in a way MTV never had. Then suddenly it was gone. Looking back there is no question we made the right choice on behalf of our investors, to whom we were accountable. When the clock struck midnight on September 21, 1986, V66 went from showing music videos to selling bracelets and juicers. It was the day our music died. 🔇

24. While You See a Chance

Steve Winwood, 1980

Vanilla Ice was one of the first artists to come to *Open House Party*. Vanilla (and his posse) shown here in 1987 at the *Open House Party* studio in the basement of my house. I'm the other white guy, sitting in the middle.

Selling V66 gave me the kind of financial freedom I'd never had before. I was forty-four years old and as long as I didn't get stupid, I'd never have to work again. It was an odd feeling, this sense that I had no responsibilities and really could do anything I wanted. I felt both free and uncertain about what lay ahead. It felt like I did back when I was lying on the hill in Vermont under a beautiful starry sky. The pressure was off but the question remained the same—what the hell did I want to do with my life?

A million ideas ran through my head. I could just take it easy and go fishing. You know, live an easy life without the stress, without wrestling with budgets or looming deadlines. That thought left my head almost as quickly as it appeared. For starters, I find fishing to be completely boring. More than that, not having a real motivation to get out of bed in the morning sounded like torture. I'd go crazy. Something in television was a possibility, but the whole V66 experience had showed me how segregated the work was, and for a hands-on guy like myself I knew it wouldn't work. There were a million people needed to produce a TV show. No one person has actual control of the final product, even the producer, whose job is like riding around on a Ouija board with all the headaches, personnel problems, and drama. It wasn't like radio where I had always enjoyed taking on multiple roles: general manager, program director, deejay, music director, the guy getting his hands dirty trying to fix the transmitter. I didn't want to be stuck in a corner office again managing budgets, people problems, and investors. I wanted to be where all the creativity was happening.

The more I thought about what I wanted, what I loved, and what I was good at, the more the answer came back to radio. Building community, creating great programming, entertaining listeners—those were things I loved doing. But it wasn't 1972. Creating another local radio station from scratch didn't make sense.

Radio was about to enter a sea change, and in big ways. National programming, where stations piped in syndicated shows, had taken over the talk show format and I was convinced it was only a matter of time before it would happen with music radio. With guys like Elvis Duran, Howard Stern, and Ryan Seacrest, it's become common now, but back then the whole concept was unheard of.

My old mentor, Jack Carlson, often told me that "in life, timing is everything." In May, 1987, I attended a Warner Brothers Records album release party at 13 Up, an alternative club across the street from Fenway Park on trendy Lansdowne Street in Boston, upstairs from Spit nightclub (we jokingly called it "Spit Up"). It was for Peter Wolf, the J. Geils Band frontman, who was putting out his first solo album, *Come As You Are*. I'd known Peter for years, going back to when he was a kid hanging around Harvard Square. Wolf is a complete character. That whacky, bee-bopping personality he presents on stage is pretty much the same guy you get off it. He's wiry and bright, and always speaking in rhythm, like he's constantly got a backup band with him.

There was the expected mass of music industry people, eating free shrimp cocktail and sucking down drinks from the open bar to the sound of his new album blasting away. I was making the rounds when all of a sudden Sunny Joe White tapped me on the back.

"Hi, there, John Garabedian!" he said exuberantly and gave me a big hug.

You couldn't help but love Sunny. He was an electric, larger-than-life person, the kind of guy who could shift the gravity in a room when he walked into it. Everyone wanted to be near him. He was also one of the big personalities in Boston radio—part diva, pure showman, and one of America's brightest radio programmers. I first met Sunny at a party in 1975 in the Back Bay apartment of "Disco" Vinny Peruzzi, a young gay club deejay who worked as an intern at the old WBZ-FM, an automated Top 40 station, which is now Magic 106.7.

Sunny had moved to Boston from his native Charlotte, North Carolina, to host the morning show on WILD (AM) in Boston. It was there that through their mutual love of jazz, Sunny became friends with Richie Balsbaugh, who was in the midst of taking over as general manager of Boston's WWEL (FM) to turn it into Kiss 108. Sunny immediately came aboard as Kiss 108's program director and was the driving force behind its initial disco format and eventual number one ratings. Radio is filled with programmers who just copy what the other guy is doing with no originality or creativity. I call them "penguins." Sunny wasn't a "penguin."

Part of it was just who Sunny was. He was smart, stylish, engaging, and had this wonderful way of talking—a kind of rolling, slightly sing-songy voice that picked up a few decibels when he got excited, which was often. He made everything he said sound interesting. Sunny was not a T-shirt-and-jeans kind of guy. One day he might be wearing a muumuu, the next, some Nehru thing. Or he might just be in an all white suit, like Don Johnson wore in *Miami Vice*. It all came packaged together in his fabulous little blue Mercedes convertible he drove around the city.

During the V66 years, we had hired him to do live Saturday night TV broadcasts from the mammoth Palace nightclub. He was great when he actually showed up. The problem with Sunny was that he liked drugs and sex way too much, and that often got in the way of him showing up on time. When he and Richie Balsbaugh launched KISS 108, Sunny hosted the morning show, as he had at WILD. Unfortunately, Sunny's nightlife conflicted with his starting time, and he was perpetually late for his 6 a.m. start. Richie was smart, though. He needed Sunny's programming genius and didn't want to take Sunny off the air, but he knew things couldn't continue as they had. So he hired the midday DJ from WBCN, tall, dry-witted Matt Segal, and moved Sunny to 10 a.m.-to-noon. Predictably, Sunny was always late for that, too, and his music director Rocky would fill in, doing Sunny Joe White impersonations until the real host arrived around 10:30 or 10:45.

It was the same thing at V66. Sunny drove our program manager David Beadle crazy. He was not only constantly late for the TV show, but he never made it to rehearsal. We finally had to make the hard decision to let him go. His lifestyle no doubt led to health issues leading to his early death in 1996 at the age of forty-two.

In true Sunny fashion, though, he went out in style. His parents asked me to deliver the eulogy at his funeral, which was held at the Concord Baptist Church in Boston's South End. It was packed. Standing room only. I had never been to an African-American church before and was just blown away by the utterly spectacular service. The soloists and choir were superb, good enough to win a recording contract. The pastor delivered a wonderfully inspiring sermon about life and death, while Sunny's close friends told warm, humorous stories about Sunny. As we all walked out of the church, Mark Parenteau remarked, "Leave it to Sunny to put the 'fun' in funeral."

At the Peter Wolf album release party, Sunny was unusually happy to see me. "I've been meaning to give you a call!" he yelled over the noise of the party.

"Really?" I said, curiously. "What about?"

Sunny motioned me over to the side of the room where we could hear each other. He looked around and shook his head. "I have to call Rick Dees and Scott Shannon tomorrow to tell them we're dropping their countdown shows," he said. "KISS gets great ratings Monday through Friday, but on the weekends we take a big drop. I got a letter from a listener asking why KISS turned into a machine on the weekends. It got me thinking and I was wondering if you'd have any interest in doing a weekend shift on KISS like you did on WBCN?"

I laughed. "Why don't you hire some college kid?" I asked.

Sunny rolled his eyes. "That's what we do now, and you know how that goes," he said. "They're weak. They have trouble putting two sentences together, let alone be entertaining." Then a smile came over his face and he put his hand on my right shoulder. "I used to listen to you on WBCN and just *loved* the stories you used to tell. You were so engaging. I'd love to bring something like that to KISS."

"Tell you what, Sunny," I said. "I understand exactly what your problem is. I don't really want to do weekends on KISS, but I think I have a better solution to your problem. Let's have dinner next week and talk about it."

"OK, I'll look forward to it!" he said, his voice rising with excitement.

The following Tuesday we met at Felicia's, a little Italian restaurant Sunny loved on Hanover Street in Boston's North End. The subject of weekend radio certainly wasn't new to me. Most every radio station faced the issue of how to maintain the same quality of programming on Saturdays and Sundays when the pro talent only works Monday through Friday.

During the time since we sold V66, I had concluded that eventually the future of radio would be in national and world programming and had actually conducted acquisition discussions with Transtar and Satellite Music Network, the two leading national 24/7 programming networks that then only served

mostly small and medium market radio stations. The solution to Sunny's
problem dovetailed perfectly with
my interest in national programming
and what I saw as the coming age
of national programming. As Sunny
mopped up his pasta sauce with a
chunk of bread, I put my fork down
and launched into my vision.

Open House Party's "moment of conception" came at a Warner Brothers release party for Peter Wolf at 13-Up, when Sunny Joe White asked me if I'd be willing to do a weekend shift
at KISS 108. (Left to right) myself, Aerosmith manager Tim
Collins, Peter Wolf, Sunny Joe White, and Mark Parenteau.
Wolf is the only straight guy. *Photo by Leo Gozbekian.*

"The solution is cranking it out
like they do in a factory," I said.
"Charlie's Diner does a great business
until McDonald's or Wendy's opens
up across the street. Suddenly everyone's going across the street to McDonald's for
faster service, better quality, and more appealing décor. They have the best real
estate people select the sites, the best restaurant designers design the stores, the
best chefs formulate the food, the best packaging people design the packaging, and
the best marketing people make the ads. What does that little diner have? Rude
waitresses, cold fries, no parking, and a dirty bathroom. Charlie's doesn't stand
a chance."

I took a sip of my Merlot and started up again. By now, Sunny had finished his
dinner and was giving me his full attention. "Today we have satellites," I continued.
"Talk radio is using them to crank out the best talk programs with the best hosts
to local stations in the biggest markets and getting great ratings. It's home movies
or Hollywood! There's no reason Top 40 stations can't do the same thing." Sunny
had shoved his plate to the side and ordered a cappuccino. He wanted to hear more.

"Top 40 has never used satellites," I said. "People work hard all week and
look forward to enjoying their weekends, yet radio programming is weakest on
the listeners' two most important days of the week. What if instead of having
some twenty-year-old kid boring everyone, there was a big national Saturday
night party?"

Sunny was hooked. "What would this party be like?" he asked.

John Garabedian

Once we sold the Nantucket radio station, David and I each bought homes on the island. Here at my house on Long Pond is David O'Leary, left, with my late, great friend, Bob Lund.

Fired up, I barreled forward. "You'd have a superstar big name guest every week, which you could promote all week to build anticipation," I said. "You'd have live call-ins from backstage at concerts and big events to put listeners in touch with the hottest social events. There would be '800' lines installed for listeners to phone in requests, and you'd accurately tabulate them to instantly determine the music people want to hear specifically on a Saturday night. You'd put callers on the air and listeners from around the country would hear them. There'd be bands in the studio playing live, and even have a live studio audience screaming in the background. There would be prizes and contests, the kind of stuff a local station could never budget for a typical weekend show." Then with a smile I added, "And of course, a superstar host," and here I paused for dramatic effect, "Me!"

Sunny was vibrating, "What would you call this show?" he asked.

I said. "I've done this show. It was called *Open House Party* at WORC in Worcester and it had a twenty-five share!"

Sunny was enraptured. "Ohh, I love it!" he said in a high pitch tone. "People listening will feel like they're a part of something *big*. If you want to build your studio and develop it before going national, we'll put it on KISS 108 right away, and you'll have time to perfect it."

I hadn't planned on jumping into something like this, but the more I thought about it, the more I realized this wasn't something someone else could do. They'd only screw it up and the idea would fail. Sunny's charm only added to my enthusiasm for the idea. If he believed in you, he made you feel like a million bucks and that anything in the world was possible. The deal we struck that night over dinner became our agreement. It was a simple handshake. No paperwork. No contracts. And for a deejay who hadn't done a live radio show since my final days at WBCN in 1984, that suited me just fine.

That whole summer of '87, I poured my life into getting the new *Open House Party* off the ground. As I looked for commercial office space to build the studio, I quickly came to the conclusion that putting it in some sterile office building with cold, fluorescent lighting would kill the spirit of the show. Then I realized I never used my basement playroom in Southborough. My studio solution had been at my house the whole time, so I brought in a carpenter and my friend and engineer Bob Lund and turned the space into a professional radio studio. I was motivated by the excitement for this next big adventure in my life, and the chance to work on this big project. Plus, I needed something to fulfill me.

◀

In the months since we sold V66, the relationship between David and me had become strained. Fragile, and sometimes tense. For the first time in the eleven years we had been together, we bickered over small things. The sudden end to the television station had hurt David's career hopes. Suddenly the fame and glory of being on TV every day was over, and his future must have felt bleak and uncertain. Looking back, I'm sure it caused him hurt. During V66's darkest days, he'd been supportive when I shared my concerns about the station's finances, but I don't think he grasped how serious the situation was. As we laid most of the staff off, it was obvious we were struggling, but the actual sale still caught him by surprise. One day he was the star of a popular TV station, the next, he was trying to figure out his next steps in life.

That summer of 1987, around the time I first started talking to Sunny about *Open House Party*, David and I were doing less and less together. It was like we were moving at different speeds. All through our relationship, things had felt extremely well-balanced. Even though I may have managed two of the places he worked at, that power dynamic never polluted our relationship. David was never afraid to express opinions and I respected and deeply valued his input.

After V66, though, something shifted. Maybe down deep David felt betrayed. Maybe I seemed uncaring about what the sale of the station had meant to him. Maybe, as often happens in relationships, the two of us changed. Perhaps our needs and interests had evolved and we wanted and needed different things. Probably it was all of that.

In late August of '87, David and I were quibbling over something stupid when I finally just said, "You know, David, if it's going to keep going on like this, we shouldn't live together." It killed me to say it, to put thought out there. Yet it hurt to be living the way we were living. And I knew David wasn't happy either.

A few days later, on a Thursday morning, he came into the kitchen. We'd hardly spoken over the last few days, and when I saw him standing in the doorway, I had a pretty good idea what he wanted to say.

"I've thought a lot about what you said, about how things can't continue the way they are," he said, nervously stuffing his hands in his pants pockets. "I think you're right. I'll be moving out at the end of the month."

I swallowed hard. "OK," I said. "There's no point in the two of us staying miserable."

A part of me wanted to hold on to him and try to recover the incredible relationship we had enjoyed. But I knew better. He was making the right decision for both of us.

Today I realize more than ever, I became a different person thanks to spending years with David. Kinder, more mellow, more understanding of other people's feelings and how they should be treated. He was the only person who really knew how to handle me in every situation. He calmed me down when I got fiery and helped me believe in my dreams. I'm forever grateful to him for that. There is no person I have ever met in my life who is a more perfect human being than David O'Leary, and today I am proud and happy that we remain best friends.

Two days after David announced he was moving out, on Saturday night, September 5, 1987, *Open House Party* debuted live on KISS 108 in Boston. During the final run-up to the launch of the show, I felt like my brain was split in two. One half consumed by what had happened with David—was he okay? Why did we end up where we were?—the other locked in on getting the new program off the ground. It was an adrenaline-filled roller coaster ride. I'd spend the day working in the basement studio, excited by how great I felt about where the show was headed, then trudge upstairs for a break and be reminded of how empty the house had become.

Open House Party studio around 1995. No more turntables (everything was on hard drive), no more editing phone calls on tape (note the Akai digital recorder), and I'd grown a mustache.

Those early years of *Open House Party* were some of my favorite. There was an exciting start-up atmosphere to the entire thing. We were always improving the program flow, adding features to the formatting, and constantly improvising. I wasn't a bit nervous about being back on the air and doing a live Top 40 show for the first time in almost a decade, but I definitely felt the rust. I wasn't as crisp in my interviews and didn't feel as quick with one-liners when the callers came in. I kept telling Sunny that, but he simply waved me off. "Nonsense, John," he'd say. "You sound great. Now we really have a fabulous Saturday night show to showcase our weekends."

Sunny wasn't just trying to be nice. He wasn't that way. If the thing had sucked, if the music was wrong, if I sounded out of touch with the culture, and more telling, if the numbers had bottomed out, he wouldn't have been so easy with the praise. After all, he hadn't taken KISS to the top of the Boston radio ratings because he settled for crap. Then one weekday a few months later after we had launched *Open House Party*, Sunny called me up.

"I thought you'd like to know that the Fall Arbitron ratings just came in," he said.

An electricity ran through me. "Great!" I exclaimed nervously. "How did we do?"

Sunny laughed. "Now sit down," he said. "Remember how we were pulling in a 4 share on Saturday nights? In the fall, Kiss finished with a 6.4 share during the weekdays, but on Saturday nights *Open House Party* racked up"—he paused, knowing the extra few seconds of waiting would drive me crazy—"a 14.2!"

John Garabedian

I nearly dropped the phone. "Sunny," I jumped to my feet. "That's incredible!" Sunny laughed again. "Yes, yes," he said. "This thing has taken off."

The request-driven music and the listener line were a big part of it. And the guests we had on the show gave *Open House Party* that extra buzz. Every minute of the show packed a special energy and excitement that drew in the listeners and kept them tuned in. In the beginning I was nervous about who we might be able to land. After all, it wasn't like I was nationally known to either listeners or program directors. But having the KISS brand and the fabulous Sunny Joe White attached to the project gave it credibility. Everyone who mattered in radio, programmers, artists, and record executives, knew and highly respected the station. It was the number one Top 40 outlet in Boston and one of the best sounding in the world. Getting on its airwaves meant good exposure and high credibility for marketing the show to other radio stations.

The very first guest I had in the studio was the group, Milli Vanilli. For a time, this two-man band, made up of a pair of handsome, chiseled-looking German singers, Fab Morvan and Rob Pilatus, were the biggest things in pop. They just exploded onto the scene, with their long dreadlocks and a hit single, "Girl You Know It's True," that went multi-platinum and eventually earned the duo the 1989 Grammy for Best New Artist. Out of the gate, they bragged about contributing more to pop music than some of the biggest names in business. That included icons like Mick Jagger, Bob Dylan, and Paul McCartney. It was so absurd, and yet people loved it.

The taped interview was scheduled for a Thursday at two at the Southborough studio. At around 2:30 they still hadn't arrived, so I went upstairs to the kitchen to grab a glass of water. All of a sudden I heard this loud "screech-crunch." I looked out and saw that a big stretch limo had bottomed out trying to get over the small hill at the top of my driveway. The driver had his head out the vehicle, not sure if he should go forward or backward. I threw open the window.

"You'll never make it," I said. "The car's too big." As I put my shoes on to step outside, the driver jumped out to open the rear door for his clients. Out of the limo emerged two tall, handsome young black men with flowing, shoulder-length dreadlocks and gray tunics that went down to the ground. They looked like a pair of Biblical prophets and the most unlikely pair of visitors to drop by my placid little white suburban neighborhood. Across the way, a neighbor mowing his lawn, stopped and stared. I smiled and waved. As they approached the house, I introduced myself.

"Ver haf ve landed?" Fab asked in a thick German accent as he looked around. "Is thees really dee radio station?"

"Sort of," I said leading them through the garage and into the basement of my house.

During the half hour or so I had them in the studio, we talked mainly about their careers and their album. The world was still a couple of years away from discovering that Fab and Rob hadn't sung a single note on their album; that they'd lip-synced the whole thing and the real work belonged to a pair of anonymous vocalists. As I listened to them answer my questions, it struck me funny, just how thick their German accents were. Finally, I asked them about it.

"Guys, when I listen to your record, I don't hear a trace of your German accents," I said. "How do you sing in such perfect English?"

Fab and Rob traded looks then turned back to me. It was sort of an awkward silence, but nothing I spent two seconds on at the time thinking about. Fab shrugged his shoulders. "Ve practice quite a bit," he said. "Ve've worked very hart to perfect our zzound."

It was one big lie. Two years later, the *LA Times* revealed the truth behind the group's debut album. The news rocked the music world, and Fab and Rob had to return their Grammy. The two tried to bounce back with a follow-up album, *Rob & Fab,* in 1993, but they had no talent and were too disgraced to gain any commercial traction. The debacle proved especially devastating to Rob, who developed a drug habit and in 1998 died of an overdose of prescription meds and alcohol in a Frankfurt hotel room. The pair had gotten the fifteen minutes of fame they'd craved and it destroyed them.

Around the same time I first met Rob and Fab, by chance I interviewed another set of fresh-faced singers who would soon explode into a major world sensation. I just stumbled on to them. On a Friday night in the fall of '87, I went to Great Woods (now the Xfinity Center), a large outdoor concert venue in

Mansfield, Massachusetts, for an interview with Tiffany, the redhead pop singer whose remake of the Tommy James and the Shondells' 1967 single, "I Think We're Alone Now," was dominating the airwaves. Heading backstage, I ran into Charlie Walk, a young record promotion rep I knew from Columbia Records.

"Hey, John, what are you up to?" he asked, looking at my recording equipment.

"Doing an interview with Tiffany after she comes off stage," I said.

Charlie flashed a big smile. "Hey, I've a got a new group here I want you to meet," he said. "They're opening up for her. Five Boston kids called New Kids on the Block. You'll love them."

It was all I could do to be polite. Charlie was persuasive so I couldn't say no, but I wanted to groan. Meeting a group of unknown kids who most likely would be out of the business in a year wasn't something I was interested in. But I felt obliged to play along.

"Follow me," he said. "The boys just came off stage."

Charlie walked me to this large dressing room where five young guys were in full teenage mode. Donnie Wahlberg, the seventeen-year-old elder statesman in the band, had fifteen-year-old Joey McIntrye in a full bear hug and was attempting to sling him over his shoulders. The others, Jonathan Knight, his brother Jordan, and Danny Wood, egged a laughing Joey on. "Take him down!" they yelled.

As the boys whooped it up, Charlie introduced me to the group's manager, a tall, well-dressed, soft-spoken guy named Dick Scott. We all watched as the bandmates bounced around the room like little puppies. Finally, Charlie attempted to get their attention. "Boys!" he shouted, which didn't do a thing. "Boys," he said again even louder. When the room quieted, he pointed to me. "We have a guest," he said. "John Garabedian, host of *Open House Party* on KISS 108."

Donnie dropped Joey on the couch like a bag of sand, walked up to me, and stuck out a hand. "I've met you before," he said. "I'm Donnie. We met at the Boston Music Awards a couple years ago."

I shot him a surprised look. "You were that kid?" I said.

We had crossed paths at the '85 Boston Music Awards event at the Wang Center in downtown Boston. Donnie had spotted me in the lobby and said hello. He had this outgoing, confident way about him, like nothing was going to get in his way. He had watched me on V66 and hoped one day the new band he had just helped start would be on it.

New Kids on the Block on one of their many visits to *Open House Party*. (Left to right) Jordan Knight, myself, Lisa Lipps, and Donnie Wahlberg.

"What's the group called," I asked during that first meeting at the awards ceremony.

"Nynuk," he answered.

What a ridiculous name, I thought to myself. Sounds like NYNEX, the phone company. But I did my best not to sound condescending. "Good luck with everything," I said. "Work hard. I hope you make it."

Now, two years later we had run into each other again. "You weren't lying about trying to make it big," I said, "Columbia's a great record company. If anyone can get you big, it's them."

Then Charlie piped up again. "I've got an idea," he said, turning to me. "Why don't we get the boys on your show. Have them come into the studio tomorrow night for a live interview."

The next night, all the New Kids on the Block except Jonathan Knight, who'd driven to Medford, mistakenly thinking I broadcast from the KISS studios, crowded into my Southborough studio for the first of several *Open House Party* visits. Even as New Kids achieved Beatle-like fame, they always made time for *Open House Party*. It's like that. Get in early with a band and support them before they've made it, when only a few people really believe they'll become big, and they'll always show you loyalty. They never forget who those early believers are. And in the next few visits they'd bring this spunky fifteen-year-old kid with them, Donnie's brother "Marky" Mark Wahlberg. He was always rambunctious and one night as they came loudly into the studio, Mark bumped into the turntable, zapping the needle across the record playing on the air. I just put it back on the same spot, gave him a look, and the show went on.

◀

John Garabedian

"Marky" Mark Wahlberg stopped by to wish us a happy fifth anniversary in 1992. He drove up through my conservative suburban neighborhood in his brother Donnie's black Mercedes convertible with the sub-woofer throbbing so loud it rattled the glass in my window.

Part of the magic of *Open House Party* has been the people who've worked there. The legends and characters who've been a part of the show. There have been so many. One of the best was Andy McLean. In the winter of '87, we'd reached a point where our producer Brian Beecher and I needed some extra hands. The work—taking phone requests, doing mailings to affiliates, show production, cataloging the songs we played—all the little tasks that take up so much time had become too much.

"Find us an intern," I instructed Brian. "Get in touch with the colleges, all the Boston schools that have a broadcasting program and see if we can find someone."

Two weeks later, a half hour before I was scheduled to go on air, I was upstairs in the kitchen prepping for *Open House Party* when the doorbell rang. I hate interruptions just before I go on air and was in no mood to deal with guests. "Why didn't they go in through the garage," I muttered under my breath as I made my way to the door. When I opened it, I was greeted by this good-looking seventeen-year-old kid with spiked blonde hair and a big smile.

"Hi," he said, sticking out his hand. "I'm Andy and I'm your new intern."

He didn't leave until Tuesday. We just got lucky, because Andy quickly proved invaluable to *Open House Party*. He loved radio, could work a computer keyboard at sixty-five words per minute, and was like a music trivia savant. He knew everything about every artist.

We also clicked on a personal level. Andy had been outed as gay his junior year of high school and dropped out. The bullying and name-calling had even pushed him to think about suicide. I could identify with his outsider status and struggles to fit in. It wasn't long before Andy graduated from intern to employee. We hired him as production assistant and then when Brian Beecher left the show, I promoted him to producer.

Andy was young and had a wild side. Decades before Grindr and other smartphone dating apps, he hit the gay sex lines in Boston, party lines which allowed callers to connect and hook up. Even though he was barely twenty-one, he'd show up at Boston and Providence gay clubs when they were holding strip contests and enter them. He loved to bring the crowd to a huge roar. He'd run around the club before the show introducing himself, asking people for their vote like he was running for office. It worked. Andy usually won first prize, an amount from $500 to $1,000.

But around 1991, Andy started complaining he was getting tired all the time. His energy level would just drop. I pushed him to see a doctor, and after a battery of blood tests, he waited nervously for the results. Because Andy had been quite promiscuous, he was scared as hell he had AIDS.

When the doctor's office called him late one Friday afternoon, his fears went through the roof. When he arrived, the doctor sat him down and told him that the blood analysis showed he had an overproduction of immature red blood cells. "We think you might have…leukemia," the doctor finally said.

To the astonishment of the doctor, Andy revealed a huge smile. "Oh, thank God!" he exclaimed. Then he fainted.

Andy went into treatment at Dana-Farber Cancer Institute in Boston. It was a brutal experience for him, which involved extensive chemo and finally a bone marrow transplant. The poor kid lost his hair and a ton of weight and looked like a shell of himself. I visited him every chance I could. But anyone visiting

My buddy, Andy McLean around 1992. He died at age twenty-seven from an opportunistic infection following chemotherapy for leukemia. He was awesome; without him I felt like I lost my right hand.

him had to be excruciatingly careful about introducing him to any germs. Visitors had to fully scrub and put on sterile surgical gowns and caps. His immune system was destroyed by the chemo drugs and the slightest infection could kill him.

Andy recovered and a year later returned to *Open House Party*. He jumped right in like he'd never left and eventually became business manager of Superadio. His personal life settled down, too. He met a nice guy and fell in love, and by the late '90s they bought a home together in Hopedale. Everything he'd been through, from feeling ostracized for being gay to being a cancer survivor, made Andy appreciate everything he had in life. The doctors at Dana-Farber told him that with his type of leukemia, if it didn't return within five years he could consider it gone forever.

But in May of 1998, he walked into my office and with a sad tone in his voice he broke the news to me. The leukemia had returned. I wish the story ended on a good note, but after Andy had undergone a second round of chemotherapy and had actually gone into remission, he acquired an opportunistic infection. With no immune system, Andy's health quickly deteriorated. Within a matter of days he was unconscious and on a ventilator. After three weeks, the decision was made to pull the plug. He wasn't coming back. There was no sense in prolonging the inevitable. He was twenty-seven.

One of the pleasures of *Open House Party* has been the many live broadcasts we've done from major events from Boston to San Francisco. There's a special energy to those shows, an electric immediacy. What's happening is happening right now and the listener can feel that. When a live broadcast is really rolling, the listener doesn't want to change the station because they're afraid they'll miss something. Even those crappy little remotes I used to do from the Crystal Room in Milford for WMRC when I first got into the business packed a buzz. No matter how good you're trying to make a pre-recorded show, it can't compare. That's one of the weaknesses of radio now. What you're listening to now, you can hear next week or the week after or next year. It's usually pre-recorded voice tracks and it doesn't make a difference.

Our first big live broadcast event came in 1994, at Woodstock II in Saugerties, New York. I'd always regretted missing the original Woodstock festival, so when it was announced there was going to be a sequel, I was excited to not only make up for that lost opportunity but also bring something to *Open House Party* we hadn't done before. It would get us out of the studio and help attract more stations to become affiliates.

Our ad sales were done by a New York company called Media America, and Ron Hartenbaum and Gary Schonfeld, their principals, had actually invested in and had become limited-partner investors in Superadio and had secured all radio rights to Woodstock. They happily licensed us to broadcast *Open House Party* live from the festival. High-speed internet didn't then exist, and a satellite truck was beyond our budget. So our plan was to record the breaks and then upload them via 56k modem through the phone line in our motel room to the automation system in Southborough. But the phone lines in Saugerties were awful. They all had a hum, which caused the modem upload speed to be mind-numbingly slow. It would take hours to get only three minutes of audio uploaded. The solution was for me to collect what we needed, hop in my plane and fly back to Southborough, then drop the files directly into the system. So that's what I did.

Flying back after dropping off the last breaks, I arrived at the festival grounds around 11 p.m. Saturday night. Winston Farm, where it was held, packed an electric pulse with 350,000 people throbbing to the Violent Femmes. The whole area was alive with energy, and the sensual odor of weed filled the air. Then Metallica took command of the North Stage and those 350,000 people exploded with excitement as they hit the first notes of "Enter Sandman."

John Garabedian

We built Superadio Network into a major national player with over 850 major market affiliates airing more than forty programs. (Left to right) President Gary Bernstein, myself, and MediaAmerica President, Ron Hartenbaum.

Backstage there was even more electricity. As Aerosmith waited to go on and close out the night, the group's manager, Tim Collins, started to get into it with John Scher, the Woodstock promoter. Bands make their money off merchandise. You know, selling seven-dollar shirts for forty bucks a pop. But the people behind Woodstock had forbid that. Only concert merchandise was to be sold. It appeared that Metallica made a special deal, was playing by different rules, and started selling T-shirts right on the festival grounds. Nobody stopped them. Not even after Tim Collins made a stink about it.

"What the fuck is going on?" Tim demanded. "They can't be doing that. If you're going to let them do it, then we should be able to sell our stuff."

When the promoter basically waved him off, Tim went ballistic. They got physical and it took a few guys to keep them apart. Meanwhile, Aerosmith was holding off going on stage and the anxious crowd was wondering what was happening.

Suddenly, out on the main stage, someone came on the microphone and made an announcement:

"We just spoke to the National Weather Service in Albany and there are severe thunderstorms headed our way. Clear the area, don't stand near the sound towers, keep away from the metal fences!"

He might as well have said, "Everyone run for your lives!" It was instant mayhem. People started a stampede for the exits, running over each other like it was a matter of minutes before they were going to be executed. Fortunately, my producer, Mike Ortolano, and I were stationed near an exit in the fence. We jumped into our rental car just as the rains started to come down. Suddenly it became a blinding downpour. As we slowly

At Woodstock II, we smuggled the un-credentialed Westwood One people into the festival, including their network announcer Mark Parenteau and NBC producer Dea Stein, whom I ended up dating. (Left to right) WBCN's Bradley Jay, Dea Stein, and Parenteau.

drove back through throngs of drenched people we kept the doors locked, because people were banging on the car windows begging for shelter and a ride. "Sorry," I said, cheerfully, as we passed through the sea of humanity. "We'd love to help you out but we've got a warm, dry hotel room to get back to."

As messy as the grounds became, there was something beautiful about the scene and the way those fans took to the atmosphere. There was this wonderful carefree spirit about the weekend that I loved. On Sunday, the skies cleared. I took Mark Parenteau, who was broadcasting live from the festival for Westwood One, up in my plane and we circled around the farm to get a view of the grounds. He and his engineer were in the back of my plane broadcasting live on one network, and my producer Mike Ortolano and I were in the front broadcasting on another. People below were milling about, many of them naked. Others were speeding down hundred-foot mud Slip 'N Slides. No amount of weather was going to dampen the spirit of the show or why they were there in the first place. It was a beautiful experience.

By the third Woodstock festival in 1999, the technology had changed enough that we could actually do an *Open House Party* broadcast live via satellite from the festival grounds. This time the concert was held in Rome, New York, at the former Griffiss Air Force Base. It was another massive event with more than two hundred thousand people attending. The promoters had also learned their lessons from the show five years earlier, when attendees overran security and gate-crashed the concerts. For the third Woodstock, a huge steel and plywood fence was constructed to keep those without tickets from breaking in. As an added precaution, five hundred New York State Police troopers were hired to guard the grounds. It was sort of comical and sad. You could have all the peace and love you wanted, as long as you could afford the $150 ticket price.

Weather was again an issue, but instead of rain, the 1999 festival suffered from too much sun. Temperatures hit one hundred degrees and dehydrated attendees nearly broke out in riot when they were clubbed with a $4 price tag for a bottle of water.

There were also problems for all radio networks and news outlets trying to access the concert. Even though we had been granted full credentials by the promoters, at the last minute the Westwood One radio network, who was broadcasting the performances, claimed it had *all* broadcast rights. Lawyers in New York City were left to fight it out. We were unsure how it was going to break but were facing the countdown to our live broadcast with no way to set up our broadcast tent and satellite uplink. Our daring and resourceful producer, Mike Ortolano, came up with a solution. He located the Turning Stone Resort Casino on the grounds of the Oneida Indian Nation about a mile away from the main gate. The Oneidas graciously let us set up our tent and satellite broadcast equipment on their back lawn and even supplied us with power and the use of five local telephone lines for listener calls. But what kind of a live broadcast would it be if you couldn't hear the music and crowds in the background? We were in a big empty parking lot next to the woods.

My Vermont spread, showing the pond and landing strip.

John Garabedian

To get around the fact that we wouldn't actually be broadcasting from Woodstock itself, we needed ambient sound from the festival. A quick call to our tech wizard, Reed Lewis, verified the concert was being aired on Dish Network and then located a local Dish Network dealer. We rushed over and bought a satellite dish. We set up the little dish outside our tent and fed the raw concert audio feed through a big Marshall guitar amp we'd brought. Voilà! We had the concert blasting in the background of *Open House Party* throughout the Saturday night show, and it sounded like we were right there next to the Woodstock stage.

The festival was also memorable for the interviews we got to do: Kid Rock, Bush, Moby, Dave Matthews, Counting Crows, Alanis Morrisette, Aerosmith, Red Hot Chili Peppers—even Carson Daly and Kurt Loder from MTV.

Luck had something to do with our backstage artist access. Westwood One had shut everyone out from getting press credentials. On Saturday, though, I happened to be wearing a yellow T-shirt which looked identical to the standard yellow T-shirts the show's security had to wear. When we approached the gate, I waved a fake press card, they saw my shirt, and we were marshaled right into the artist enclave.

After a very successful broadcast, I woke up Sunday morning, grabbed some coffee and a muffin and headed to the airport to fly my Maule to the airstrip at my Vermont home. The rest of the crew was still sleeping after staying up tearing down our equipment and loading the truck. I had grabbed the Dish Network satellite dish and receiver to take with me to Vermont so I could watch the last day of the festival. That night when I turned it on, I couldn't believe what I was watching; the place was on fire! MTV reporter Kurt Loder was announcing, "They're telling us it's too dangerous and we have to leave right now." During the Red Hot Chili Peppers set, people began lighting piles of empty plastic water bottles on fire, then turned to rip apart and burn the plywood fences, vendor booths, and even a sound tower. The ugly ending assured there will probably never be another Woodstock festival.

It was always interesting meeting new musicians and building those relationships. But if it was only that, I wouldn't have lasted a quarter century as the host of *Open House Party*. Doing the show meant much more. The interviews, the music, the production, the callers, the big, live party feel—*Open House Party* packed together every great thing that had made me first fall in love with radio. Along with that came a certain responsibility. I didn't just show prep for four or five days be-

A rare photo together of DJ Jazzy Jeff and the Fresh Prince, aka Will Smith. With all the fame, money, and success anyone could ever have, Smith remains down-to-Earth, kind, fun, and totally relatable. On my list of the nicest people I've ever met, he is at the top.

cause I had to. The legwork became a 24/7 thing I lived with. Radio is forgiving. You can actually get away without a second of show prep and still deliver a decent-sounding product. But I wanted to create something edgy, something that jumped out of the speakers and sounded larger than life. I thought about young people who might be tuning in to *Open House Party* for the first time and how it might spark something in them, like Dick Biondi, Joey Reynolds, Dan Ingram, Joe Smith or Arnie Ginsburg had done for me.

As *Open House Party* strengthened on KISS 108 and the ratings remained strong, I began the work of rolling the show out nationally. The two biggest radio networks at that time were ABC Radio Network and Westwood One. I had thought all along that one of them would jump to pick up a new show with proven success in a top ten market, but both showed little interest. The problem was that it was a new programming concept and the "suits" at both networks lacked any kind of imagination. They never got what I was proposing, the potential of the show, or the programming problem it solved for Top 40 programmers. *So it's a countdown show?* No, it's a party. It's a big live party with big-name guests and listener requests. *So then it's a dance show?* No. We play the most requested hits and put listeners on the air. Thirty years after WORC had first introduced the concept of an interactive radio program to the airwaves, it still needed explaining. It was frustrating.

It went on like this for months. Trips to New York, meetings with network presidents, ABC's Aaron Daniels and Westwood One's Norm Pattiz, and phone calls, follow-ups, then more meetings. It was endless, and quite obvious they didn't "get" the concept and the problem it would solve for Top 40 radio stations. "Is it a countdown?" "Is it a dance show?" they'd ask. It was obvious that whatever talent these guys had, it was not in understanding the art of radio programming.

Finally, in late winter of '88, I was sitting in my kitchen having coffee when it hit me—screw it, I said to myself. I'll just start my own network! Maybe it was risky, but it wasn't rocket science. It also seemed like my only path forward if I wanted to take *Open House Party* national.

I got to work. I buried myself in spreadsheets and laid out the business plan. Creating a new network involved hiring someone to sell the show to radio stations, leasing satellite time to deliver the program to those stations, and putting in place a national advertising sales team. I tried to be realistic in my time frames. A year to contract enough affiliates to air *Open House Party* to get a big enough national rating so advertisers would buy us, another four months to sell advertising based on the ratings, and then maybe two more months to collect payment from advertisers.

When I hit the final "enter" button on my spreadsheet and saw the bottom line cash needs I groaned. To get to the place where we'd have more money coming than going out, we'd need a million dollars in investment money. How was I going to raise that kind of cash? It took about two minutes to figure I could turn to the 140 limited partners who had received a big payoff with their investment in V66 and offer them a chance to participate. Within two months I had prepared an offering memorandum, and three months after that I had the capital.

The name of this new network was important. I wanted something that sounded big and fun. Something with impact. I remembered that in the late 1970s, ABC Radio was about to launch a new national Top 40 network based upon the success of WABC/New York. They had planned to call it "Superadio."

I loved that name the moment I had heard it. ABC spent two million dollars in preparation for its launch, before the network's chairman, Leonard Goldenson, killed it. He did so after the head of the ABC Entertainment division told him it wouldn't make money for five years.

I boldly called the general counsel of ABC Radio and asked him if they had any plans to ever repurpose the Superadio name. "Not a chance," I was told. "That name is a bad word around here."

To sell the network to other stations, I turned to a well-known Boston radio fixture, Sam Kopper. Sam had been the program director Ray Riepen hired to lead WBCN after I turned him down in 1968. Later, he built a successful concert recording business, turning an old school bus into a mobile recording and broadcast facility that he used to sell live broadcasts of major rock concerts to FM stations around the country. He eventually sold the company for a handsome profit to Westwood One. Sam lived in the Boston area and understood the process of recruiting radio station affiliates.

One of the major hurdles that immediately hit us in the face was that in the forty largest radio markets, less than half the Top 40 radio stations had any satellite capability. To deliver a live radio show, we had to somehow get our audio feed delivered into every market or we wouldn't have any affiliates. The "C-band" radio satellite system used in 1987 required a fourteen-foot dish at each station. For radio stations with studios in downtown office buildings, that would require expensive structural engineering to mount the equipment on the building roof. The price tag was somewhere between $20,000 and $50,000, an amount no station was going to fork over just for a weekend show.

I had read about a new satellite system that used the "Ku" band. Operating in the eleven-gigahertz frequency band, Ku signals only required a little three-foot dish for reception, which could easily be placed anywhere. The entire satellite package could be delivered to each new affiliate for $1,800. Suddenly we would be able to get our programming into major markets that national network radio advertisers previously couldn't reach.

We rented office space in the Boston World Trade Center, and Sam hit the phones hard. We budgeted $100,000 for travel expenses to actually visit major

Behind my home in Southborough, are an airplane hangar and satellite uplink dishes.

market stations, which I felt was a far more effective way to tell our story than trying to do it by telephone.

We installed satellite dishes and built a satellite uplink along the runway behind my house and launched 24/7 satellite transmissions in April of 1988 with several stations lined up to take our signal. The lineup included Albany/Troy/Schenectady, New York's G-98 (WGFM), WINK 104 (WNNK-FM) in Harrisburg, Pennsylvania, and Magic 102 (WMGC) in Buffalo. Other stations like WABB/Mobile, WKMX/Dothan in Alabama, Q92 in (KKHQ) Cedar Rapids, Iowa, K-92 (WXLK) Roanoke, Virginia, and 95 Triple-X (WXXX) in Burlington, Vermont, soon followed. K-92 and 95 Triple-X continue to air *Open House Party* today.

Canadian stations became a part of the mix, too. In looking for investment money I took a step I would later regret when I gave my friend, Robert Whyte, a call. Robert and I first met several years before at a radio convention cocktail party at the Marriot Embarcadero in San Francisco. Killer handsome and twenty-three years old, he was standing by himself on the side of the room when I walked past him and noticed his name tag: It read "CHOM-FM, Montréal," the radio station I listened to constantly when I was in Vermont. Then I looked again and saw that his title said "sales manager."

We hit it off, hung out the rest of our time in San Francisco, and became good friends. He'd visit me in Boston often because his girlfriend Janice was studying at Boston University, and I'd visit him in Montreal. Robert was charming and fun.

Ten years later, as I was gearing up to launch Superadio, Robert was sitting on a fortune and doing nothing. Around the time I sold V66 to the Home Shopping Network, Robert, who by this time had become sales manager at CFCF-TV in Montreal, put in a call to V66's new buyers and convinced them that he should launch a similar shopping network in Canada, and they should be his investors. He then skillfully navigated the ridiculously tough Canadian TV regulations, won the license, and when he sold it a few years later, made millions.

Robert shared my belief that national networking was the future of radio programming and immediately became one of the founding investors in Superadio. I then suggested he start Superadio Canada and use *Open House Party* as the lead product. Bored in Toronto where he now lived, sitting on stocks and bonds and looking for a challenge, Robert became excited about the idea. Soon, Robert hired a staff and succeeded in getting *Open House Party* aired both Saturday

By 1990, *Open House Party* was on the air both Saturday and Sunday nights in every major Canadian city. Here I am visiting the "Rob and Crew" morning show team at Canada's heritage Top 40 station CHED, Edmonton, Alberta.

day and Sunday nights in every major Canadian city from Vancouver to Calgary, Edmonton, Toronto, Montreal, and East into Labrador and Newfoundland.

As Robert's Canadian business boomed, so did things on the American side. In most markets, we were consistently outperforming the station's ratings on nearly every station we were on. In Atlanta, Power 99 (WAPW), the leading station in the market, usually delivered a six share of audience during the week. On both Saturday and Sunday nights we had a 14 share. "You know it's kind of depressing," Power 99 program director Rick Stacy once told me, "We work really hard every day programming our station locally, then on the weekends we just push a button and get the highest ratings."

By 1990, Superadio had more than one hundred affiliates for *Open House Party* in the United States and over thirty in Canada. Ad sales were starting to rock; we had turned profitable. Growth looked unstoppable.

And then it didn't. 🔇

John Garabedian

25. Here I Go Again

Whitesnake, 1987

'N SYNC visits were always fun; they were trained to be "radio-friendly," and understood that everything had to move fast in interviews. The guys were always willing to perform live for us, which they did superbly. (Left to right) Joey Fatone, Justin Timberlake, JC Chasez, Lance Bass, and Chris Kirkpatrick.

Houston's KRBE was one of the first to go. Then WHYI, Miami. KQKS, Denver came shortly after. Followed by WIOQ, Philadelphia, WYTZ, Chicago, and then WAPW, Atlanta. In early 1991, stations around the country began canceling *Open House Party*. It was like watching a set of dominoes fall. A few early ones went down, a momentum built, and the cancellations poured in.

The economy was the culprit, and it was near collapse. Following the Lincoln Savings Bank failure, the American economy collapsed into financial crisis. By 1991, more than a thousand savings and loan banks had failed out of three thousand. Real estate fell off a cliff. Wall Street was a roller coaster ride and the unemployment rate began to soar. There wasn't a sector of the economy that wasn't affected, including radio. We had started to see advertising budgets tightening up in late 1990. A year later, they were getting slashed. Major radio stations were going broke and into bankruptcy. By 1993, Superadio was on life support.

It wasn't just revenues that were tanking. The music industry itself had taken a turn, too, and Top 40 had fallen to an unprecedented low. It wasn't hard to see why. Payola had become common currency for getting records played on the air. Program directors received free trips, laptops, TVs, drugs, sex, and even cash for playing, favoring, or even reporting airplay on records they weren't actually playing. As a result, mediocre new music that should never have made it on the air flooded the Top 40 airwaves, driving listeners to other radio formats. It was the same kind of pay-to-play thing that had nearly destroyed Top 40 three decades before. But it was worse in a way, because everyone seemed to be in on it. This time it wasn't just a few rogue deejays. The whole industry was at fault.

Added to all this was the emergence of polarizing, angry gangsta rap and hard-edged alternative rock songs. Everybody under twenty-one loved the new music and everyone over twenty-one hated it. Top 40 radio makes money selling

The B-52s!

advertising to eighteen to thirty-four-year-olds. With poor adult ratings, Top 40 stations couldn't sell advertising and stations by the hundreds switched from Top 40 to other music formats. Country emerged from the Hank Williams/Waylon Jennings era with a new modern generation of stars like Vince Gill and Garth Brooks. Alternative rock was emerging as a hot new format, along with classic rock. Top 40 wasn't dead, but it was barely struggling to breathe.

In 1988, when we launched *Open House Party*, there were over 1,200 Top 40 stations in America. By 1992, the number had dropped to three hundred. It was like McDonald's being in the hamburger business and all of a sudden it's announced that red meat causes cancer. By 1992, *Open House Party* was down to just thirty-six affiliates.

In July, 1995, Superadio president Gary Bernstein and I flew to Los Angeles for a meeting at KPWR with Rick Cummings and Doyle Rose, the two heads of Emmis Communications, one of the large radio conglomerates. We were there to discuss airing our Urban mix shows, but the session soon morphed into a discussion about how they believed the Top 40 format was dead and that it would never dominate again.

"The days of the big stage, all-inclusive Top 40 station are over," Rick pronounced. "Today you have to go after niche audiences."

Emmis's own KPWR, a rhythmic urban station in L.A., had proven that by soundly beating KIIS/Los Angeles, a legendary Top 40 powerhouse that for years had been the city's number one station. The problem wasn't the Top 40 format. It had simply lost its focus. Pop music had completely disappeared, and Top 40 stations had become polluted by highly polarizing music that turned off massive numbers of adults.

I was disheartened by the whole thing. The magnificent Top 40 format I'd grown up with and believed in, and the one that had been so crucial in shaping my life, was falling apart. For nearly five decades, Top 40 was the big stage; the central place with the biggest audiences where music variety was the key. It didn't cater to niche audiences or one kind of music. It was a variety flow of the very best of every current genre of music.

The guys in Green Day reminded me of three wacky college kids who took nothing seriously. When the group visited *Open House Party*, the guys had smoked so much weed at WAAF ahead of their visit that my studio smelled like pot for three days after they left.

By late 1992, I was a wreck. Superadio was faltering so badly that it was hard to keep faith that it could rebound. I was still hosting *Open House Party*, but it was the only stretch of the workweek that offered any pleasure, or gave any sense of achievement and satisfaction.

The low point came when I got a call from Paula Woodworth, office manager at the Superadio headquarters in Southborough. "The plant rental company is here," she said. "They're taking back the office plants because we haven't paid our bill." Everyone on the staff, laughing about it later, agreed that watching the plants roll out the door was the most depressing event they remembered about that dark time.

The day before New Year's Eve, 1992, I was in Vermont, just trying to unwind from all the business stress, when I got an unexpected call from Arnie Ginsburg. He had returned from our V66 adventure to Pyramid Broadcasting as senior vice president, which owned a chain of radio stations including KISS 108 in Boston. Arnie was with Brian Stone, another VP at the company who was heading up a new division working for banks that had taken over foreclosed radio stations. For a fee, they managed them, keeping them on the air until they could be sold.

Arnie handed the phone to Brian. "John, we're having to chop expenses and let everyone go at these stations to save money until the banks figure out what to do with them," he said. But we still need programming. "Could you produce

John Garabedian

Columbia Records threw a lavish party at Boston's Copley Plaza Hotel to debut Mariah Carey. No one told us she was married to the president of the record company. (Left to right) KISS GM Lisa Fell, myself, Sunny Joe White, Mariah, promo execs Jerry Brenner and Carl Strube. *Photo by Leo Gozbekian.*

twenty-four hours of satellite programming that we could air? We're looking for a kind of a bright adult contemporary format."

I was excited. We certainly had all the satellite equipment from the stations we lost. We also had the infrastructure because of our cutting-edge automation system. "Sure," I said enthusiastically. "We can deliver you great sounding programming that would even sound local. But how much per station could you pay?"

Brian was intrigued. "I figure about three grand a month," he said. "Why don't we get together in the next couple of weeks and talk it over?"

"A few weeks?" I said. "How about tomorrow?"

I drove the 220 miles back to Boston that afternoon. The next morning I was in the KISS 108 headquarters in Medford, finalizing a deal that immediately landed us on a half-dozen stations. Within a few weeks we were operational. We named the service CITY-FM. And it had to sound "major-market" great. Through the brilliant programming skills of our IT genius Reed Lewis, we adapted the same voice-tracking system we invented at WGTR twenty years before. That creation enabled us to afford a top shelf crew of Boston DJs to host. Station owners loved it. As we marketed CITY-FM, we kept getting asked if we also had a country format. So we added a second format called "Super Hit Country" that aired on another batch of stations, using air talent from WSIX in Nashville.

Yet due to the long sales cycle, even when we reached fifty affiliate stations it didn't completely stop the cash-bleeding. Every Friday I was down at the phone company, paying the bill, just to keep our lines on. I even threw in another couple hundred grand of my own money to meet payrolls and keep the company running, but it all proved to be just a temporary fix. To beat back the pressure, I began going to the gym three times a week. I wanted to de-stress. But it rarely worked. By 3 a.m., my eyes shot open and I'd stare at the ceiling, running through mental spreadsheets to try and figure a solution.

The operation of Superadio involved use of highly advanced computer programs. None existed for radio at the time, so we designed and wrote them ourselves, thanks to the incredible genius of our IT master Reed Lewis, shown here at Cape Canaveral atop a rocket preparing to launch the AMC-11 satellite.

Then who shows up again but good old Kris Carlson, my nephew who pushed me out of WGTR a dozen years prior. By now, I had let bygones be bygones. Still always the charmer and dressed in a dark suit with a white pocket handkerchief ("it gives the impression of trustworthiness," he once said), Kris was now holding himself out as a financial wizard and advisor. And although he was operating without a broker's license or required registration and his activities were legally questionable, he assured me he could raise money to help Superadio through the crisis. Kris set up meetings with potential investors, and I furnished him with five-year business projections and other materials.

Then I learned that he was telling the potential investors that if they invested, he would be running the company, and he presented them with a modified business plan giving himself a big cut of ownership and profits. I was outraged. He endeared

John Garabedian

himself to me by coming in as a fundraiser, and now he was pulling his old act of trying to take over and push me aside. But karma has a funny way of working.

One April morning, returning from the gym, I received an unexpected phone call from a guy named Chris Devine, president of a radio group in Chicago. "We're interested in buying your twenty-four-hour formats," he said. "Do you have any interest in selling?"

I did my best to not laugh out loud. "You're calling at just the right moment," I answered. "We are in the middle of a refinancing, and this could work out perfectly."

Chris's call was like a dream. We could've plodded forward with what we were doing, but at the current growth rate we were still months away from turning a profit and being able to generate enough cash to survive until we were in the black.

The next day, a Friday, I faxed him a value calculation I'd prepared based on a five-year "discounted cash flow" projection, a standard means of valuing a business. The valuation came in at $2 million for "CITY-FM" and "Super Hit Country." But I told him, "I'll knock off twenty-five percent as 'closing insurance' to make this a really good deal." I figured it was exactly the infusion of cash Superadio needed to keep *Open House Party* going and cut expenses until market conditions improved.

But to sell major assets, I needed the approval of Superadio's limited partner investors. So I sent a letter explaining the deal and expected them to green-light it. I canvassed them by phone and got the impression they were all on board with the arrangement. But behind my back, my old friend Robert Whyte had also contacted them and scheduled a meeting to convince them that they should get a bigger cut of the cash proceeds, an undeserved cut which would have stolen Radiocraft's payback for delivering the formats which made the sale possible.

The original deal was structured so that Radiocraft, Inc., the company I'd founded prior to Superadio, which owned and produced *Open House Party*, would split all revenues with Superadio fifty-fifty. This had been clearly disclosed in the original investor prospectus. Since Radiocraft had financed and produced the CITY-FM programming under the same arrangement, it deserved and was entitled to get repaid its fifty-percent share of the proceeds. The remaining chunk would stay in Superadio's bank account to fund the short-term losses as we continued the business's recovery. Robert didn't agree and lobbied the other investors to push for a hundred percent cash distribution to the limited partners, screwing Radiocraft and me out of any money for producing the format that had brought half the sale price. Two days before the closing, he called me up and sprung a surprise.

The once-charming Robert Whyte in better days back when we were friends and business partners at his former home in Toronto. Last I heard of him, he had left Canada for California where he now runs a company producing "Bob & Stacy's Cocktails," premixed alcoholic drinks in juice pouches.

"John," he said tersely. "I've spoken to the other partners and we're having a meeting at the Four Seasons Hotel in Boston this Thursday at four. You're welcome to join us, but if you choose not to come the meeting will happen without you."

I was pissed. "Robert," I said, "that's the day of the closing. You know I can't miss that."

Robert didn't care. "It's going to happen, John," he said. "The partners want out and they want their money."

From there it just got ugly. Sale of the two formats closed, but the funds were deposited in escrow until the matter was settled. I knew I was right, so we filed a lawsuit against the partners with the Worcester Superior Court asking for a declaratory judgment based on the facts. In the end, five of the partners, including my now former friend Robert Whyte, agreed to be bought out for fifty cents on the dollar. It meant a business expenditure I wasn't expecting, but it also ended up giving me ninety-percent equity in Superadio. As Craig Howard used to say, "Every misfortune is a fortune in disguise."

It was a somewhat risky bet that Top 40 could bounce back, but I just completely believed it had to. As market conditions improved and pop music returned with boy bands like the Backstreet Boys and 'N SYNC, my confidence in

John Garabedian

The Backstreet Boys first came by along with their roly-poly manager Lou Pearlman. Six months after they hit it big, Pearlman reappeared with another bunch of cute boys called 'N SYNC. Something about him felt slimy to me. Lou is currently serving twenty-five years in federal prison for a 300 million dollar Ponzi scheme.

the format was finally proven right. The Nick Carters and Justin Timberlakes of the industry had saved the Top 40 format by returning variety to the format. *Open House Party's* reach exploded too. By the turn of the century, *Open House Party* was flourishing, airing on 150 major market stations across the country and bringing in one third of Superadio's revenue. We developed programming in new formats such as gospel, oldies, country, and our Urban division driven by Gary Bernstein had made Superadio the world's largest producer of Urban radio programming. Once again, Superadio was pumping out lots of cash.

But the radio business is fluid. Change is a constant and after 2000, following government deregulation, the rise of the Internet, and a barrage of consolidation deals that had pretty much put nearly all of the country's major market stations in the hands of three monstrous companies, the future looked uncertain. I remembered what a wealthy friend of mine had once said about investments. "It's best to leave the party while the music's still playing." After thirteen years, the longest I've ever worked at one place, I felt the best move we could make was to lock in the value we had created and cash out.

A fifteen-year-old kid from Raleigh started calling the *OHP* request lines, and eventually got through to me: "How do I get into radio?" he asked. At nineteen, he moved to Boston and became our mixer. Now "Kannon" hosts Sunday *OHP* plus mornings on KVIL in Dallas. Photo shot at the Rabbit Hill Inn in Vermont visiting with his family at Thanksgiving.

In 2001, I retained Deutsche Bank to explore a deal to sell the network. A year later Access One Communications, a company in New York City that owned WWRL in New York and half of the American Urban Radio Network, bought Superadio. One bizarre piece of synchronicity was that the founder and chairman of Access One was Sidney Small. During negotiations, I kept thinking "I've met this guy before." Then I remembered: He was the business manager of ABC Radio whom I met thirty years before in 1972 when buying the WABC-FM automation system we used at WGTR.

The sale proved to be a validation to me and to the four other limited partner investors who had bucked Robert Whyte's advice, stayed with me, and walked away with a handsome return on their original Superadio investment. More important, the deal didn't include the sale of Radiocraft and *Open House Party*. I could now return to just playing deejay, having fun, and playing great music. I was done with the daily headaches of running a radio network business.

That was my plan, anyway. 🔇

John Garabedian

26. Something New

Axwell-Ingrosso, 2015

With David O'Leary recently at the Harvard Club for an Aero Club of New England function. David is now happily married with three grown children and hosts the morning show on Boston's most listened to radio station, Magic 106.7. We remain best friends.

On the morning of September 12, 2014, I was headed to the Boston Marriott Quincy for the annual induction ceremony of the Massachusetts Broadcasters Hall of Fame. It was a beautiful blue sky day and the crisp air packed just a bit of a bite, an early reminder of the coming New England fall. For weeks I had been anticipating this event and dreading it. Not that I wasn't familiar with the affair—I'd been to other induction ceremonies, even presenting my friend Arnie Ginsburg in 2008. But now, only one year after being named "Broadcaster of the Year" by the Massachusetts Broadcasters Association, I was being inducted into the Broadcasters Hall of Fame. The thought of speaking in front of hundreds of my fellow radio and TV colleagues made me nervous.

Don't get me wrong. I was deeply gratified for the recognition. It meant everything to be placed among so many legendary Massachusetts broadcasters I had admired. But for weeks, I anguished over what I was going to say. I wanted to say something substantial but not come off like a televangelist.

It's an odd thing. Behind a radio studio mike, I can speak to a national audience of millions of people effortlessly for hours. Hand that same mike to me and put me on a stage in an auditorium full of people and I tighten up and feel stupid. Perhaps it's because that kind of "PA system;" public speaking has none of the intimacy that you get when you're talking, one-on-one with a radio listener. The whole thing dredges that old feeling of not wanting to stand out and be the center of attention.

"Be warm and charming and keep it simple," I kept telling myself as I pulled into the hotel parking lot.

Inside the Marriott, the big event room where the ceremony was to be held had already swelled with people. Boston's biggest media personalities were there. Retired WCVB-TV news anchor Natalie Jacobson; KISS 108 morning

Broadcaster of the Year award to John Garabedian from the Massachusetts Broadcasters Association.

man, Matt Siegel; and longtime TV sports reporter, Bob Lobel, mingled and found their seats. Off to the side, WBZ's Jordan Rich, the event's emcee, joked around with his former WBZ colleague and my former young New Hampshire newsman, a now-mature and retired Gary LaPierre.

Near the center of the room, sitting at a table not far from the stage was my lifetime friend and former business partner, Arnie Ginsburg, who at the age of eighty-seven had made the two-hour journey from his home in Ogunquit, Maine, to be here for me. Arnie nursed a glass of water and did his best to quietly fit in. But that was impossible. Even among all these heavyweights, Arnie was treated like a god. A stream of people came up to him, many previous and current fellow Hall of Fame inductees, to introduce themselves, shake his hand, and let him know what kind of impact he'd had on their lives.

Outside the big room in the lobby, I tried to keep a low profile. For the next hour, my life became a blur of new and familiar faces, interviews, and congratulations. I put on a good face. I smiled and said "Good to see you" even when I didn't quite recognize who it was I was talking to, but none of it was enough to distract me from worrying about my damn acceptance speech. Every so often, a panic ran through me and I checked my suit coat pocket to make sure the sheet of paper on which I'd scribbled down a few talking points, was still there. At my side stood my best friend, David O'Leary, whom I suggested to introduce me. As I sorted through the hellos, David occasionally looked over and flashed a warm smile. He knew me better than anyone else and the discomfort level I was feeling.

It's a strange thing to watch your career edited down into a single sixty-second spot. To see a telescoped air check of all the triumphs and losses—a fifty-five-year career mashed together into a tightly scripted highlight reel. Did that all really happen? Do people even care about what did happen? It's another, thing, too, to look across a room and see a sea of faces who've had a hand in bringing that career together. On this day those people included my two older sisters, eighty-six-year-old Doris and eighty-two-year-old Jackie, who'd turned out to celebrate their little brother. After the highlight reel with some of my air work, David took the podium microphone and read his introduction.

Dr. Leo Beranek founded WCVB-TV, Boston, as well as consulting firm Bolt, Beranek, and Newman, which developed the Arpanet and TCP/IP, which became the Internet. He is also a world renowned sound engineer and has tuned most of the world's great opera houses.

"John is what many of us in radio can only aspire to," he told the crowd. "He is the whole package. Entrepreneur, innovator, programmer, air talent, engineer, even a pilot for your traffic reports. In any area of our industry you'd have to look long and hard to find someone with higher standards for the work that we do and what we can accomplish as broadcasters." David's introduction calmed me down. His Zen-like persona is unbelievably credible, and what he said was humbling but gave me confidence to go up and deliver my acceptance speech.

The first thing I did when I took the stage was honor the man who'd been inducted just prior to me. I had first met Dr. Leo Beranek years before when we served together on the board of the Massachusetts Broadcasters Association. I've always been in awe of him. Now spry and sharp, just three days before his one hundredth birthday, he was being inducted for founding Boston's WCVB-TV and building it into what became the most acclaimed local television station in America. But in lauding that accomplishment, Natalie Jacobson, his introducer, had omitted his most significant innovation, founding Bolt, Beranek and

John Garabedian

Newman, the Boston company that developed Arpanet, the digital networking system that became the Internet. I couldn't let the omission go by, so I saluted Dr. Beranek's monumental achievement, then I went into my speech.

Adding my Leo Beranek salute didn't quite fit in the two minutes I was allotted on the stage. So the exit music fired up just as I launched into the meat of what I wanted to say. About perseverance. About following your dream. About life's beautiful bouts of unpredictability. About turning misfortune into fortune.

The music got louder so I got louder, and then more philosophical: "Nothing is more important than being happy," I said. "You want money? No. You want money because you think it will make you happy. You want power? No. Power is what you want because you think it will make you happy. But what you really want is 'happy'."

The "get off the stage" music ended as I hit my closing with three lines from Robert Frost's poem, "Two Tramps in Mud Time":

My object in living is to unite
My avocation and my vocation
As my two eyes make one in sight.

As those last words came out of my mouth, a rush of emotion went through me and my voice tripped up a little. The specialness of the moment, the gratitude of being in that place in front of so many fellow broadcasters whose careers I respected, of having had a fantastic career journey, and of standing up there in front of many old friends, got to me. When I finished I stepped down from the stage and found my seat. I then took in a deep, relieved breath. It was finally over.

The great Sunny Joe White once said, "Just because a person turns thirty doesn't mean they want to listen to oldies." Sunny always looked at things the way they actually were, beyond the way they may have been generally accepted. His bold, unconventional thinking enabled him to build KISS 108 into a unique

OHP live from the Billboard Awards in Orlando. Our guest was Casey Kasem, who talked just like he sounds on the radio. (Left to right) intern Neil "Romeo" Paris (now at KISS/Boston), Kasem's daughter, Mike "Kannon" Hershberger, Kasem, producer Mike Ortolano, myself, and engineer Steve Riggs.

radio station that stood out and dominated Boston radio listening for nearly fifteen years.

When I was a kid, many of the rules and customs of life didn't make sense and drove me to try to figure out what was real. Rather than following traditional paths, I struggled to discover the real rules of right and wrong, rather than be obedient to traditional thinking. My obsession with seeking reality transformed me into who I have become and what I believe. Every single thing I have achieved stems from being true to myself, doing what I believe is right, and passionately pursuing what I love.

My work is a real privilege: to be able to entertain millions of people all over the country, to showcase the greatest music of our time, to get to meet and know talented performing artists, and to do it all completely live in my stocking feet from the basement of my own house.

The evolving rainbow of contemporary music reflects contemporary life, and life is now. I never wanted to be one of those people who can only relate to "oldies." To me, that's a sign of "psycho-sclerosis," the hardening of the brain. The

John Garabedian

shawnmendes ● 3h

● 210006 likes

shawnmendes Had the pleasure of hanging out with radio legend John Garabedian, thanks for showing me your planes !! So cool 😃

Shawn Mendes.

world keeps changing. Music keeps changing. One of the most enjoyable parts of my work is meeting the musicians who create it while pursuing their dreams.

The first time I interviewed Taylor Swift was at the Xfinity Center in Mansfield, Massachusetts. Her career had just begun, but she wasn't at all drunk in her fame. We spent an hour in her tour bus, Taylor, her mom, and me. She was so grateful and appreciative of how far she had come. We talked about the artists she listened to growing up in Pennsylvania, her life after getting signed by RCA Records as a songwriter and the support her parents gave her to advance her career, moving to Nashville when she was fourteen. She was as unfiltered and open as anyone I'd ever met. At one point she recalled driving around Nashville one hot summer night and hearing a listener request her first hit, "You Belong To Me," on *Open House Party*. She'd never heard her song on the radio before, and she said when it came on the air she screamed. Other stars like Katy Perry Justin Bieber, Rihanna, Bruno Mars, and Adam Levine are the same. They're grounded, real, and just fun to be around. Beyond all their fame and glamour, most of them are down-to-earth: real people with insecurities, dreams, hopes, and disappointments.

Of course, sometimes watching someone's career evolve can make me groan. In early spring of 2009, I came across a new song by an unknown artist from New York City. No radio stations were playing "Just Dance," but the song blew me away and I knew the audience would love it. So we started playing it heavily on *Open House Party*. Requests for it soon poured in. "Just Dance" by Lady Gaga became our most requested song and stayed that way for weeks. Despite urging her label, Interscope Records, to make it a promo-

My dear John,
(I love you with
all my gaga heart.
Thank you for believing in me.
You are really special
Lady Gaga

Lady Gaga was a frequent *Open House Party* guest, allowing us to broadcast the world premiere of "Poker Face." It had a surprise ending.

tional priority, the company put its focus on singles by other artists. Still, the requests poured in, keeping it our top request. The stations that aired *Open House Party* were also getting massive requests for "Just Dance" and started playing it. With this radio feedback now coming from everywhere, Interscope prioritized it and finally, with their promotional horsepower, "Just Dance" became the number one most-played song on the radio in America. During her second visit to *Open House Party* in 2010, an appreciative Lady Gaga told listeners on the air, "If it weren't for John Garabedian, no one in America would know who I am."

During that same visit, Lady Gaga brought us her unreleased brand new album, *The Fame*, for us to premiere. "Play cut four, 'Poker Face,'" she urged during a commercial break. I had never heard it, and since the FCC had just increased the fines for broadcasting profanity from $10,000 to $300,000, I was hesitant to blindly air a song I hadn't screened for language. "Are there any bad words in it?" I asked.

Gaga shook her head. "Oh, no, don't worry," she said. "It's nothing like that," she replied. So we put it on. I was immediately impressed by it. But as the song progressed through the chorus where it was presumed to sing "pa-pa-pa-pa-pa-pa-pa-pa-poker face," it seemed the chorus really sang something that sounded like "fa-fa-fa-fa-fa-fa-fa-fa-fuck-her-face." Since she had assured me it was clean I thought, Oh well, maybe I was hearing things. The next morning I went back into the studio and played it at half speed, then full speed several times. It really sounded like "fuck-her-face." I complained to the record company, and within a week we had a new, unmistakably "pa-pa-pa-pa," unmistakably clean version.

Following that hugely successful debut album and a second "deluxe" version of the album called, *Fame Monster* (the same album repackaged with a couple of new songs added), she released in 2011, *Born this Way*. Radio stations jumped on the title cut due to anticipation that had been built up after the success of *Monster*. Yet the album ended up a semi-flop. While it sold 1.1 million albums the first week, 449,000 of those were sold for ninety-nine cents on Amazon, greatly inflating the early numbers. Airplay on songs "Judas" and "The Edge of Glory" was disappointing. Listener test scores quickly buried the tunes and Gaga's rule of the pop airwaves suddenly fell apart. Today, with the exception of "Just Dance" and "Poker Face," her songs receive almost no air-time on the radio.

Lady Gaga's career choices troubled me. She earned the super success she had lusted for, but then she became entranced by the aroma of her own perfume. Suddenly, it wasn't enough to be an A-list pop star. She wanted to become an "artiste," a legend, the next Edith Piaf: exotic, abstract, hyper avant-garde.

The problem is an old one. When an artist is unproven, they are hungry and their career is shaped and controlled by a seasoned professional management team. They eagerly follow the guidance of those who control the money and run the show at the record label. Those people are only interested in producing big hits that make them money, not in creating great art. So label personnel usually decide which songs should be on an album, who produces it, and which are good enough to be released as a

Chris Brown was fun to have over, playfully starting a snowball fight in my driveway on the way out.

single. Unfortunately, once the artist achieves superstar status, they frequently contract a disease I call "big-head-itis," an over-confidence and belief they can do everything well and largely do it themselves. The dictionary example of a superstar artist imploding was Prince, who changed his name to an unpronounceable symbol and began choosing which songs he would release, none of which ever became hits. His career evaporated.

Once she was consumed by her sense of infallibility, Gaga no longer respected the opinions of those who had guided her previous success. After the total disaster of her third album, *Artpop*, she fired Troy Carter, her manager of seven years, along with other highly talented members of her creative team who had shaped her initial success. 🔇

John Garabedian

27. Heading Up High (Years Remix)
Armin Van Buuren, 2016

The outermost point of Cape Cod, with a departing PBA DC-3 over Race Point, Provincetown. This is the starting point for U.S. Route 6 which ends in Bishop, California, the longest transcontinental highway in the United States *(artist: Ray Crane)*.

Open House Party evolved over the years, but the essence of it, a big Saturday night party with callers from around the country featuring the biggest stars, remains. Thanks to technology, the party's reach exploded. With the rise of the Internet, fans across the country and in every part of the world began streaming the broadcast. We hear from listeners in Europe, China, Russia, Canada, the Middle East, and even parts of Africa where Open House Party was recently broadcast live every Saturday night on Capital FM, Nairobi. For many years, Open House Party aired every Saturday night throughout Turkey. A century after my Armenian grandparents had fled the Ottoman Turkish massacres for a new life in America, their grandson had returned via satellite to entertain thousands of Turks with "the biggest party on the planet."

In early 2012, I started receiving form letters from a Philadelphia law firm representing creditors who were pressing for a declaration of bankruptcy of a company called Nassau Broadcasting. I usually skimmed random junk mail and tossed them in the wastebasket. But one cold February morning in 2012, I was again going through my mail and came across another, much thicker envelope from the same Philadelphia law firm. This one announced that the Delaware bankruptcy court had ordered an auction sale of all of Nassau Broadcasting's radio stations. That got my attention.

As I scanned the list of fifty radio stations to be auctioned, I noticed it included a "Cape Cod cluster," which consisted of two stations, Classic Rock "PIXY 103" (WPXC), and Classic Hits "Frank-FM." Cape Cod is a place I've loved since I was a teenager, and where I now own a home. This looked like a great opportunity for my sought after "next move."

Shot for an *OHP* magazine ad, four of the kids in this shot became major radio stars: Behind blonde left is Kannon, KVIL, Dallas; behind blonde right is Neil "Romeo" Paris, KISS, Boston; behind me right is Kidd O'Shea, WMYX, Milwaukee; to right is Sarah Meany, WFLZ, Tampa.

In August of 2012, we finalized the purchase of the Cape stations. The key management team also included an old friend. While shopping at the Westborough Stop & Shop one night, I heard someone call out "John!" Wheeling around, there was my former V66 business manager, Merril Buchhalter. After we sold the TV station to Home Shopping Network, they had named Merril as general manager. We'd lost touch, and without either of us realizing it she now lived a half mile from my Southborough home. I immediately recruited her to be my CFO and business manager of the Cape stations. Working with great people you respect and enjoy is one of life's pleasures.

The year 2012 became my twenty-fifth year hosting *Open House Party*. While I still loved doing it every Saturday night, I now felt I needed to relieve myself of the daily responsibilities of running Radiocraft, the network which owned and distributed *Open House Party* and several other shows. A wise friend once told me, "When you cut away the dead branches on a tree, you make way for new growth."

Selling Radiocraft proved to be a snap. United Stations Radio Network, which had been handling our advertising sales, moved quickly to buy it. The company's president, Jim Higgins, and I made a deal in two days, and we closed at the end of 2012. Their purchase came with one important requirement: They would only buy it if I remained as host of *Open House Party* for several more years. I was highly complimented by the requirement and agreed to continue hosting the show, which I enjoy tremendously.

Since taking over Cape Cod radio stations PIXY 103 and Frank-FM, we did some engineering sleight-of-hand and launched two brand new stations, Y-101 ("Today's Hits"), and Koffee-FM. It put me back in the local radio station business and returned me to the fun and satisfaction of building great local radio stations with an outstanding team of professionals. Best of all, I get to create something excellent and beautiful with value to a community in one of the most beautiful places in America. ◀×

28. Just Be (Antillas Mix)

Tiesto, 2012

Flying to Vermont high above the clouds.

It was pushing 1:30 in the morning before I'd been able to relax enough to hit the sack and get some sleep after my Saturday night show. Now, ten hours later, walking across the back lawn toward the airplane hangar behind my Southborough home, I replayed the show in my head. I love a Sunday that comes on the heels of a great show. It resets the week and is made even better when it includes a trip to Vermont to chill and hang out with some friends.

Reaching the hangar, I opened the big electric door and gave a welcome look to my classic 1961 Navion Rangemaster. Pulling it outside with the PowerTow, its crimson finish shimmered like a jewel in the late morning sunlight.

Carefully inspecting the outside, I climbed into the cockpit and ran through the pre-flight checklist, starting the engine, and letting the Continental IO-520 purr for a couple of minutes as it warmed to minimum takeoff temperature. With everything ready, I taxied into position on the runway and pushed the throttle forward to full power. The lines of the runway became a blur as I picked up speed. Faster and faster I accelerated, hitting rotation speed of sixty-five knots before pulling the yoke back, raising the nose, and moving into a good climb over a bank of trees. From there, it was like riding an elevator. As the view opened up, I moved above the clouds and life below grew smaller, quieter, more still. My own life receded into the distance, too. Up there, there are no problems to deal with. It's just me, the airplane, stunning stretches of blue sky, and beautiful New England.

I leveled off at a smooth 6,500 feet, cruising at 160 mph over southern New Hampshire, past mountains and lakes, small towns and freshly greened farms. After passing Lake Sunapee and Mount Kearsarge, the mighty Connecticut River came into view along with the lush, rolling farmland that epitomizes the Vermont landscape. The journey took me over Grafton State Forest, Signal Mountain

John Garabedian

in Marshfield, Joe's Pond in West Danville, and then, finally, Cabot. Among all those hills and farms, my airstrip and Vermont home now came into sight. Descending, I dropped the landing gear as I flew a ninety-degree crosswind over the grass runway. Then I banked left into downwind over Birmingham's Farm, a picture postcard mass of pastures and horses. On final approach, I slowed down over the trees, then cut power as I flared, letting the main wheels touch at the same moment on the grassy strip for a soft, quiet, and welcoming landing.

Taxiing up to the hangar, I shut down the engine and opened the door. The crisp Vermont spring air washed over me like a long lost friend. With the plane put away, I closed up the hangar and stood in the sunlight, gazing at the forty-mile view from the mountaintop airstrip. Below was the eleven-room expansion of that original cabin I built with my own hands, forty years before. Around it the valley landscape—the Green Mountains, those open fields—that keep calling me back, even now, nearly a half century after Angus McPherson first introduced me to Vermont.

What did I want to do with my life? That was the question this setting had inspired me to ask all those years ago when I sat in that mountain field staring up at the stars. It's a question that many people either never ask or, if they do, it baffles them as it did me. And many never resolve it. Like every mystery about the rules of life I had questioned since childhood, I was determined to figure it out. Finally, one night I turned it around and looked at it from the other side: How should I spend my life so that on my dying day I would be proud of what I'd done and who I had become?

The ultimate achievement would be to figure a way to fix the world. Seriously. Imagine if we could end crime, war, hatred, misery, and live in a world where people do the right thing, treat others fairly, and don't lie, cheat or steal. Imagine a beautiful world of happy people, enjoying each other, chasing their dreams, and finding fulfillment.

Under those Vermont stars it became so obvious to me that every single thing you do creates a chain of both tangible and invisible events that inevitably shape your future. Therefore your life becomes the product of what you do and have done.

Navion Rangemaster parked outside my backyard hangar.

It was here on this mountain I eventually realized that the supreme goal of living is simply working to achieve the highest state of happiness. Nothing trumps happy. To a tree, happy is fertile soil, rain, sun, and wind. To a bee, it's sweet nectar to take to the hive, and to a dog, it's a meaty bone. But to a person, it should be developing your life to become your best, to passionately pursue the dreams that bring you joy and fulfillment, eliminating negative elements that pull you down. The ideal is to become the person you most respect and admire.

So many people have miserable lives, which only erode further as they get older and lead to horrible endings. They do dumb things when they're young and never change. And they never realize that their misery is one of their own creation. Power, money, glory, popularity—these superficial aims become their target goal. But what they breed is dissatisfaction and disappointment and separate themselves even more from the desired goal of achieving happiness with an authentic life they can be proud of.

I see it all the time with musicians and for so many of them I feel sad. They have a huge first hit, millions of YouTube hits, do the big TV shows, and go on tour. Then when the second or third song doesn't do well, their joy turns to quiet desperation as they are no longer hot, the record company doesn't return their

John Garabedian

This area of Vermont is called the "Northeast Kingdom" because of its majestic unspoiled views and natural beauty.

phone calls, and no one cares about them anymore. For them it is abandonment, a sentence in purgatory, and they try anything they can for months and years to get back the former fame that is now just a memory. It's a superficial world where you're only as relevant as your last hit.

A happy life comes when you open your mind up and give yourself permission to honestly learn who you are and what you need in life. There is endless opportunity and fulfillment for those who seek it.

With its quiet, open space, Vermont allowed me to find that. I've never forgotten my mother's advice to "weed out the takers." Life's too short and filled with possibilities to be brought down by negativity and those who waste your time, bring you nothing, and drag you down.

I feel so fortunate to have many long-time close friends. Recently, I made a list of close friends I have who've told me that they love me in the past month. I hit eleven. Earning that deep appreciation from people whom I respect and care about is certainly one of my greatest life achievements.

The world has changed dramatically since I first came to Vermont in 1969. It's bigger, louder, more connected. Gazing out across the mountains, I often think about my early struggles to fit in, the early coming-to-terms I had with figuring life out and determining what was right and wrong. All that questioning I did of who I was, what kind of world we lived in, was challenging. But it made me stronger, too. Those internal battles, and later some of the battles I waged with those around me, forced me to know myself, know who I was, and what I

Tommy Nicoletti shortly before he died at age fifty-three.

was capable of taking on. It built my backbone, gave me a clearer vision of reality and instilled self-confidence. If you don't give up, life has a wonderful way of taking you where you want to go.

So many important people in my life didn't live long enough to achieve all their dreams. In fifth grade, I returned to school from Christmas vacation to learn a ten-year-old classmate named Eddie Novak had drowned when he fell through the ice on Claypit Pond in Belmont. He was the first. Later, close friends like Bob Lund, who died of a heart attack at forty-three; Wally Rouleou and Jimmy Mack, both from complications from AIDS at age twenty-seven; Roger Elswick committed suicide in my barn at forty-two; my nephew, Phillip, was just thirty when killed in an auto accident.

Sunny Joe White died from heart failure at forty-two; cancer claimed my *Open House Party* producer Mike Ortolano when he was fifty-two; and at fifty-three, life finally caught up with ex-boyfriend Tommy Nicoletti.

Andy McLean was another. He was twenty years old when he was diagnosed with leukemia. A year after chemo and a bone marrow transplant, he was in remission. But the cancer returned when he was twenty-seven and took his life. Like it does for many cancer patients, it opened him up to a new world of wonder and admiration for every moment of life. When you realize you may not be around for long, every day is precious. Every sunrise, every cool breeze, every blooming garden, feels like a new and wonderful gift. I marveled not just at

Andy's positivity, but his embrace of a life he knew was so fleeting. From Andy I learned to really appreciate how precious life is, how special each day is, and how lucky we are just to be alive.

They and others helped shape me into the person I became. I was also very lucky to have great parents. They gave me a strong conscience, and the confidence to make good decisions, and not to be afraid of taking risks. They laid the foundation for me to question everything and to learn the difference between what's really right and what's really wrong. Every person in your life, every decision you make, channels you toward your destiny.

One Sunday in 1971, I was having brunch with Don Law at his home in Cambridge. Don was then on his way to becoming the country's biggest concert promoter and was talking about the mechanics of successfully promoting concerts. He always had a profound way of saying things and muttered something which included the phrase, "…the harmony of parts." That phrase rang in my head like a note from heaven. It crystallized everything I'd thought about regarding the goal of happiness and achieving serenity by working the elements in your life to fit together in balance. When every part of your life fits together in harmony, you have achieved nirvana, the perfect life and the perfect you. Striving to arrive at that place has been my life's effort.

As I made my way from the hangar to my house, built on the spot where I once laid on a blanket under the stars dreaming of the life I wanted for myself and the world I wanted to live in, I was reminded of all those early trips and close friendships where I bonded with my most intimate friends. Those were the uncertain, unconditional journeys we made up here to find something, to find ourselves, to find our place in the universe. Did I unlock the answers to all those life mysteries the crew of us seemed determined to figure out? Not completely. But this story isn't over. Have I possibly planted seeds for future generations? Who knows?

On a summer evening, when the day and season feel like they will go on forever, I can take some satisfaction at this journey I've been on, the fulfilling relationships I've experienced, the wisdom I've acquired, and the place I've arrived at. I feel so grateful to have reached this point.

For over forty-five years, my final words on the air at the end of every show is a message I've used to guide my own life. Many people have told me their lives were greatly inspired and changed by it:

> *Learn from yesterday,*
> *live for today,*
> *dream for tomorrow,*
> *but most important,*
> *be* your *dream.* 🔇

John Garabedian

Epilogue

The first thing everyone asks when they learn I'm a radio DJ is, "Have you ever met [fill in the blank]?" So here are some photos of musical artists I have met.

Actually, except for Michael Jackson, John Lennon, and Elvis Presley, I have met or interviewed every major pop artist since the early sixties. Some are surprisingly short—Prince, Billy Joel, Bruno Mars, Eminem—most are really nice, and a few are assholes.

We Five at *Open House Party*, 1965.

Beatles concert at Boston's Suffolk Downs racetrack.

Paul Stanley and Gene Simmons of KISS.

Lou Gramm of Foreigner.

Laura Branigan

Tiny Tim

Peter Frampton

Liza Minnelli

Billy Joel *©Ron Pownall/RockRollPhoto.com*

Janet Jackson *Photo by Leo Gozbekian.*

John Garabedian

Vanilla Ice

Cher

The Bee Gees *Photo by Leo Gozbekian.*

Elton John

Steven Tyler of Aerosmith.

Sinéad O'Connor *Photo by Leo Gozbekian.*

Donna Summer

TLC and *OHP* producer Mike Ortolano.

Jon Bon Jovi

Matchbox Twenty

John Garabedian

Aaron Carter with RCA's Joe Daddio, me,
and producer Mike Ortolano.

Alicia Keys

Enrique Iglesias

Mariah Carey

Lionel Ritchie

Christina Aguilera

Jessica Simpson, Nick Lachey, and Mike Ortolano.

DJ and producer Paul Oakenfold.

Gwen Stefani

The Black Eyed Peas

John Garabedian

Mary J. Blige

Carey Hart and Pink

Maroon 5

Rihanna

Pete Wentz of Fall Out Boy.

Hulk Hogan and family.

Kanye West

The Jonas Brothers

Justin Bieber

Hayley Williams

John Garabedian

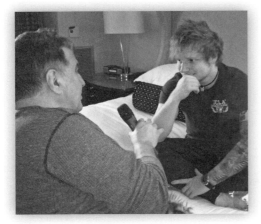

Ed Sheeran

Jason Derulo

Flo Rida

Bruno Mars

Zedd

Miley Cyrus

Demi Lovato

Herb Kelleher, founder of Southwest Airlines. You are now free to move about the country.

Shawn Mendes

Selena Gomez

John Garabedian

Index

Remos N66NX at Barre-Montpelier Airport, 2015.

John Garabedian

About the Author

Ian Aldrich's work has appeared in numerous publications and been recognized by the *Best American Sports Writing* anthology. He is currently a senior editor at *Yankee Magazine*. Ian lives with his wife and son in southern New Hampshire.